ENGLISH PRACTICE GRAMMAR

With answers

Michael Macfarlane

Garnet
EDUCATION

Published by Garnet Publishing Ltd.
8 Southern Court, South Street,
Reading RG1 4QS, UK

First edition 1999
Reprinted 2008, 2009

British Library Cataloguing-in-Publication Data
A catalogue record for this book is available from the
British Library.
ISBN: 978-1-85964-131-6

Editors: **Jane Hobbs and Jane Rollason**
Additional material: **Elizabeth Oliver**
Design: **David Rose and Mark Slader**
Illustration: **Mark Stock and Janette Hill**
Typesetting: **Samantha Abley**

Printed in Lebanon

Contents

Introduction to the student

Is *English Practice Grammar* the right level for me?

- Yes, if you are no longer a beginner.
- Yes, if you are not yet an advanced user of English.
- Yes, if you find examples of English in context useful.

How can this book help me?

Study *English Practice Grammar* when you have a problem with a particular point. It will help you to understand it, see it in context and practise it.

Do not try to read the book from the beginning to the end. It is not a coursebook!

What does the book contain and why?

The Contents on pages 3 to 5 and the Index on pages 217 to 224 help you to find the grammar point you want.

The 88 Units on pages 8 to 205 explain the essential grammar of English and provide practice exercises for each point. Most of the Units have two pages – a page of grammar and contextualised examples and a page of practice exercises. Some important grammar points have two pages of explanation and two pages of exercises.

The Answer key on pages 225 to 245 allows you to check the answers to the exercises.

The Appendix sections on pages 206 to 216 give you information about irregular verbs, spelling rules, punctuation, numbers, days, dates and times.

What's in a Unit?

Grammatical forms

Illustrated grammar situation

Explanations and examples

Exercises

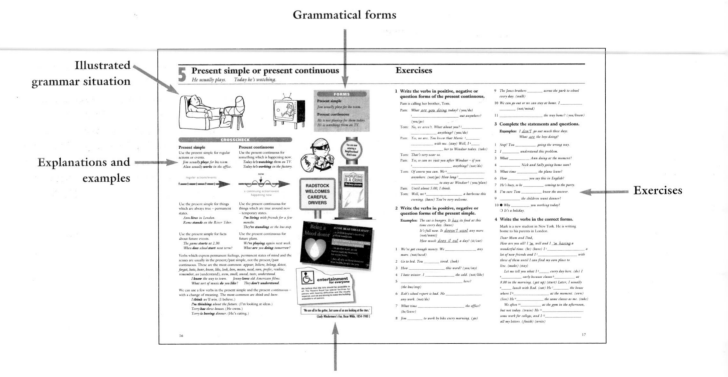

Everyday examples in context; some are highlighted for easy identification, others are for you to find

How do I use the book?

1 Find the grammar point you want to study in the Contents or the Index.

2 Turn to the correct Unit. Study the illustrated grammar situation, the grammatical forms and the explanations and examples of different uses. Look to the right – at the everyday examples in context. Read and think. Which uses do they show?

3 Do the exercises.

4 Check your answers in the Answer key.

5 If you have made any mistakes, read the grammar explanation again to understand what you did wrong.

6 Study the Appendix sections if you want information about irregular verbs, spelling rules, punctuation, numbers, days, dates and times.

Introduction to the teacher

English Practice Grammar is designed mainly for self-study by students who may be learning at secondary school, college or adult levels. You may want to recommend that students study particular Units to supplement, reinforce or revise work that has been done in class. The exercise material can of course also be used in class, the reference materials then being used as a reminder and summary of your own language presentations.

Acknowledgements

To my many students who have helped me find ways of explaining that thing that is so difficult to explain – English grammar; my Editor, **Jane Hobbs**, and **Tony Hobbs** for all their help and encouragement over a very long period; **Elizabeth Oliver** for her work on examples of language in context; **David Rose** and **Mark Slader** for the design; **Mark Stock** and **Janette Hill** for the illustrations; **Samantha Abley** and **Vicky Henriksen** for preparing the typescript.

Bibliography

The publishers would like to thank the following for permission to reproduce copyright material: *p.8* item 2 and *p.86* item 4 **Tesco Stores Ltd**; *p.16* item 4 and *p.126* item 4 **National Blood Service**; *p.18* item 2 reproduced by permission of **English Heritage**; *p. 74* item 1 **Driver and Vehicle Licensing Agency**; *p.78* item 4 and *p.146* item 3 reproduced by kind permission of **The Donkey Sanctuary, Sidmouth, Devon**; *p.112* item 1 **Pain Trust Publicity Literature**; *p.116* item 2 **Plymouth Pavilions**; *p.122* item 2 **The Tate Gallery**; item 3 **National Marine Aquarium**, a Registered Charity committed to education, conservation and research; *p.134* item 1 and *p.138* item 5 **Central School of Speech and Drama**; *p.144* item 4 **Open College of the Arts**; *p.182* item 4 **Thelma Hulbert Gallery** *p.192* item 2 **Sustrans**

1 Imperatives

Light the firework.

Light the firework ... and stand back!

The basic imperative is the infinitive, or dictionary form of a verb.
Use a main verb infinitive for an action.

> **Light** *the firework ... and* **stand back**!

Make a formal or written negative imperative with *Do not*.

> **Do not hold** *the firework.*

Make an informal spoken negative with *Don't*.

> **Don't hold** *the firework.*

Use *be* + adjective.

> **Be careful**! **Don't be stupid**!

Use imperatives to give orders.

> **Be** *quiet*! **Don't talk**!

Use imperatives to give instructions, eg for operating machines and in cookery books.

> **Turn** *the handle to the left and* **press** *the red button.*
> **Chop** *an onion and* **fry** *it in oil until it is brown.*

Use imperatives for polite instructions.

> *Please* **turn** *to page 15.*

Use imperatives for warnings.

> **Look out**! *It's going to fall!* **Be** *careful not to hurt yourself.*
> **Don't play** *with that knife or you'll hurt yourself.*

Use imperatives for friendly advice.

> **Relax**! **Don't worry**! *Everything will be all right.*

Use imperatives for invitations.

> **Come** *and* **have** *dinner on Saturday.*
> *Hello!* **Come in** *and* **sit down**. **Make** *yourself at home.*

Use imperatives for directions.

> **Go** *straight on,* **take** *the first turning on the left,* **cross** *the bridge, and the bank is on the right.*

Use *Let's* + imperative to suggest doing something together.

> **Let's buy** *some fireworks.*

Form the negative with *Let's not*.

> **Let's not go out** *today.*

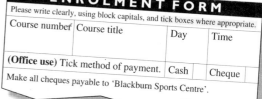

Healthy Eating *for kids*

1. Only buy the foods you want your children to eat. Then let them make their own choices from the careful selection you provide.

2. Encourage children to get involved in planning and preparing meals. For example, children who help make their packed lunches are more likely to eat them.

3. Set an example by eating the right foods and having regular meal times. Make all meal times an occasion and avoid distractions such as television.

When you get to the Hangar Lane roundabout, take the third exit - that's the North Circular Road going east. Stay on the North Circular until you pass the junction with the M1. Don't take the first left, but take the second left after the M1 junction, follow that road for about a kilometre, then look for an Esso garage. Turn right after the garage, and we're the fourth house on the right.

Let me catch your cobalt eye
Among the piercing rival glares
And light your fingers with my touch.
Let's dance beneath those icy stares

(Anonymous)

Exercises

1 Complete the imperative sentences.

Example: *The bus leaves at exactly 4.00, so* <u>*don't be*</u> *late.*

1 _____ *quiet, everyone. You're too noisy.*

2 ● *Is the plane going to crash?*
  ○ *Oh, _____ silly. Of course it isn't.*

3 _____ *careful with that knife. It's sharp.*

4 _____ *mean, Joe. Give Sam the toys.*

5 _____ *quick, Larry. There isn't much time.*

6 *Drive carefully. _____ such an idiot!*

7 _____ *helpful to your mother. She's very busy.*

8 *Why are you crying? _____ so sad.*

2 Complete the imperative sentences with these verbs.

drive, forget, go, play, press, take, talk, turn off, write

Example: <u>*Go*</u> *home now. It's late.*

1 _____ *with matches. They're dangerous.*

2 _____ *this money to the bank, please.*

3 *It's time to sleep now. _____ the lights.*

4 _____ *to your sister like that. It's rude.*

5 _____ *to collect the air tickets on your way to the airport.*

6 *To open the machine, _____ this button.*

7 _____ *so fast. You'll have an accident.*

8 _____ *your name, age and address here, please, madam.*

3 Complete the instructions with these verbs.

choose, enjoy, place, press, pull down, push, put, put in, take

Ben: *How do I work this drinks machine, Sam? I'd really like some coffee.*

Sam: *It's easy. Do you want milk and sugar?*

Ben: *Sugar, please, but no milk.*

Sam: *OK, first* <u>*pull down*</u> *a plastic cup from this hole on the right. Then* ¹ _____ *your money. Now* ² _____ *the cup under here and*

³ _____ *the sugar button. Now*

⁴ _____ *your drink – black coffee.*

⁵ _____ *your cup under here,*

⁶ _____ *the button and the coffee comes out.*

And now just ⁷ _____ *your coffee and*

⁸ _____ *it!*

Ben: *Thanks, Sam.*

4 Study the map and complete the directions to May's Garage. Use these verbs.

cross, drive, follow, go, pass, take, turn

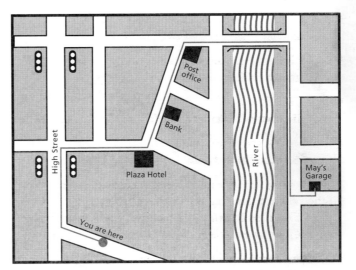

1 *To get to May's Garage,* <u>*go*</u> *to the end of this road.*

2 _____ *right into the High Street.*

3 _____ *right again at the first traffic lights.*

4 _____ *the second left opposite the Plaza Hotel.*

5 _____ *the bank on the right.*

6 _____ *the road to the end and _____ right at the post office.*

7 _____ *the bridge and _____ right.*

8 _____ *along the side of the river and _____ the third left. May's Garage is near the corner, on the left.*

2 Present simple

Ann works at A.B.C.

Ann works from 8.00 to 4.30 every day.

In positive statements a verb usually has no ending.
> *I **work**.   You **talk**.   We **write**.   They **go**.*

The 3rd person singular is different. The verb usually ends in *s*.
> *He **works**.   It **moves**.*

If the verb ends in *y*, change the *y* to *ies*.
> *cry → cries, fly → flies, try → tries*

If the verb ends in *o, ch, sh, ss* or *x*, add *es*.
> *go → goes, watch → watches, wish → wishes,*
> *miss → misses, box → boxes*

Verbs in negative statements and most questions have no ending.
They all need the auxiliary verb *do/does*. (See Unit 21 for
information about *do/does* as a main verb and auxiliary verb.)
> *I **don't like** this music.   She **doesn't talk**.*
> *Do you **know** him?   Does it **work**?*
> *When **do** they **start**?   Where **does** he **live**?*

Use the present simple for permanent states and situations.
> *I **live** in London.   I **have** two sisters.*

Use the present simple for things which always happen.
> *The sun **rises** in the east.   Water **boils** at 100° C.*

Use the present simple for repeated actions and events.
> *I **get up** at 7.00 most days.   Ann often **has** coffee at 11.00.*

Use the present simple for facts about future events.
> *Flight 765 **leaves** at 10.30.*
> *The President **arrives** at midday tomorrow.*

Some verbs usually take the present simple and not the present
continuous. (See Unit 5 for a list of these.)
> *I **know** what to do next.   Susan **doesn't like** cold weather.*
> *Do they **understand** English?*

A nice cup of tea

Tea bushes grow in warm, wet countries like China, India, Sri Lanka and Kenya. Tea pickers harvest the tea by hand. They take just the top two leaves and bud from each branch of each tea plant. The leaves are then dried and crushed and sorted into different grades. The tea is ready to use when it turns black.

WIMBLEDON OPENS TOMORROW

The British, and even world, tennis event of the year gets underway tomorrow once again at the famous Lawn Tennis Association grounds in West London.
  The weather promises to be kind this year, after last year's wash-out. Forecasters predict a warm, south-westerly breeze and sun with light cloud.

Amazing Bone Facts!

Some people have more than 206 bones. People who spend most of their time riding horses often develop extra bones in their thighs. Some people have an extra pair of ribs and a few people even have extra fingers and toes!

Listen to this ...

Whatever your problem, we can help

My parents don't let me go out in the evening, although I'm 15 years old. All my friends go to parties and discos, but I have to stay in. What can I do?

Mike, a bored teenager

Exercises

1 Write the verbs in the correct forms.

Example: Rob often _watches_ TV. (watch)

1 We _____ in London. (live)

2 I really _____ this picture of you. (like)

3 That baby _____ every night! (cry)

4 Ann and Mary _____ work at 8.30. (start)

5 Ann _____ home at 4.30. (go)

6 Mary's husband _____ her from work at 5.00. (fetch)

7 Our cat _____ fish for lunch every day. (have)

2 Write the verbs in positive or negative forms.

Examples: We _need_ to explain again. (need) She _doesn't understand._ (not/understand)

1 I _____ to visit Rome again. (want) I really _____ the city. (love)

2 We sometimes _____ the stereo, but it _____ very well. (use) (not/work)

3 Charlie's fat! He _____ any exercise, and he _____ too much! (not/get) (eat)

4 They aren't interested in sport. They _____ football, and they _____ volleyball either. (not/like) (not/enjoy)

5 Roy _____ very often, but Andy _____ swimming every day. (not/swim) (go)

6 I _____ coffee before bed time because it _____ me awake. (not/drink) (keep)

7 Sally _____, so she always _____ to work. (not/drive) (walk)

3 Write the questions for the answers.

Example: (come/from Britain)
● _Do you come from Britain?_
○ Yes, I do. I'm from London.

1 (Tom/drive)
● _____
○ Yes, he does. He's got a blue Nissan.

2 (you/know/Ann Smith)
● _____
○ Yes, I do. She's an old friend.

3 (the TV/work)
● _____
○ No, it doesn't. It's broken.

4 (you/go out/much)
● _____
○ No, we don't. We usually stay at home.

5 (Marie/speak/French)
● _____
○ Yes, she does. She's fluent.

6 (Fred and Mary/live/near here)
● _____
○ Yes, they do. They live in the next road.

4 Change the statements into questions.

Example: I go swimming. (How often)
How often do you go swimming?

1 Tom goes to work. (How)

_____

2 Sally visits her parents. (When)

_____

3 They go on holiday every year. (Where)

_____

4 I get home in the evening. (What time)

_____

5 We always make mistakes. (Why)

_____

6 The children watch TV after school. (How long)

_____

7 The cat has lunch at 1.00. (What)

_____

3 Present simple: *be*

Jim is a really good player.

> Jim is a really good player.

Use the present simple of *be* for any state.

Age:	I'm 22. Carol isn't 10. She's 11.
Description:	Jim *is* tall and dark. How tall *is* Ann?
Height:	She's 1 metre 70. *Is* he as tall as me?
Weight:	Jim *is* 78 kilos. How heavy *is* the parcel?
Feelings:	We're tired, hungry and angry!
Distance:	The town *is* about five kilometres away.
Size:	The room *is* five metres by six.
Price:	How much *are* these shoes, please?
Time:	What time *is* it? What's the time?

Use the present simple of *be* in *there is/there are.*

- ● *Is there* a post office near here?
- ○ Yes, **there's** one in the next street.

Use *Yes/No* questions to check information. Form them like this.
> She *is* clever. → *Is* she clever?
> The students *are* in Room 1. → *Are* the students in Room 1?

You can answer *Yes/No* questions with short answers.

- ● *Is* she clever?   ○ Yes, she *is*.
- ● *Are* the students in Room 1?   ○ No, they **aren't**.

We always use full forms in *Yes* answers, when the verb is the last word.
> Yes, I **am**.   Yes, he *is*.   Yes, they **are**.

We usually use short forms in *No* answers.
> No, she **isn't**.   No, we **aren't**.   (But *No, I'm not.*)

Use *Wh* questions to get more information.

- ● Who *is* she?   ○ Her name *is* Pam Woods.
- ● Where *is* she now?   ○ She's in Room 1.

> Is it a bird?
> Is it a plane?
> No. It's Superman.

LOOKING AFTER YOUR BONES -
your questions answered

Q Is calcium important for strong bones and teeth?

A Yes, it is. Ninety-nine per cent of the calcium in our bodies is found in the skeleton.

Q I'm 75 years old. Am I too old to exercise?

A No, you aren't. No one is too old to exercise. Exercise strengthens our bones and reduces the risk of developing osteoporosis.

There's more choice at

SUPERWAYS

Where there's always a welcome

> What's about three centimetres long, with eyes on stalks, ten legs and purple spots?

> I don't know.

> Neither do I, but there's one crawling up your back.

Exercises

1 Complete the statements and questions.

Examples: *This _is_ my book.*
          Are these your books?

1 *Those _____ your shoes.*
2 *_____ that your teacher?*
3 *The time _____ 10.30.*
4 *_____ I late for the bus? Oh, no!*
5 *_____ they the new students?*
6 *Ann _____ Rosie's best friend.*
7 *_____ you from Japan?*
8 *Dear Sir,*
   My brother and I are writing in reply to your
   advertisement today in the Daily Times. I _____ 20
   years old, and he _____ 19. We _____ both experienced
   drivers.

2 Write the short forms.

Examples: *she is _she's_*
          *we are not _we aren't/we're not_*

1 *I am _____*   5 *I am not _____*
2 *he is _____*   6 *he is not _____*
3 *they are _____*   7 *they are not _____*
4 *you are _____*   8 *you are not _____*

3 Correct the statements.

Example: *Sue is a nurse. (doctor)*
         Sue isn't a nurse. She's a doctor.

1 *I'm 80 kilos. (85)*
   I _____
   _____

2 *Alan is in Berlin. (Paris)*
   Alan _____
   _____

3 *You're 1 metre 75. (1 metre 80)*
   You _____
   _____

4 *They're at home. (school)*
   They _____
   _____

4 Answer the questions. Use short forms.

Examples: ● *Are you from Britain? (Yes)*
          ○ *Yes, I am.*
          ● *Is Sam from LA? (No) (Miami)*
          ○ *No, he isn't. He's from Miami.*

1 ● *Is Sally from London? (Yes)*
   ○ _____

2 ● *Are we on time? (No) (very late)*
   ○ _____

3 ● *Is it 1st May today? (No) (30th April)*
   ○ _____

4 ● *Are there any people on the beach? (Yes)*
   ○ _____

5 ● *Are you 30? (No) (only 28)*
   ○ _____

5 Read. Then write questions and answer them.

Example: *(What/name)*
         ● *What's his name?*
         ○ *Nick.*

Nick is 25. He is a designer at A.B.C. His office is on
the second floor. There are six other people in the same
room. Nick's desk is the one by the window.

1 *(How old)*
   ● _____
   ○ _____

2 *(What/job)*
   ● _____
   ○ _____

3 *(Where/office)*
   ● _____
   ○ _____

4 *(How many people)*
   ● _____
   ○ _____

5 *(Which/desk)*
   ● _____
   ○ _____

4 Present continuous
I'm flying!

Look! I'm flying!

Statements

I	am am not	flying.
He She It	is is not	moving.
We You They	are are not	stopping.

Yes/No questions

Am	I	flying?
Is	he she it	moving?
Are	we you they	stopping?

Wh questions

What is he doing?
Why are we stopping?

Full answers

He is swimming.
We are stopping for lunch.

Short forms: *I am = I'm   he/she/it is = he's, she's, it's*
we/you/they are = we're, you're, they're   I am not = I'm not
he is not = he isn't, he's not   we are not = we aren't, we're not

Form the present continuous with *am, is, are* + main verb + *ing*. (See Unit 21 for information about *be* as a main verb and auxiliary verb.)

> Peter **is flying** to New York now.
> **Are** the boys **stopping** for a rest?

If the main verb ends in *e*, leave it out.

> *move → moving, come → coming, drive → driving*

If the main verb ends in a single consonant after a short vowel, double the consonant.

> *stop → stopping, run → running, swim → swimming*

If the main verb ends in *ie*, change *ie* to *y*.

> *die → dying, lie → lying*

Use the present continuous for things which are happening now.

> *Look! I'm flying!*
> *Listen! Something is moving over there.*

Use the present continuous for temporary states and activities.

> **I'm staying** with friends for a month.
> Paul **is painting** his house this week.

Use the present continuous for future plans.

> Sam **is playing** football tomorrow.
> **Are** you **doing** anything on Saturday?

Some verbs usually take the present simple and not the present continuous. (See Unit 5 for a list of these.)

> *I **know** what to do next.*
> *Susan **doesn't like** cold weather.*
> ***Do** they **understand** English?*

On Saturday Manchester United are playing at Anfield Park.

music on the move
ALL OUT RIOT

After outselling every other rap band in the UK, this Manchester-based band are now recording their second album. Not even taking time out from recording, Raze O'Dwigher spoke to *Buzz* magazine at the studio.

BM: Are you expecting to win the 'UK Rapper of the Year Award' for your next album?

RO'D: Yes, we are the best rappers

NEW SPACE * NEW IMAGES * NEW ARTISTS * NEW SPACE * N

The New Space Gallery

is opening its doors for the first time next week.
For our inaugural exhibition we are showing a group of local West London artists. The artists themselves are presenting their work to the press on Saturday 12 April.

What are you jumping up and down for?

I've just taken my medicine but I forgot to shake the bottle first.

Exercises

1 Write the short forms.

Examples: *She is going.* <u>She's going.</u>
We are not going. <u>We aren't/'re not going.</u>

1 *I am going.* _____

2 *You are not going.* _____

3 *He is not going.* _____

4 *They are going.* _____

5 *It is not going.* _____

2 Write the verbs in positive or negative forms.

Examples: *You <u>'re talking</u> too much. (talk)*
Let's go out. It <u>isn't raining</u> now. (not/rain)

1 *Stop the car. I _____ well. (not/feel)*

2 *Be careful! You _____ too fast. (go)*

3 *It's dark! The lights _____ (not/work)*

4 *The phone _____, but Cathy*
_____ it. (ring) (not/answer)

5 ● *I _____ Tim. Is he here? (look for)*
○ *I'm sorry. He _____ here this week.*
(not/work) He _____ our Paris
office. (visit)

6 ● *Hello. Can I speak to Alice, please?*
○ *I'm afraid not. She _____ a bath at the*
moment. (have)

7 *Paul and Pat _____ television.*
(not/watch). They _____ to some
of their favourite music. (listen)

3 Complete the questions and answers.

Examples: ● *What <u>are you doing?</u> (you/do)*
○ *I <u>'m mending</u> the door. (mend)*

1 ● *What _____*
(the children/do)
○ *_____ in the garden. (they/play)*

2 ● *_____ the film? (you/enjoy)*
○ *Yes, I _____ It's really good.*

3 ● *Why _____ so much? (Bill/train)*
○ *_____ to get into the team. (he/try)*

4 ● *_____ to the party? (Sally/go)*
○ *No, she _____ She's very tired.*

5 ● *How fast _____ (we/fly)*
○ *_____ 700 kph. (we/do)*

6 ● *_____ the car?*
(the boys/wash)
○ *No, they _____ . _____*
the grass. (they/cut)

7 ● *What _____*
(the cat/eat)
○ *_____ fish. (it/eat)*

4 Write these verbs in the correct forms.

choose, cut, get, have, leave, make, plan, write

Example: *She <u>'s having</u> a cup of tea.*

1 *He _____ his tools from the garage.*

2 *The boys _____ a library book.*

3 *_____ a new book,*
Professor?

4 *I _____ to visit Canada next year.*

5 *We _____ in a minute. Give me your*
case.

6 *Why _____ the wood into*
pieces, Dad?

7 *Sarah _____ a cake. (make)*

5 Write these verbs in the correct forms.

build, do, go, start, study, train, work
Two old college friends meet by chance.

Nina: *Hello, Alan! What <u>are</u> you <u>doing</u> here?*

Alan: *Oh, hi! I [1]_____ for my uncle's*
construction company. We [2]_____
some offices here in London. Tell me, [3]_____
you still [4]_____ at college?

Nina: *No, I [5]_____ . I [6]_____ to be*
a banker.

Alan: *And [7]_____ your brother still [8]_____ to*
school?

Nina: *No, he's left school now. He [9]_____*
at college next month.

5 Present simple or present continuous

He usually plays.   Today he's watching.

CROSSCHECK

Present simple	**Present continuous**

Present simple

Use the present simple for regular actions or events.

*Jim usually **plays** for his team.*
*Alan usually **works** in the office.*

regular actions/events

Present continuous

Use the present continuous for something which is happening now.

*Today he's **watching** them on TV.*
*Today he's **working** in the factory.*

now

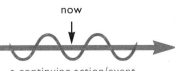

a continuing action/event
happening now

Use the present simple for things which are always true – permanent states.

*Ann **lives** in London.*
*Rome **stands** on the River Tiber.*

Use the present continuous for things which are true around now – temporary states.

*I'm **living** with friends for a few months.*
*They're **standing** at the bus stop.*

Use the present simple for facts about future events.

*The game **starts** at 2.30.*
*When **does** school **start** next term?*

Use the present continuous for future plans.

*We're **playing** again next week.*
*What **are** you **doing** tomorrow?*

Verbs which express permanent feelings, permanent states of mind and the senses are usually in the present/past simple, not the present/past continuous. These are the most common: *appear, believe, belong, detest, forget, hate, hear, know, like, look, love, mean, need, own, prefer, realize, remember, see* (understand), *seem, smell, sound, taste, understand.*

*I **know** the way to town.   Jenny **loves** old American films.*
*What sort of music **do** you **like**?   They **don't understand**.*

We can use a few verbs in the present simple and the present continuous – with a change of meaning. The most common are *think* and *have.*

*I **think** we'll win. (I believe.)*
*I'm **thinking** about the future. (I'm looking at ideas.)*
*Terry **has** three houses. (He owns.)*
*Terry **is having** dinner. (He's eating.)*

You are now entering a Neighbourhood Watch area

RADSTOCK WELCOMES CAREFUL DRIVERS

SHOPLIFTING IS A CRIME
We always prosecute

Being a blood donor

AS YOU READ THIS LEAFLET ..
...a child in hospital is receiving a blood transfusion.
...a girl is learning how to smile again, as she recovers from leukaemia.
...on another ward, an old man is receiving treatment for severe burns.
...they all rely on blood donations from healthy people like you.

entertainment
for everyone

We believe that the Arts should be accessible to all. The Theatre Royal has special facilities for patrons with hearing difficulties and the visually impaired, and we are striving to make the building accessible to all patrons.

'We are all in the gutter, but some of us are looking at the stars.'

(*Lady Windermere's Fan*, Oscar Wilde, 1854-1900)

Exercises

1 Write the verbs in positive, negative or question forms of the present continuous.

Pam is calling her brother, Tom.

Pam: *What __are you doing__ today? (you/do)*
¹_____ out anywhere?
(you/go)

Tom: *No, we aren't. What about you? ²_____*
_____ anything? (you/do)

Pam: *Yes, we are. You know that Marie ³_____*
_____ with me. (stay) Well, I ⁴_____
_____ her to Windsor today. (take)

Tom: *That's very near us.*

Pam: *Yes, so can we visit you after Windsor – if you*
⁵_____ anything? (not/do)

Tom: *Of course you can. We ⁶_____*
anywhere. (not/go) How long ⁷_____
_____ to stay at Windsor? (you/plan)

Pam: *Until about 5.00, I think.*

Tom: *Well, we ⁸_____ a barbecue this*
evening. (have) You're very welcome.

2 Write the verbs in positive, negative or question forms of the present simple.

Examples: *The cat is hungry. It __has__ its food at this*
time every day. (have)

It's full now. It __doesn't want__ any more.
(not/want)

How much __does it eat__ a day? (it/eat)

1 *We've got enough money. We _____ any*
more. (not/need)

2 *Go to bed. You _____ tired. (look)*

3 *How _____ this word? (you/say)*

4 *I hate winter. I _____ the cold. (not/like)*

5 *_____ here?*
(the bus/stop)

6 *Rob's school report is bad. He _____*
any work. (not/do)

7 *What time _____ the office?*
(he/leave)

8 *Jim _____ to work by bike every morning. (go)*

9 *The Jones brothers _____ across the park to school*
every day. (walk)

10 *We can go out or we can stay at home. I _____*
_____ (not/mind)

11 *_____ the way home? (you/know)*

3 Complete the statements and questions.

Examples: *I __don't__ go out much these days.*
What __are__ the boys doing?

1 *Stop! You _____ going the wrong way.*

2 *I _____ understand this problem.*

3 *What _____ Ann doing at the moment?*

4 *_____ Nick and Sally going home soon?*

5 *What time _____ the plane leave?*

6 *How _____ you say this in English?*

7 *He's busy, so he _____ coming to the party.*

8 *I'm sure Tom _____ know the answer.*

9 *_____ the children want dinner?*

10 ● *Why _____ you working today?*
○ *It's a holiday.*

4 Write the verbs in the correct forms.

Mark is a new student in New York. He is writing
home to his parents in London.

Dear Mum and Dad,
How are you all? I __'m__ well and I __'m having__ a
wonderful time. (be) (have) I ¹_____
a lot of new friends and I ²_____
with three of them until I can find my own place to
live. (make) (stay)

Let me tell you what I ³_____ every day here. (do) I
⁴_____ early because classes ⁵_____ at
8.00 in the morning. (get up) (start) Later, I usually
⁶_____ lunch with Rod. (eat) He ⁷_____ the house
where I ⁸_____ at the moment. (own)
(live) He ⁹_____ the same classes as me.
(take)

We often ¹⁰_____ at the gym in the afternoon,
but not today. (train) He ¹¹_____
some work for college, and I ¹²_____
all my letters. (finish) (write)

6 Past simple
I washed them yesterday.

Speech bubble: *I washed your jeans yesterday.*

FORMS

Statements		Yes/No questions		
I	washed it.	Did	I	wash it?
You			you	
He	did not wash it.		he	
She			she	
It			it	
We			we	
They			they	

Wb questions

When did she do it?
What did she do?

Full answers

She did it yesterday.
She washed his jeans.

Short form: *did not = didn't*

Use the past simple for actions which started and finished in the past. Look for past time markers such as *yesterday*.

> *Ann **phoned** us yesterday.   Leo **arrived** home last night.*

In past simple statements the verb usually ends with *ed*.

> *She **washed** his jeans.   He **played** with his friends all morning.*

If the verb ends in *e*, add *d*.

> *We **moved** to our new house a month ago.*

If the verb ends in a *y*, we usually cut *y* and add *ied*. (But not in *say, pay* and *lay*. See Appendix 1 for the past forms of these verbs.)

> *I **hurried** to catch the bus.   She **carried** her baby to bed.*

If the verb ends in a single consonant after a short vowel, double the consonant.

> *We **stopped** work for lunch.   They **fitted** the pieces together.*

A lot of important verbs are irregular, and their past forms do not end in *ed*. You have to learn these one by one. (See Appendix 1 for a list of these.)

> *come → came, go → went, drink → drank, eat → ate*

Positive statements need only a main verb.

> *I **went** to the cinema last night. I **enjoyed** the film.*

Most questions and negatives need the auxiliary verb *did*. (See Unit 21 for information about *do* as a main verb and auxiliary verb.)

> ● *What **did** you **see**? **Did** you **enjoy** it?*
> ○ *I **saw** Robocop 4. I **didn't enjoy** it much.*

Some verbs usually take the past simple and not the past continuous. (See Unit 5 for a list of these.)

> *I **knew** what to do next.   Susan **didn't like** cold weather.*

We can use the form *used to* + verb for something that often happened in the past, but does not happen now.

> *I **used to go** training every day.   I **didn't use to smoke**.*
> *How often **did** Alan **use to go** abroad?*

A team of experts fought yesterday to stop toxic mud polluting one of Europe's most important bird reserves after the waste reservoir dam at a Spanish mine gave way, leaking acidic chemicals into a river.

Environmental organizations said rising tides could send the mud flooding back into the park, and argued that the spill, which took place on Saturday, was a disaster waiting to happen. They demanded the resignation of the Spanish environment minister. She replied, "What did they expect me to do?"

ENGLISH HERITAGE
JIMI HENDRIX
1942 - 1970
Guitarist and Songwriter lived here
1968 - 1969

POLICE NOTICE
Accident
Monday 16 February
Did you see anything?
Phone the police

Ancient Egypt

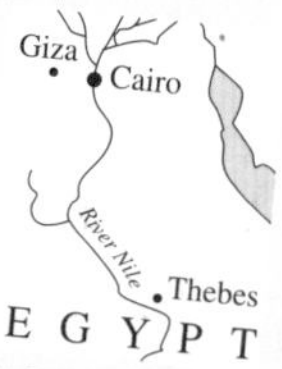

Egyptian civilization developed on the banks of the Nile about 5,000 years ago. It was a single nation and, unlike other civilizations which came before, had a single ruler. Egypt had a strict class system. The lowest class, slaves, didn't have rights and did all the hard, manual work. All the great Egyptian

Map labels: Giza, Cairo, River Nile, Thebes, E G Y P T

THE SIMPSONS, created by cartoonist Matt Groening, first appeared in 1987 as a series of 30-second spots for the FOX series, The Tracey Ullman Show. The response was so positive that THE SIMPSONS had its première on FOX as a half-hour Christmas special in December 1989 and then it began as a regular series in January 1990.

Exercises

1 Write the past forms.

Examples: *clean* <u>cleaned</u> *sell* <u>sold</u>

1 *ask* _____
2 *be* _____
3 *break* _____
4 *call* _____
5 *do* _____
6 *drive* _____
7 *eat* _____
8 *find* _____
9 *go* _____
10 *have* _____

11 *invite* _____
12 *jump* _____
13 *keep* _____
14 *leave* _____
15 *meet* _____
16 *need* _____
17 *open* _____
18 *run* _____
19 *see* _____
20 *wake up* _____

Which verbs are irregular?
Which verbs can be main verbs and auxiliary verbs?

2 Complete the paragraph with verbs from Exercise 1.

This morning, I <u>woke up</u> *late. When I* [1]_____
the time, I [2]_____ *out of bed, and I*
[3]_____ *downstairs. I* [4]_____ *a piece of*
bread, and I [5]_____ *a glass of orange juice. I*
[6]_____ *the house at 8.00, and I* [7]_____
at 100 kph all the way to work!

3 Write statements with positive and negative forms.

Example: *(see/his parents ✓) (see/his sister ✗)*
Sam <u>saw his parents</u> *last night, but he*
<u>didn't see his sister.</u>

1 *(find/my old suit ✓) (find/my new one ✗)*
I _____ *yesterday, but I*
_____

2 *(clean/her red shoes ✓) (clean/her black ones ✗)*
Tina _____ *this*
morning, but she _____
_____

3 *(call/their mother ✓) (call/their sister ✗)*
They _____ *the other*
day, but they _____
_____

4 Write questions and short answers.

Example: *I went to the beach. (Ben) (Yes)*
● <u>Did Ben go to the beach too?</u>
○ <u>Yes, he did.</u>

1 *Andy visited Paris last year. (Tim and Fred) (No)*
● _____
○ _____

2 *Sue ran well in the race. (Ann) (Yes)*
● _____
○ _____

3 *They had a Maths test. (French) (No)*
● _____
○ _____

4 *Peter practised the violin. (piano) (Yes)*
● _____
○ _____

5 Read. Then write questions for the answers. Use these question words.

How, What time, When, Where, Who, Why

Example: ● <u>Where did Susan Hill go?</u>
○ *She went to London.*

Susan Hill went to London last Thursday because she wanted to buy a wedding present for her sister. She went by train and she got there at 10.30. She met an old school friend at the station and they went shopping together.

1 ● _____
○ *She went there last Thursday.*

2 ● _____
○ *She went by train.*

3 ● _____
○ *Because she wanted to buy a wedding present.*

4 ● _____
○ *She got there at 10.30.*

5 ● _____
○ *She met an old school friend.*

6 ● _____
○ *They met at the station.*

7 Past simple: *be*

They were by my bed.

Where were they?

They were by my bed all the time!

Statements			Yes/No questions		
I	was	there.	Was	I	there?
He				he	
She	was not			she	
It				it	
We	were	at home.	Were	we	at home?
You				you	
They	were not			they	

Wh questions

What was that noise?
Where were they?

Full answers

It was an animal.
They were at home.

Short forms: was not = wasn't   were not = weren't

Use the past simple of *be* for any state.

Age: The boys **weren't** 15. They **were** 16.
Description: She **was** beautiful with fair hair.
Height: He **was** only 1 metre 50 when he was 13.
Weight: I **was** 80 kilos last week.   How heavy **was** the parcel?
Feelings: **Were** you sad at the end of the holiday?
Distance: How far **were** they from the sea?
Size: The house **was** about 2,000 square metres.
Price: **Was** that watch expensive?
Time: What time **was** your lesson yesterday?

Use the past simple of *be* in *there was/there were*.
- **Was there** a big match on Saturday?
- Yes, and **there were** thousands of fans at the match.

Use *Yes/No* questions to check information. Form them like this.
    She **was** clever. → **Was** she clever?
    The students **were** in Room 1. → **Were** the students in Room 1?

You can answer *Yes/No* questions with short answers.
- **Was** she clever?   Yes she **was**.
- **Were** the students in Room 1?   No, they **weren't**.

We always use full forms in *Yes* answers, when the verb is the last word.
    Yes, I **was**.   Yes, he **was**.   Yes, they **were**.

We usually use short forms in *No* answers.
    No, she **wasn't**.   No, we **weren't**.

Use *Wh* questions to get more information.
- Who **was** she?   Her name **was** Pam Woods.
- Where **was** she?   She **was** in Room 1.

25

Dinosaurs were reptiles and lived on land. There were hundreds of different types, divided into two main groups. Some dinosaurs, such as Tyrannosaurus (right), were carnivores (meat eaters); others, such as Stegosaurus, were herbivores (plant eaters). Tyrannosaurus Rex was the largest carnivorous dinosaur.

Competition News!
Last week's lucky winner was Margaret
Richards from north London, who won a
fabulous weekend for two in Paris.
The answer to the question was
Marie Antoinette.

UFO SIGHTED

John Male of Fleet, Hampshire, had the shock of his life when he saw a UFO land in his back garden.

'It was really big.' said Mr Male. 'It was bright blue and there were lots of flashing lights.'

He showed our reporter the burn marks on his lawn. 'It was only there for about two minutes,' he recalled. 'Then it took off and vanished.'

Exercises

1 Complete the statements and questions.

Example: ● How old <u>were</u> you in 1989?
○ I <u>was</u> 13.

1 It _____ late, and the children _____ tired.

2 The Johnson brothers _____ at the same college. Rod _____ a medical student, and Harry and Tony _____ law students.

3 We _____ 30 minutes early for the party and there _____ nobody there. The room _____ empty!

4 ● How long _____ you and your wife in Cairo?
○ I _____ there for three years, but she _____ there for only two.

2 Complete the conversation.

Two friends meet after a party.

Jenny: We <u>were</u> sad that you <u>weren't</u> at the party.

Robin: I ¹_____ sorry to miss it too. ²_____ it a good one?

Jenny: Yes, it ³_____ There ⁴_____ a lot of old friends there. Where ⁵_____ you and the family?

Robin: Dad ⁶_____ away on business, and Mum ⁷_____ very well. And my brothers ⁸_____ back from holiday. They ⁹_____ still away.

3 Read. Then write questions and answer them.

Example: (When/they/at the house)
● <u>When were they at the house?</u>
○ <u>Last night.</u>

We saw a lovely house yesterday. We were there last night. It was about 100 years old, and we wanted to buy it immediately. There were four bedrooms upstairs. Downstairs, there was a beautiful dining-room, and the living-room was very big – 12 x 5 metres. The kitchen at the back of the house was large too, and very modern. Outside there was a beautiful garden with a stream. We loved the house! The only problem was the price. It was £200,000!

1 (How old/the house)
● _____
○ _____

2 (How many bedrooms)
● _____
○ _____

3 (How big/the living-room)
● _____
○ _____

4 (Where/the kitchen)
● _____
○ _____

5 (What/outside)
● _____
○ _____

6 (What/the only problem)
● _____
○ _____

7 (How much/the house)
● _____
○ _____

4 Complete the statements.

Example: Maria <u>wasn't</u> good at English at school, but she <u>'s</u> excellent now.

1 Go and see the old city. There _____ thousands of old buildings there. Some of them _____ over 500 years old.

2 Simon _____ at home yesterday, but he _____ there now.

3 We _____ wrong to leave the main road. Now we _____ lost!

4 The children _____ tired after the party, but I _____ nearly asleep.

5 Alan _____ at work yesterday, but he _____ at home today. Here _____ his phone number. You can call him.

21

8 Past continuous

It was raining again.

They looked out of the window. It was raining again.

Form the past continuous with *was, were* + main verb + *ing.* (See Unit 21 for information about *be* as a main verb and auxiliary verb.)

> I **was reading** all last night.   What **were** you **doing** at 2.00?

Remember the spelling rules with *ing.* (See Unit 4.)

> *move → moving, stop → stopping, die → dying*

Use the past continuous for things which were continuing at a certain moment in the past.

> ● *What **were** you **doing** at 12.00?*   ○ *I **was going** home for lunch.*

Use the past continuous for emphasizing that something was continuing for a long time – often something unwanted.

> *The baby **was crying** all night.*

Use the past continuous for things which were continuing (a continuing action) when something else suddenly happened (a short action).

a short past action/event
(past simple)

now

a continuing action/event (past continuous)

When the two actions are in one sentence, use the connectors *when, as* or *while* to join the two sentence parts.

> *Jenny **was reading when** Ann **phoned**.*
> *The truck **hit** my car **as** I **was turning**.*
> *The policeman **arrived while** we **were having** dinner.*

Do not confuse these two different ideas.

> *When Tom **arrived**, we **were having** tea.* (Tea was continuing.)
> *When Tom **arrived**, we **had** tea.* (Tom arrived. Then tea started.)

Some verbs usually take the past simple and not the past continuous. (See Unit 5 for a list of these.)

> *I **knew** what to do next.*   *Susan **didn't like** cold weather.*

Chapter 1
The Nightmare Begins

Sam looked out of the window at the street below. He didn't want to be here but Inspector Caldwell had insisted. Suddenly he heard his name.

'What were you doing at ten o'clock last night, Mr Wright?' Inspector Caldwell was looking at him and waiting for an answer.

'I wasn't doing anything special,' he replied. 'I was at home,' he added lamely.

The inspector looked at him without interest.

'So you were doing nothing – at home.' He paused. 'And what were you doing when your wife phoned you from the Grand Hotel?'

Sam tried to remember that night but he could only think of what had happened later.

'There was a party upstairs,' he began. 'People were dancing all night. I was listening to some music to drown the noise. I couldn't have heard the phone when it rang.' Sam broke off. It sounded as if he was incriminating himself out of his own mouth.

Here is some traffic news at midday. Traffic on the M5 is moving again northbound. Police have cleared the accident which was blocking the northbound side earlier today.

PLEASURE BOAT RESCUE

A pleasure boat from Greatlington Beach sank yesterday in rough seas following a collision with rocks off Steer Point. The boat was carrying 15 passengers. Luckily all those on board including the two crew were recovering last night in hospital after a dramatic rescue by the Greatlington lifeboat.

GAUMONT CINEMA
While you were sleeping
A film with Sandra Bullock

Exercises

1 Write the verbs in the correct forms.

The Carter family all remember what they were doing when the last Californian earthquake happened.

Example: Sally: *I _was cooking_ lunch for John. (cook)*

1 John: *I _____ my boss in New York. (call)*

2 Ron and Sue: *We _____ at the lake with Paul. (swim)*

3 Tom: *I _____ a football game on TV. (watch)*

4 Ann and Carol: *We _____ a Pepsi at the Corner Café. (have)*

5 Flo: *I _____ ready to go out with some friends. (get)*

6 Tim and Bill: *We _____ our bikes in the park. (ride)*

2 Complete the questions and answers.

Examples: ● *_Was_ Sally _cooking_ dinner? (cook)*
○ *No, she _wasn't_. She _was cooking_ lunch.*
● *What _were_ Ann and Carol _doing_? (do)*
○ *They _were having_ a Pepsi at the Corner Café. (have)*

1 ● *Who _____ Ron and Sue _____ with? (swim)*
○ *They _____ with Paul.*
● *_____ at the swimming pool?*
○ *No, they _____ They _____ _____ at the lake.*

2 ● *_____ Tom _____ to the radio? (listen)*
○ *No, he _____ He _____ TV. (watch)*
● *What _____*
○ *He _____ a football game.*

3 ● *Where _____ Tim and Bill _____ their bikes? (ride)*
○ *They _____ their bikes in the park.*

4 ● *Who _____ John _____ (call)*
○ *He _____ his boss.*

3 Write the verbs in the correct forms.

Examples: *I _was making_ lunch when the earthquake _happened_. (make) (happen)*
What _were the children doing_ at this time last week? (the children/do)

1 *What _____ at this time yesterday? (you/do)*

2 *Why _____ along the street at 10.00 last night? (he/run)*

3 *She _____ home when her new car _____ (drive) (break down)*

4 *I _____ the window. (open) The sun _____ (shine)*

5 *They _____ in the garden when the phone _____ (work) (ring)*

6 *The storm _____ the boat as it _____ to reach the harbour. (hit) (try)*

7 *The plane _____ to land when it _____ (try) (crash)*

4 Write the verbs in the correct forms.

When I _went_ out at 9.00 the sun _was shining_. (go) (shine) It [1]_____ a beautiful spring day and the birds in the park [2]_____ (be) (sing) I [3]_____ along the road beside the park when suddenly I [4]_____ my old friend, John. (walk) (notice) He [5]_____ football with his son in the park. (play) I [6]_____ to him and he [7]_____ round in surprise. (call) (look) Then he [8]_____ back and [9]_____ me to join them. (shout) (invite) Soon all of us [10]_____ _____ football together. (play) Then we [11]_____ to get some ice-creams. (stop) While we [12]_____ them, we [13]_____ to go to the lake and hire a boat. (eat) (decide) Then something terrible [14]_____ (happen) Just as I [15]_____ into the boat, it [16]_____ to move away, and I [17]_____ straight into the water between the boat and the shore. (get) (start) (fall) Hundreds of people [18]_____ , and they all [19]_____ (watch) (laugh) I [20]_____ really embarrassed! (feel)

9 Present perfect 1

I've washed the car.

Look, Dad! I've washed the car.

Great! It's really clean now.

Form the present perfect with *have, has* + past participle. With regular verbs the past participle is the same as the past simple form – main verb + *ed*.

> *I've **washed** the car. I've just **finished**.*
> ● ***Has** she **finished** dinner?* ○ *No, she **hasn't**.*

If the verb ends in *e*, add *d*.

> *The train **has arrived**. There it is! Let's run.*

If the verb ends in *y*, change the *y* to *ied*.

> *Mary **has carried** the case for an hour. She's tired.*

These are different.

> *say → said, pay → paid, lay → laid*

If the verb ends in a single consonant after a short vowel, double the consonant.

> *The bus **has stopped**. We can get off now.*

A lot of important verbs are irregular, and their past forms do not end in *ed*. The verbs *be, do* and *have* are all irregular. (See Unit 21 for information about *have* as a main verb and auxiliary verb.)

Infinitive	Past form	Past participle
be	*was/were*	*been*
do	*did*	*done*
have	*had*	*had*

Many common main verbs are irregular too. You have to learn these one by one. (See Appendix 1 for a list of these.)

Infinitive	Past form	Past participle
hit	*hit*	*hit*
make	*made*	*made*
speak	*spoke*	*spoken*
give	*gave*	*given*

The Aliens Have Landed

Starring
Jill Turner and Ralph Lauder

VOICE 1   *(from upstairs)* Have you put the breakfast scraps in the bin, dear?

VOICE 2   *(from downstairs)* Yes, dear.

VOICE 1   Have you fed the budgie, dear?

VOICE 2   Yes, dear.

VOICE 1   Have you made a cup of tea, dear?

VOICE 2   Yes, dear.

VOICE 1   I'm bringing up your cup of tea now, dear.

VOICE 2   Have you put the sugar in?

VOICE 1   Yes, dear. *(whispers)* And the rat poison and the superglue. *(shouts)* I hope you enjoy it, dear.

Beach Car Park

HAVE YOU PAID AND DISPLAYED?

Tickets available from machine

Use the present perfect when something happened in the past, and affects us now.

> *Tom **has cleaned** the car.* (So now it's really clean.)
> *Ann **has broken** her arm.* (So now she can't write.)

Use the present perfect when something started in the past and continues to the present. Look out for the words *yet* and *just*.
yet means 'up to now'.

> ● ***Have** they **repaired** the car **yet**?*
> ○ *No, they **haven't had** time **yet**. They're going to do it tomorrow.*

just means 'only a very short time ago'.

> *The water **has just boiled**. Would you like a cup of tea?*
> *Our new car **has just arrived**. Come and look.*

We sometimes use *yet* and *just* together.

> ● ***Have** you **finished** your homework **yet**?*
> ○ *Not **yet**. I**'ve just finished** question 1, but I **haven't finished** question 2.* (I'm doing it now.)

Use *still ... not* for something that happens late.

> *I started this last week and I **still haven't finished**.*

Use *already* for something that happens early.

> *It's only 8.00 in the morning and they**'ve already done** three hours work.*

We sometimes use *still ... not* and *already* together.

> ● *I suppose Joe **still hasn't started** work!*
> ○ *You're wrong. He**'s already finished**!*

The *'s* short form can mean *is* or *has*, so check the main part of the verb. Study the different meanings.

> *She**'s come** home.* (*'s come* = *has come*)
> *She**'s coming** home.* (*'s coming* = *is coming*)

Exercises

1 Write the past participles.

Example: *buy* <u>bought</u>   *happen* <u>happened</u>
          meet <u>met</u>

1 *ask* _____   11 *keep* _____
2 *be* _____   12 *leave* _____
3 *choose* _____   13 *make* _____
4 *do* _____   14 *need* _____
5 *eat* _____   15 *open* _____
6 *find* _____   16 *put* _____
7 *give* _____   17 *run* _____
8 *have* _____   18 *start* _____
9 *invite* _____   19 *take* _____
10 *join* _____   20 *wake up* _____

Which verbs are irregular?
Which verbs can be main verbs and auxiliary verbs?

2 Complete the paragraph with verbs from Exercise 1 (including the examples).

Dear Mum,

Well, a lot of things have <u>happened</u> *since our move to Australia. Larry has* [1]_____ *a good job at a bank, and we have* [2]_____ *a small house outside town for $70,000. Peter and Sally have* [3]_____ *at their new school, and they're very happy there. Peter has*
[4]_____ *the football team and Sally has* [5]_____ *a lot of good friends in her class. I have* [6]_____ *all the neighbours now, and they have* [7]_____ *very kind. In fact, our next-door neighbour has* [8]_____ *all of us to a barbecue lunch on Sunday.*

3 Write these verbs in the correct forms.

arrive, break, catch, get, paint, win

Example: *Tom* <u>has cleaned</u> *the car. Now it looks like new.*

1 *They* _____ *the TV. It doesn't work.*
2 *The police* _____ *the bank robbers. They're at the police station now.*
3 *Ann* _____ *the room. It's pink now.*
4 *My parents* _____ *Their car is outside.*
5 *Mark* _____ *the race. He's the new champion.*
6 *Dad* _____ *the tickets, so we can go in.*

4 Write statements with positive and negative forms.

Example: *(find/a job ✓) (find/a house ✗)*
          Alan <u>has found a job,</u> *but he* <u>hasn't found a house.</u>

1 *(join/the school drama group ✓) (join/the tennis club ✗)*
Tony _____
_____ *but he* _____
_____

2 *(make/a cake ✓) (make/any sandwiches ✗)*
Julie _____ *but she*
_____

3 *(bring/their books ✓) (bring/their pens ✗)*
The boys _____ *but*
they _____

4 *(choose/the carpets for their new house ✓) (choose/any furniture ✗)*
Ian and Sue _____
_____ *but they*
_____
_____

5 *(wash/the car ✓) (wash/the children's bikes ✗)*
I _____ *but I*
_____
_____

6 *(invite/Alan to the party ✓) (invite Joe ✗)*
We _____
but we _____

5 Write questions and and short answers.

Examples: *Lisa has cleaned her shoes. (boots) (Yes)*
          ● <u>Has she cleaned her boots too?</u>
          ○ <u>Yes, she has.</u>

          Peter has eaten his lunch. (Bill) (No)
          ● <u>Has Bill eaten his lunch too?</u>
          ○ <u>No, he hasn't.</u>

1 *The boys have done their Maths homework.*
(French homework) (No)

● _____
_____

○ _____

2 *Vicky has been busy all day. (Mark) (Yes)*

  ● _____

     _____

  ○ _____

3 *Barry has learnt to fly. (you) (Yes)*

  ● _____

  ○ _____

4 *Petra and I have brought our books. (Sally) (No)*

  ● _____

  ○ _____

6 Re-order the words to make questions.

Example: *(gone/where/girls/have/the)*
      Where have the girls gone?

1 *(lived/Emma/how long/London/has/in)*

   _____

2 *(late/come/you/why/so/have/home)*

   _____

3 *(my/what/you/have/with/shirt/done)*

   _____

4 *(the/has/Andy/where/put/bike)*

   _____

5 *(kilometres/you/how many/today/driven)*

   _____

7 Write the answers. Use *just* or *yet*.

Examples: ● *Is the TV working? (Yes) (mend/it)*
      ○ _Yes, I've just mended it._

      ● *Have you seen your picture in today's newspaper? (No) (buy/one)*
      ○ _No, I haven't bought one yet._

1 ● *Has Ruth moved? (Yes) (go to/Rome)*

   ○ _____

2 ● *Do you know the Smiths? (No) (not/meet/them)*

   ○ _____

3 ● *Does Bob like sweet things? (Yes) (buy/some chocolate)*

   ○ _____

4 ● *Are we going home now? (No) (not/finish/work)*

   ○ _____

5 ● *Have the boys had lunch? (No) (not/come/home)*

   ○ _____

6 ● *Have you got enough petrol? (Yes) (buy/some)*

   ○ _____

7 ● *Have you moved my books? (Yes) (put/them/in your case)*

   ○ _____

8 Write statements. Use *already* or *But . . . still . . . not*.

Examples: *Tom's boots are dirty. (clean/them ✗)*
      But he still hasn't cleaned them.
      Ann works very fast. (do/her Maths ✓)
      She's already done her Maths.

1 *I asked you to talk to Bill yesterday. (call/him ✗)*

   _____

2 *We're planning to go to Spain. (buy/the tickets ✓)*

   _____

3 *I asked you to get ready. (pack/your bag ✗)*

   _____

4 *She's saving for a CD player. (get/£50 ✓)*

   _____

5 *Number 33 is moving fast now. (do/300 kph ✓)*

   _____

6 *I write three weeks ago. (have/a reply ✗)*

   _____

I've lived here for 35 years.   *Have you ever visited Scotland?*

Present perfect + *for/since*

Use the present perfect when something started in the past and it continues to the present. We often use *for* and *since*. *for* shows how long something has continued. *since* shows when something started.

since
(a point in the past)   *for*
                    (a period of time)   now

*Karen **has been** a nurse **for 15 years**. OR **since 1980**.*

Present perfect + number of times

Use the present perfect when things have happened in a period of time that started in the past and continue to the present. We often use *ever* and *never* and time expressions such as *this year, this week, today, since 1960*.

a point in
the past   a period of time   now

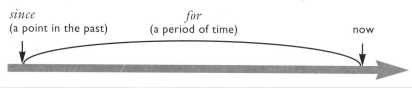

actions/events in a period of time

● ***Have** you **ever been** back to Sydney?* (In the 35-year period.)
○ *Three times.*
● ***Have** you **ever visited** Scotland?*
○ *Yes, I've **been** there many times. OR No, I've **never been** there.*

Study the different meanings of *been* and *gone*.

*He's **been** to India. He went there last year.* (And now he's home again.)
*He's **gone** to India. He's working in Calcutta.* (He's there now.)

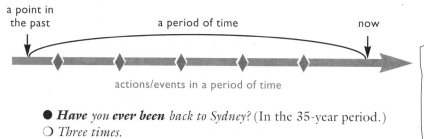

Exercises

1 Write statements.

Examples: *(Charlie/live/there/35 years)*
<u>*Charlie has lived there for 35 years.*</u>

(he/be/there/20 years old)
<u>*He's been there since he was 20*</u>
<u>*years old.*</u>

1 *(this land/belong to/Mr Hill/1950)*

_____
_____

2 *(Sally/have/the same car/five years)*

_____
_____

3 *(we/live/in this house/I was 25)*

_____
_____

2 Complete the questions and answers.

Example: ● *I live in London.*
○ *How long* <u>*have you lived*</u> *there?*
● <u>*Since*</u> *1985.* OR <u>*For*</u> *ten years.*

1 ● *Nick and Sue have a Mercedes.*
○ *How long* _____ *it?*
● _____ *last month.*

2 ● *My brother works for IBM.*
○ *How long* _____ *for them?*
● _____ *three years.*

3 ● *The Carter family want to move house.*
○ *How long* _____ *to do that?*
● _____ *Mr Carter got a job in London.*

4 ● *Nick Ellis lives on a small island.*
○ *How long* _____ *there?*
● _____ *most of his life.*

3 Write negative answers for the questions.

Example: ● *When was the last time you had an*
ice-cream? (ages) OR *(last week)*
○ <u>*I haven't had an ice-cream for*</u>
<u>*ages.*</u> OR <u>*since last week.*</u>

1 ● *When did Tim last see Susan? (three weeks)*
○ _____
_____

2 ● *When did the whole family last meet? (Claire's wedding)*
○ _____
_____

3 ● *When was the last time we had fish for dinner? (months)*
○ _____

4 Write questions. Use *ever* where possible. Then answer the questions.

Examples: *(you/stay/in Miami) (three times)*
● <u>*Have you ever stayed in Miami?*</u>
○ <u>*Yes, I've stayed there three times.*</u>

(How often/he/stay/there) (once)
● <u>*How often has he stayed there?*</u>
○ <u>*He's stayed there once.*</u>

1 *(you/study/English/before) (once)*
● _____
_____
○ _____

2 *(How many times/he/see/Superman) (seven times)*
● _____
_____
○ _____

3 *(they/try/Indian food) (a few times)*
● _____
_____
○ _____

4 *(How often/it/rain/today) (twice)*
● _____
○ _____

5 Complete the questions and answers.

Example: ● *Does Susan like sailing?*
○ *She loves it! She* <u>*'s been*</u> *sailing every*
weekend this year. She <u>*'s gone*</u> *again*
this weekend.

1 ● _____ *you ever* _____ *to Rome?*
○ *No, but my brother* _____ *just* _____ *there*
this week. He's there now.

2 ● *Where's Alan?*
○ *He* _____ *to the bank to get some money.*

3 *Sue* _____ *never* _____ *to China.*

11 Present perfect or past simple

It has opened.   It opened last week.

CROSSCHECK

Present perfect

Use the present perfect when something happened in the past, but you do not know when.

*The new sports shop **has opened**.*

Use the present perfect when something happened in the past, but it affects us now.

*He's **broken** his leg.* (The leg is still broken.)

Use the present perfect when something started in the past and it continues to the present.

*Mary **has lived** in London for seven years.* (And she still lives there now.)

Use the present perfect when something has happened in a period of time up to the present, eg *today, this year.*

*She's **written** three letters today.*
__Have__ you __had__ exams this year?

Use the present perfect to find out if something has happened, not when.

__Has__ Peter __gone__ home yet?

We often start to talk about an event at an unstated time in the past.

● *__Have__ you ever __visited__ Japan?*
○ *Yes, I've **been** there three times.*

Past simple

Use the past simple when something happened completely in the past.

*It **opened** last week.*

Use the past simple when something started and finished in the past and you know when.

*He **broke** his leg last year.* (His leg is OK now.)

Use the past simple when something started and finished in the past.

*Mary **lived** in London for seven years.* (But she doesn't live there now.)

Use the past simple when something happened in a period of past time, eg *yesterday, last year.*

*She **wrote** five letters yesterday.*
__Did__ you __have__ exams last year?

Use the past simple to find out when something happened.

When __did__ Peter __go__ home?

We then fix the details of the event in the past with the past simple.

● *When **were** you last there?*
○ *I **stayed** there last summer.*

Meet the Chef!
Liz Bailey is the main chef at Ludlow's. She started catering when she was 15. She worked at the Three Bridges for a number of years and at the Lakeside Bakery in Bampton. She has worked at Ludlow's since 1993 when the Old Farmhouse restaurant opened.

Star Interview

How many films have you made this year?

Just two. It wasn't a busy year. I made *The Waiting Game* in January. Then I had to wait seven months for Warner to offer me *Starman*.

What have you enjoyed most this week?

It was a very busy week and the best thing was when I stayed in bed the whole of Friday morning.

Dear Mrs Oliver,

It's true - a short time ago your name was entered into the Vauxhall pre-draw which has now taken place. As you have come through the first stage of the draw, I am notifying you now that you could already be the WINNER!

Exercises

1 Write the verbs in positive, negative or question forms of the past simple.

Rob: *You know, last night <u>was</u> terrible. (be) I <u>locked</u> myself out of the house. (lock)*

Lyn: *Oh, no! What [1]_____ (you/do)*

Rob: *I [2]_____ round the house and I [3]_____ for an open window. (go) (look)*

Lyn: *[4]_____ one? (you/find)*

Rob: *There [5]_____ any on the ground floor, but there [6]_____ one upstairs. (not/be) (be)*

Lyn: *It's a pity you [7]_____ us. (not/call) You're always welcome to stay here.*

Rob: *Thanks, but I [8]_____ to give you any trouble. (not/want)*

Lyn: *So what [9]_____ after that? (you/do)*

Rob: *I [10]_____ the police. (phone)*

2 Write the verbs in positive, negative or question forms of the present perfect.

Tina and Bill are getting ready for school.

Example: Mum: *<u>Have you had</u> enough to eat? (you/have)*

Tina: *Thanks, Mum. I <u>'ve eaten</u> lots. (eat)*

Bill: *Well, I <u>haven't</u>. I'm still hungry.*

1 Tina: *Bill, where _____ my coat? (you/put)*

Bill: *I _____ your coat since last week. (not/see)*

2 Mum: *_____ your bag for school, Tina? (you/pack)*

Tina: *Yes, but I _____ my pencil case upstairs. (leave)*

3 Mum: *_____ you your lunch money, Bill? (Dad/give)*

Bill: *No, he _____ Can you give me some?*

4 Dad: *I _____ the car to the front door. (bring) Are you ready to go?*

Bill: *I am, but Tina _____ upstairs for her pencil case. (go)*

3 Write the past forms and past participles.

Examples: *write <u>wrote</u> <u>written</u>*

1 *ask* _____ _____
2 *be* _____ _____
3 *cut* _____ _____
4 *do* _____ _____
5 *find* _____ _____
6 *go* _____ _____
7 *have* _____ _____
8 *invite* _____ _____
9 *join* _____ _____
10 *keep* _____ _____

Which verbs are irregular?
Which verbs can be main verbs and auxiliary verbs?

4 Complete the statements and questions.

Examples: *Helen <u>has</u> never been to Canada.*
<u>Did</u> you spend much money yesterday?

1 *How long _____ Ann been at home?*
2 *I'm sure Peter _____ make a mistake.*
3 *Tom _____ finished work yet.*
4 *_____ anybody see the news at 1.00?*
5 *We _____ found the way, but we're trying.*
6 *_____ anybody seen my sweater?*
7 *When _____ the accident happen?*
8 *How many times _____ you seen that film?*

5 Write the verbs in the correct forms.

Mark is writing home to his parents in London.

6th November

Dear Mum and Dad,

Well, I <u>arrived</u> here in New York on 6th September, so I <u>'ve been</u> here for two months. (arrive) (be) I'm sorry I [1]_____ to you since last month, but life [2]_____ very busy. (not/write) (be) Classes [3]_____ and I [4]_____ a lot of things to do. (begin) (have) I [5]_____ you about Rod in my last letter. (tell) He [6]_____ me stay at his place since I first [7]_____ here. (let) (get) But, at last I [8]_____ a place of my own. (find) I [9]_____ the agreement with the owner last night, and he [10]_____ me a key. (sign) (give)

12 Present perfect continuous
I've been waiting for an hour.

FORMS

Statements			Yes/No questions		
I	have	been waiting.	Have	I	been waiting?
You				you	
We	have not			we	
They				they	
He	has	been playing.	Has	he	been playing?
She				she	
It	has not			it	

Wh questions

What have you been doing?
How long has he been waiting?

Full answers

I have been watching TV.
He has been waiting for an hour.

Short forms: I/you/we/they have = I've, you've, we've, they've
he/she/it has = he's, she's, it's   have not = haven't   has not = hasn't

We often use the present perfect continuous instead of the present perfect. We use it to emphasize that something has continued for a long time.

> *I've been waiting for an hour!*
> *Tom has been building that boat since 1985. Will he ever finish?*
> *How long have you been learning English?*

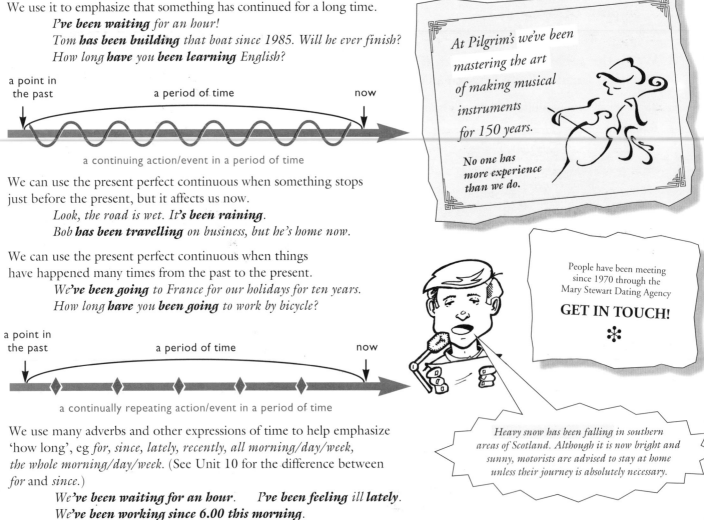

a point in the past — a period of time — now

a continuing action/event in a period of time

At Pilgrim's we've been mastering the art of making musical instruments for 150 years.

No one has more experience than we do.

We can use the present perfect continuous when something stops just before the present, but it affects us now.

> *Look, the road is wet. It's been raining.*
> *Bob has been travelling on business, but he's home now.*

We can use the present perfect continuous when things have happened many times from the past to the present.

> *We've been going to France for our holidays for ten years.*
> *How long have you been going to work by bicycle?*

a point in the past — a period of time — now

a continually repeating action/event in a period of time

People have been meeting since 1970 through the Mary Stewart Dating Agency

GET IN TOUCH!
✳

We use many adverbs and other expressions of time to help emphasize 'how long', eg *for, since, lately, recently, all morning/day/week, the whole morning/day/week*. (See Unit 10 for the difference between *for* and *since*.)

> *We've been waiting for an hour*.   *I've been feeling ill lately*.
> *We've been working since 6.00 this morning*.

Heavy snow has been falling in southern areas of Scotland. Although it is now bright and sunny, motorists are advised to stay at home unless their journey is absolutely necessary.

Exercises

1 Complete the answers.

Example: ● *Why are you so tired?*

○ *I 've been studying all night. (study)*

1 ● *Hello! Where have you been recently?*

○ *I _____ in London. (work)*

2 ● *Why are the children so dirty?*

○ *They _____ in the garden. (play)*

3 ● *I can't find my Walkman. Where is it?*

○ *John _____ it upstairs. (use)*

4 ● *Why haven't you washed the car yet?*

○ *I _____ jobs for Mum. (do)*

5 ● *Maria speaks very good English.*

○ *Yes. She _____ very hard. (study)*

2 Complete the answers.

Example: ● *Have the children been helping Mum?*

○ *No, they haven't been helping her. They 've been watching TV. (watch)*

1 ● *Has Tony been spending all his money?*

○ *No, he _____ it.*

He _____ it. (save)

2 ● *Have we been going the wrong way?*

○ *No, we _____ the wrong way. We _____ the right way. (go)*

3 ● *Has Ann been doing her homework?*

○ *No, she _____ that. She _____ to her new CD. (listen)*

3 Complete the questions.

Examples: You meet an old friend who is now at college.

● *How have you been getting on at college? (you/get on)*

You ask about your friend's brother. He's recently started at a new school.

● *Has your brother been enjoying his new school? (your brother/enjoy)*

1 You meet a friend. You haven't seen her for a month.

● *What _____ recently? (you/do)*

2 You ask Tom's sister about him. He's been studying Spanish in Spain.

● *How _____ in Spain? (he/get on)*

3 You want to know about Tom's studies.

● *_____ a lot of Spanish? (he/learn)*

4 Your small brother's hands and mouth are dirty.

● *_____ chocolate? (you/eat)*

5 Someone tells you about some friends. They're working in London.

● *How long _____ there? (they/work)*

4 Write questions and answer them.

Examples: Joe is travelling round the world. He left at the end of last year OR six months ago.

● *What has Joe been doing recently?*

○ *He's been travelling round the world.*

● *How long has he been doing that?*

○ *Since the end of last year. OR For six months.*

1 Pam is looking for a new job. She started last month

● *What _____ recently?*

○ *_____*

_____

● *How long _____ that?*

○ *_____*

2 Nick and Andy are training for the London Marathon. They began three months ago.

● *What _____ recently?*

○ *_____*

_____

● *How long _____ that?*

○ *_____*

13 Past perfect and past simple

When they arrived the film had started.

When they arrived the film had started.

Form the past perfect with *had* + past participle.
> The film **had started** before we arrived.
> **Had** it **begun** before you arrived?

Use the past perfect for a past event before another past event. Use it to show the time connection between two events.

| 1st past action/event (past perfect) | 2nd past action/event (past simple) | now |

> At the airport I couldn't find my passport. **I'd left** it at home.
> The rain **had** just **stopped**, so we decided to go out for a walk.
> I got to the party at 8.00. My friends **had** already **gone**.

The past perfect shows the end of one past event before the start of another past event. We can talk about these two events in one sentence. Use these words to connect the two sentence parts: *when, after, before, once, until, as soon as*.
> **When** the last person **had** finally **come**, the meeting started.
> Susan cried for ages **after** her brother **had gone**.
> We went out **as soon as** the rain **had stopped**.

Do not over-use the past perfect. Use the past simple for two events that happen quickly after one another.
> I **saw** Peter and I **said** hello.
> When I **got** home, I **sat** down and **turned on** the TV.

Note the difference in meaning between the following.
> When the Director **arrived**, the meeting **started**.
> (First the Director arrived and then the meeting started.)
> When the Director **arrived**, the meeting **had started**.
> (First the meeting started and then the Director arrived.)

DRIVER WAS BLIND AND DRUNK

Police called to breath test a suspected drunk driver were astonished to find he was registered blind. Roger Bolton, 40, could not see the end of his bonnet, but had managed to drive two miles before crashing into a parked car. Magistrates at Exeter heard that Bolton's sight had worsened until he was registered blind in March. He had been at the pub with his girlfriend, who normally drove, but this time she had had several drinks too. Magistrates imposed an immediate driving ban on him.

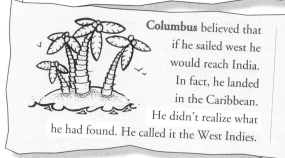

Columbus believed that if he sailed west he would reach India. In fact, he landed in the Caribbean. He didn't realize what he had found. He called it the West Indies.

'Welcome to my house! Enter freely and of your own will!'

He did not step forward to meet me, but stood like a statue, as though his welcoming words had fixed him in stone. The instant, however, that I had stepped over the threshold, he moved impulsively forward. Holding out his hand, he grasped mine with a strength which made me wince and with a hand as cold as ice – more like the hand of a dead man than a living one.

'Count Dracula?' I asked.

(*Dracula*, Bram Stoker, 1847–1912)

Exercises

1 Write the verbs in the correct forms.

Example: *It was a strange house. Nobody <u>had lived</u> there for years. (live)*

1 *The town was empty. Everyone _____ (go)*

2 *The car wasn't there. A thief _____ it. (take)*

3 *The biscuit tin was empty. Tim _____ them all. (eat)*

4 *I didn't recognize old Mr Jarvis. He _____ a lot. (change)*

5 *We decided to buy a sofa which we _____ the weekend before. (see)*

6 *We went back to the shop to get the sofa, but somebody else _____ it. (buy)*

7 *I wanted to speak to Mr Jones, so I phoned his office. Unfortunately he _____ five minutes before. (leave)*

8 *Bob was late for football practice and they _____ without him. (start)*

2 Write the verbs in the correct forms.

Example: *We <u>'d only been</u> at home for a few minutes when the phone rang. (only/be)*

1 *I invited Pat, but she _____ to go out. (already/arrange)*

2 *They were amazed. They _____ such a beautiful place. (never/see)*

3 *Celia _____ dinner when the police called. (just/start)*

4 *Mrs Spear was worried. She _____ _____ her son's accident. (recently/hear about)*

5 *I phoned the garage, but they _____ _____ my car. (still/not/repair)*

6 *Tony wanted to buy a bike with the money, but Tina _____ it. (already/spent)*

7 *The Grant family _____ their house for a year when it burned down. (only/have)*

3 Write the verbs in the correct forms.

Example: *Alan <u>had lost</u> his key, so he <u>broke</u> a window to get in. (lose) (break)*

1 *I _____ at the party at 8.00, but my friends _____ (arrive) (go)*

2 *The horses _____ before we _____ the gate. (get away) (close)*

3 *Once we _____ the river, we _____ to move faster. (cross) (be able)*

4 *The manager _____ us all there until we _____ everything possible. (leave) (do)*

5 *They _____ because they _____ food and water. (turn back) (run out of)*

4 Join each pair of statements to make one statement. Use *when*.

Example: *We went out. We had breakfast.*
We <u>went out when</u> we <u>'d had</u> breakfast.

1 *We drove out of town. We loaded the jeep.*
_____
_____

2 *We stopped for a rest. We drove into the hills.*
_____
_____

3 *We started again. We had a good rest.*
_____
_____

4 *We stopped for the night. We were on the road for ten hours.*
_____
_____

5 *We started to cook dinner. We unpacked the jeep.*
_____
_____

6 *We went to sleep. We finished dinner.*
_____
_____

14 Future with *going to*

We're going to drive.

We're going to drive across Australia.

Use *going to* to explain future plans.
- ● *What **are** you **going to do** on Saturday?*
- ○ *I'**m going to visit** my grandparents.*

Use *going to* to talk about a decision to do something in the very near future.
> *I'm just **going to make** some salad. Then we can have dinner.*
- ● *Dad, can you help me with my homework?*
- ○ *Sure, I'**m** just **going to watch** the news. I'll help you when it's finished.*

Use *going to* when it is clear that something must happen soon.
> *Look at the clouds. It'**s going to rain**.*
> *Listen to the car! It'**s going to break down**!*

Use *going to* with *go*, just like any other verb.
> *We'**re going to go** to the cinema.*

CROSSCHECK

Present continuous

We often use the present continuous to talk about future arrangements.
- ● *Are* you *doing* anything tomorrow?
- ○ *Yes, I'**m seeing** Sally. We'**re meeting** at 3.00.*

going to

When we use *going to*, the arrangements sound more carefully planned.
- ● *What **are** you **going to do**?*
- ○ *First we'**re going to take** a trip on the river. Then we'**re going to see** a film.*

Virgo

With the planet Jupiter in your house, this is going to be a very exciting year for Virgoans. Your practical, down-to-earth nature is going to help you deal with the many changes that await anyone born under this sign.

At a press conference held by the lottery organizers, winner Peter Morgan, an unemployed miner with four children, sprayed reporters with champagne. 'It's going to be a great Christmas!' he told them. Mr Morgan, aged 39, who netted £2.3 million, went on to say, 'It's going to change my life!'

I'm looking forward to running in next Sunday's marathon. Apparently it's going to be the biggest race ever, with more than 32,000 runners! I'm wearing number 9345, so watch out for me on television. The weather forecast says the sun is going to shine all day – oh dear!

Exercises

1 Complete the answers.

Example: ● *Have you had dinner yet? (later)*
○ *No, not yet. I 'm going to have it later.*

1 ● *Have you washed the car yet? (after lunch)*
○ *No, not yet. I* _____
_____

2 ● *Has Tessa cleaned her shoes yet? (now)*
○ *No, not yet. She* _____
_____

3 ● *Have the boys mended their bikes yet? (this evening)*
○ *No, not yet. They* _____
_____

4 ● *Has the cat had its food yet? (in a minute)*
○ *No, not yet. It* _____
_____

2 Write the verbs in positive or negative forms.

Example: Your local football team are in the cup final, but they're playing badly.
● *They 're going to lose. (lose)*
○ *They aren't going to win. (not/win)*

1 You're in the hills. There are black clouds.
● *It* _____ *(rain)*
○ *We* _____ *very wet. (get)*

2 Alan should be on his way to the airport to catch a plane, but he's still in bed.
● *He* _____ *there in time. (not/get)*
○ *He* _____ *his plane. (miss)*

3 Your car is very low on petrol, and you're still a long way from the petrol station.
● *We* _____ *petrol. (run out of)*
○ *We* _____ *the petrol station in time. (not/reach)*

4 Your friend is in a marathon race. He's very tired, but he's very near the end of the race.
● *He* _____ *now. (not/give up)*
○ *He* _____ *for sure. (finish)*

3 Write questions and short answers.

Example: *(we/be/late) (No)*
● *Are we going to be late?*
○ *No, we aren't.*

1 *(Sam/pass/his exams) (Yes)*
● _____
_____
○ _____

2 *(your parents/take/you out) (No)*
● _____
_____
○ _____

3 *(you/watch/TV this evening) (Yes)*
● _____
_____
○ _____

4 *(Sally/buy/a newspaper) (No)*
● _____
_____
○ _____

4 Write questions.

Example: ● *I'm planning to go on holiday.*
○ *(Where/you/go)*
Where are you going to go?

1 ● *Ann has bought some lovely flowers.*
○ *(Where/she/put them)*
_____

2 ● *The Smith family have sold their house.*
○ *(When/they/move out)*
_____

3 ● *I'm making some cakes for the party.*
○ *(How many/you/do)*
_____
_____

4 ● *Bill is planning to go to the cinema.*
○ *(What/he/see)*
_____

15 Future with *will*

People will live in space.

Use *will* to express future facts.

> Sam **will be** 20 next month.   The new road **will be** eight lanes wide.

Use *will* to predict something in the future – something that you know or believe will happen.

> One day soon people **will live** in space.
> Don't worry! I'm sure you**'ll pass** your exams.

Use *will* to say what you decide to do at the time of speaking.

> I've left the window open. I**'ll go back** and **close** it.

Use *will* to offer, promise or threaten to do something.

> That looks heavy. I**'ll help** you.   I promise I **won't be** late.

Use *will* to ask somebody to do something and to agree or refuse to do it.

> ● **Will** you **post** this card for me?   ○ Yes, I**'ll post** it on my way home.

We use *will* to predict the future, so we often use it with words such as *sure, certain, probably, definitely* and *certainly*. Note that the *ly* words change position in *will* and *won't* sentences.

> He**'ll definitely love** Rome. He **probably won't want** to come home.

Do not use *will* to express plans and arrangements.

> I can't see you tomorrow as I**'m visiting/going to visit** my parents. (not *will visit*)

will often goes with verbs like *expect, think* and *know*.

> I **expect** I**'ll be** late home tonight.
> I **don't think** he**'ll agree** to the idea.

We sometimes use *shall/shall not (shan't)* instead of *will/will not*, but only with *I* or *we*. We usually use it for suggestions, offers and asking for instructions or suggestions.

> You look terrible! **Shall** we **call** a doctor?
> I've finished this job. What **shall** I **do** next?

New Relationships

Dr Arthur Brookes

This book will definitely change your life

Exercises

1 Write the verbs in positive or negative forms.

Examples: The film _will start_ at 8.00. (start)

It _won't finish_ until 11.00. (not/finish)

1 I've hidden the presents, so the children

_____ them. (not/find)

2 The bridge _____ the river here. (cross)

3 The road _____ until next year. (not/open)

4 Ask the boys. They _____ the job for you. (do)

5 Paul _____ 20 until next year. (not/be)

2 Complete the offers and promises with positive or negative forms of these verbs.

be, buy, close, forget, look after, lose, make, wash

Example: ● Please look after my jewellery.

○ Don't worry. I _'ll look after_ it. OR

○ Don't worry. I _won't lose_ it.

1 ● We haven't got any milk.

○ All right. I _____ some at the shop.

2 ● Be sure to get there on time.

○ Don't worry. I _____ late.

3 ● The car is very dirty.

○ OK. I _____ it.

4 ● Look, the windows are open.

○ All right. I _____ them.

5 ● Try to get everything right this time.

○ No problem. I _____ any mistakes.

6 ● Remember to take this letter and post it.

○ Don't worry. I _____ it.

3 Complete the answers with these verbs. Use the correct pronouns.

be, carry, cut, get, give, phone

Example: ● Please give your parents a call.

○ Yes, _I'll phone_ them now.

1 ● Is Simon at work now?

○ No, not yet. _____ to the office at 9.00.

2 ● I'm thirsty.

○ Ask Sue. _____ you a Pepsi.

3 ● This case is very heavy.

○ Give it to me. _____ it for you.

4 ● Dad's very late.

○ Don't worry. _____ home soon.

5 ● We need some wood for the fire.

○ OK. _____ some pieces now.

4 Write questions and short answers.

Example: (Joe/win/the competition) (No)

● _Will Joe win the competition?_

○ _No, he won't._

1 (Ann/be/ten next week) (Yes)

● _____

○ _____

2 (the boys/like/their new school) (No)

● _____

○ _____

3 (Mr Hall/arrive/tonight) (Yes)

● _____

○ _____

4 (next term/start/on 15th April) (No)

● _____

○ _____

5 Write the verbs in the correct forms.

Luke and his friends are planning a class river trip.

Luke: Here's my idea. We _'ll take_ some boats and go up the river. (take)

Andy: OK, but how much _will it cost?_ (it/cost)

Luke: I don't know. I [1]_____ the boat company and ask. (phone) But I'm sure it [2]_____ too expensive. (not/be)

Andy: [3]_____ to go? (everybody/want)

Luke: Yes, I'm sure they [4]_____

Tony: What [5]_____ to take? (we/need)

Luke: We [6]_____ take a picnic. (have to)

Andy: [7]_____ raincoats? (we/need)

Luke: No, we [8]_____ Don't worry. The TV weatherman says we [9]_____ a lovely day tomorrow, and he promises it [10]_____ (have) (not/rain)

39

16 Future continuous

I'll be swimming.

Just think! At this time tomorrow, I'll be swimming in the Indian Ocean.

Use the future continuous to say that something will be continuing at a certain point in the future.

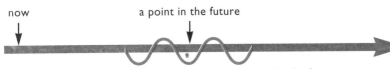

a continuing action/event happening at a point in the future

- What **will** you **be doing** in five years?
- ○ **I'll be travelling** round the world.

Use the future continuous to show that something will continue for a long time.

> There's so much to do! We**'ll be working** all day.
> We're having a party tomorrow evening, so we**'ll be cooking** all afternoon.

These uses of the future continuous are similar to uses of other continuous tenses. Compare the following.

> It's 9.00 now. Harry **is watching** TV.
> At 9.00 yesterday he **was watching** TV too.
> At 9.00 tomorrow he**'ll be watching** TV again.

Use the future continuous to talk about something that is already arranged.

- Will you be free after school?
- ○ No, **I'll be playing** basketball then.

This use is like the present continuous for future arrangements and *going to* for expressing plans.

I'll be calling	at the supermarket on my way home.
I'm calling	Can I get you anything?
I'm going to call	

8.00-10.15 Olympic Special

This live action Olympic coverage will include the final of the 100 metres. At 9.15 this evening, everyone in Britain will be sitting on the edge of their seats hoping that we can once again win Olympic gold.

MEMO

To: *All Staff*
From: *The Management*
Date: *15/11*

Staff are reminded that they will be working a full day on Christmas Eve. Anyone wishing to do Christmas shopping should arrange for an afternoon off during the coming week.

Dear Tony

Sorry I can't come to your wedding on the 16th, but I'll be flying out to South Africa next Saturday to cover the elections there.

Good luck to you both. I look forward to seeing you and Sarah when I get back.

Love, George

Exercises

1 Read. Then answer the question. Use these verbs.

do, have, learn, study

John's timetable

9.00	9.45	10.30	11.15	12.00	12.45
Science	Art	French	Maths	English	Lunch

What will John be doing at these times?
9.30, 10.00, 10.45, 11.20, 12.20, 1.05

Example: *At 9.30 he'll be having Science.*

1 _____

2 _____

3 _____

4 _____

5 _____

2 Read Jack's and Lisa's diary pages for next week. Then complete the conversation.

	Jack Hill	**Lisa Bell**
Mon. 1	Morning – Talk to customers from Japan.	Afternoon – Meet the Sales Manager.
Tues. 2	Morning – Visit the factory.	Afternoon – Have meetings with the sales team.
Wed. 3	Show visitors round London all day.	–
Thur. 4	–	Spend the day in Paris.
Fri. 5	–	–

Company directors Jack and Lisa need to have a meeting next week, but when?

Lisa: *Can we meet on Monday morning?*

Jack: *No, sorry. I 'll be talking to customers from Japan. Are you free on Monday afternoon?*

Lisa: *I'm afraid not. I ¹_____ _____ Are you free on Tuesday morning?*

Jack: *No, I'm afraid not. I ²_____ _____ Can we meet on Tuesday afternoon?*

Lisa: *No, sorry. I ³_____ _____ Are you free on Wednesday?*

Jack: *No, sorry. I ⁴_____ _____ Are you free on Thursday?*

Lisa: *I'm afraid not. I ⁵_____ _____ Can we we meet on Friday?*

Jack: *Yes, I'm free then.*

3 Read. Then write questions and answer them.

Roger Barnes is a traveller. On his next trip he will be travelling round the world by bicycle. He will be flying to Florida next Monday. Then he will be riding across America on his bike for the next two months. He will be arriving in California in ten weeks. From there he will be going up the west coast to Alaska. Then he will be crossing to Asia by ship.

Example: *(How/he/travel/round/the world)*
● *How will he be travelling round the world?*
○ *By bike.*

1 *(When/he/fly/Florida)*
● _____
○ _____

2 *(How long/he/ride/across America)*
● _____
○ _____

3 *(Where/he/arrive/in ten weeks)*
● _____
○ _____

4 *(Where/he/go/from there)*
● _____
○ _____

17 Future perfect
We'll have done it by 4.00.

I need it at 4.00 tomorrow. Will it be ready?

Oh, yes. We'll have done it by then.

24-HOUR DRY CLEANING SERVICE

Form the future perfect with *will* + *have* + past participle.
> We**'ll have cleaned** it by 4.00.
> We**'ll have done** it before closing time.

Use the future perfect to say that something will happen *before* or *by* a future time. In the negative we often use *not ... until/till*.

```
                 an action/event before
                 a point in the future
  now                                      a point in the future
   ↓                                              ↓
  ──────────────────◆──────────────────────────────────────►
```

> The new manager **will have started** work **before/by** 1st May.
> The new manager **won't have met** all the staff **before/by** 1st May.
> The new manager **won't have met** all the staff **until/till** 30th May.

Do not use *until/till* after a positive future perfect form. Use *before* or *by*.

Yes/No questions are unusual in the future perfect. *Wh* questions in the future perfect are very unusual.
- ● We need to arrange a meeting for tomorrow afternoon. **Will you have had** your lunch by 1.30?
- ○ Yes, I **will**.
- ● Good. Let's have the meeting then.

We often use the future continuous to say that something will be happening at a certain time in the future. We use the future perfect to say that something will happen before a certain time in the future. Compare the following.
> I**'ll be doing** the work at midday.
> I**'ll have done** the work by 1.00.

TIME FOR A CHANGE
From our Sports Editor

When England play in the World Cup in Australia in six months' time, Andy McNee will have been manager of the England team for exactly four years. Whatever the outcome of the championship, many believe it is time for him to move on.

Intermediate Swimming Courses
CHALLENGE AWARDS

Bronze challenge

By the end of the course, you will have learned how to:

1. jump into the deep end.
2. swim 10 metres, surface dive and swim underwater for 5 metres.
3. tread water in a vertical position for 3 minutes.

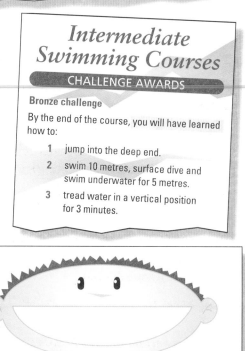

By the time they are five years old, nearly half the children in the UK will have had some dental treatment.

Try to think of alternatives to sweets as presents and treats!

Exercises

1 Read. Then write statements.

Tessa Black is 16. She wants to be a famous writer. These are her ambitions.

By the age of:

18 – sell some short stories
20 – write a book of short stories
25 – produce a play in London
30 – publish a best-seller novel
35 – win an important international prize
40 – make a lot of money

Example: *By the age of 18, she hopes she* <u>*'ll have sold*</u> <u>*some short stories.*</u>

1 *By the age of 20, she hopes she* _____

   _____

2 *By the age of 25, she hopes she* _____

   _____

3 *By the age of 30, she hopes she* _____

   _____

4 *By the age of 35, she hopes she* _____

   _____

5 *By the age of 40, she hopes she* _____

   _____

2 Write the verbs in positive or negative forms.

Example: ● *Could you record the 9.00 news?*
   ○ *All right. I* <u>*'ll have mended*</u> *the video by then. (mend)* OR
   ○ *I'm sorry. I* <u>*won't have mended*</u> *the video by then. (not/mended)*

1 ● *Could I have the report by 5.00, please?*
   ○ *I'm afraid I* _____ *it by then. (not/finish)*

2 ● *Let's buy the red sofa which we saw.*
   ○ *The shop* _____ *it by the time we get there. (sell) It was very cheap.*

3 ● *Ask everyone to come here at 6.00.*
   ○ *I'm sorry, but they* _____ *by 6.00. (go)*

4 ● *Will she know the results by the 15th?*
   ○ *Yes, she* _____ *them before then. (get)*

5 ● *Will Alex bring a present to the party?*
   ○ *No, he* _____ *time to get one. (not/have)*

3 Read. Then complete the questions and answer them.

This is a schedule for building a house.

	Schedule
Finish putting up the walls	10/6
Finish putting on the roof	20/6
Finish putting in the windows	12/7
Finish fitting the doors	29/7
Finish doing the wiring	6/8
Finish laying the floors	18/8
Finish plastering the walls	10/9
Finish painting the house	25/9

Example: ● <u>*What will they have finished*</u> *by 15/6?*
   ○ <u>*They'll have put up the walls, but*</u> <u>*they won't have put on the roof.*</u>

1 ● _____
   by 15/7?
   ○ _____
   _____
   _____

2 ● _____
   by 15/8?
   ○ _____
   _____
   _____

3 ● _____
   by 15/9?
   ○ _____
   _____
   _____

18 Future review

I'll be 18 next week.   I'm going to have a party.

I'll be 18 next Sunday, so I'm going to have a party. Please come, everyone!

CROSSCHECK

will

Use *will* to express things that you know or believe will happen.
> *Susan **will be** 18 next Sunday.*

Use *will* to say what you decide to do at the time of speaking.
> *I know! I'll **have** a party!*

Use *will* to offer, promise or threaten. Use *will* to request or refuse to do it.
> ● *I'll **pay** you £100 to do the job.*
> ○ *All right. I'll **do** it tonight.*

going to

Use *going to* when it is clear that something must happen soon.
> *That's a big shopping list. It's **going to be** an expensive party!*

Use *going to* when you explain future plans.
> *I'm **going to make** a huge cake.*

Present simple

Use the present simple for facts about future events and times.
> *The party **starts** at 6.00.*
> *Susan's school **finishes** next Thursday.*
> *When **does** school **start** next term?*

will

Use *will* to express a complete action in the future.
> *The party **will start** at 6.00.*

Future perfect

Use the future perfect for an action that will be complete before a certain point in the future.
> *Don't worry! The party **will have finished** long before midnight.*

Present continuous

Use the present continuous for future plans.
> *She's **having** a big cake.*
> *Susan **is having** a party next Sunday.*
> *All her friends **are coming** to the party.*

Future continuous

Use the future continuous for something continuing in the future.
> *They'll **be dancing** for hours.*

Future continuous

Use the future continuous for something continuing at a certain point in the future.
> *At lunchtime next day they'll still **be cleaning up** after the party!*

Exercises

1 Write the verbs in future forms. Use *going to* or *will*.

Example: ● *We 're going to run out of milk soon. (run out of)*
○ *I 'm going to get a newspaper, so I 'll buy some milk too. (get) (buy)*

1 ● *Slow down! We _____ (crash)*
○ *Don't worry. We _____ all right. (be) I promise.*

2 ● *_____ out this evening? (we/eat)*
○ *Yes, we _____ to the Café de Paris. (go)*

3 ● *What would you like – tea or coffee?*
○ *I _____ some coffee, please. (have)*

4 ● *The phone is ringing. _____ it, please? (you/answer)*
○ *Yes. It _____ Harry. (probably/be)*

5 ● *You _____ 18 soon, so _____ _____ school? (be) (you/leave)*
○ *Yes, I _____ engineering at college. (study)*

6 ● *What time _____ ? (the meeting/start)*
○ *At 6.00 exactly, so be there on time.*
● *I _____ late. (not/be) I promise.*

2 Write the verbs in present tense forms for future meanings.

Examples: *The Stone family are going to Cyprus for their holidays. (go)*
Their train leaves at 18.15. (leave)

1 *They _____ a train to the airport. (take)*

2 *It _____ the airport at 19.45. (reach)*

3 *They _____ with KLM. (fly)*

4 *The plane _____ at 21.30. (take off)*

5 *It _____ in Cyprus at 00.30. (arrive)*

6 *The family _____ in a villa near the beach. (stay)*

3 Write the verbs in future forms. Use *will* or the future continuous.

Example: ● *Will you be at home at 5.00? (you/be)*
○ *No, I won't. I 'll be playing tennis then. (play)*

1 ● *At this time tomorrow, I _____ to Australia. (fly) What _____ _____ ? (you/do)*
○ *I _____ here, as usual. (work)*

2 ● *Do you think she _____ her exams? (pass)*
○ *I don't know. She certainly _____ very well if she doesn't work harder. (not/do)*

3 ● *What time _____ home from college? (Sam/be)*
○ *At lunchtime. I expect you and Sam _____ _____ a lot to talk about. (have)*
● *Yes, I expect we _____ all afternoon. (talk)*

4 ● *Hurry up, or we _____ here all day. (wait)*
○ *Don't worry. I _____ everything ready in five minutes. (have)*

4 Write the verbs in future forms. Use the future perfect or future continuous.

Example: *By this time next week, I 'll have left London, and I 'll be travelling to Africa. (leave) (travel)*

1 *By the time they finish the new offices, 2,000 builders _____ 30 million bricks. (lay)*

2 *In two months from now, 1,000 people _____ _____ in the new offices. (work)*

3 *Don't worry. Your washing machine _____ _____ again in a minute. (work)*

4 *I _____ my exams in June. (take)*

5 *By this time next year, I _____ school, and I _____ as a pilot. (leave) (train)*

6 ● *Could you come soon after 5.00? The others _____ _____ between 5.00 and 5.30. (arrive)*
○ *I'm sorry, but I _____ work by then. (not/finish)*

have and *have got*

He has a huge pack.   *He's got a huge pack.*   *He's having a rest.*

He's got a huge pack.
He's having a rest.

FORMS

***have* and *have got* for possession**

	have			*have got*	
Present					
I	*have* / *do not have*	*a huge pack.*	*I*	*have got* / *have not got*	*a huge pack.*
He	*has* / *does not have*		*He*	*has got* / *has not got*	
Past					
I	*had*	*a huge pack.*	*I*	*had*	*a huge pack.*
He	*did not have*		*He*	*did not have*	

have for an action

He is having a rest.   *He is having a Pepsi.*

Short forms: *I/you/we/they have got = I've got, you've got, we've got, they've got*   *he/she/it has got = he's got, she's got, it's got*   *have not got = haven't got*   *has not got = hasn't got*

have and *have got*

We use both *have* and *have got* to mean 'own' or 'possess'. Both forms are usually possible, but *have got* is less formal than *have*.

    ***Does* he *have* a pack?**   **Has he *got* a pack?**

We use *have* (own) in simple tenses, and not continuous tenses, eg present simple, not present continuous.

    ● ***Do* you *have* any fruit juice?**   ○ No, I ***don't***. I only ***have*** Pepsi.

The verb form *have got* is the present perfect form of *get*, but the meaning is present.

    ● ***Have* you *got* any coins?**   ○ No, I ***haven't***. I've only ***got*** notes.

Auxiliary verb *have* and main verb *have* often go together. Auxiliary verb *have* often shortens, but main verb *have* does not shorten. (See Unit 21 for more information about *have* as a main verb and auxiliary verb.)

    *He's **had** that car for 11 years.*   *They've **had** that house since May.*

When we use the past simple, we usually use the form *had*, not *had got*. When we use the present perfect, we always use the form *had*.

    *He bought that car 11 years ago. He's **had** it for 11 years.*

have for an action

We use this form of *have* in continuous tenses as well as simple tenses.

    *He's **having** a rest now.*   *He **has** a swim every day.*

We use this form of *have* in a lot of very useful expressions. These are the most common.

    have a swim/wash/bath/shower   *have a walk/run/ride*
    have (a cup of) coffee/tea   *have breakfast/lunch/dinner*
    have a meal/snack/break/rest   *have a look*
    have a talk/chat/discussion/fight/an argument

Exercises

1 Write the correct forms of *have got*.

Example: ● <u>*Have you got*</u> any free time later? (you)
○ No, I <u>*haven't got*</u> a minute. Sorry.

1 ● _____ any coins for the phone? (you)
   ○ No, sorry. I _____ any money at all. Ask Tom. I think he _____ some.
   ● No, he _____ any. I've already asked him.

2 ● What does your brother look like?
   ○ He's tall and he _____ red hair.
   ● _____ a moustache? (he)
   ○ No, he _____ You're thinking of someone else.

2 Write the correct forms of *have*.

Example: ● <u>*Do you have*</u> any free time later? (you)
○ No, I <u>*don't have*</u> a minute. Sorry.

1 ● _____ any stamps for this letter? (you)
   ○ No, sorry. I _____ any stamps at all. Ask Sue. I think she _____ some.
   ● No, she _____ any. I've already asked her.

2 ● What does your sister look like?
   ○ She's thin and she _____ dark hair.
   ● _____ glasses? (she)
   ○ No, she _____ You're thinking of someone else.

3 ● _____ a bike when you were young? (you)
   ○ Yes, I _____ , but it was very heavy. I _____ a good bike until I was 15. That was a great bike. It _____ a special light-weight frame.

4 ● Alan, what kind of car _____ (you)
   ○ I _____ one. I walk everywhere. I _____ one for three years. I sold it.
   ● What kind of car _____ (you)
   ○ It was a Toyota.

5 ● Nick, _____ a holiday home in Spain.
   ○ Lucky man! How long _____ it? (he)

3 Write the correct forms of *have* and *have got*. Use *have got* where possible.

Example: Ann <u>*has got*</u> a new TV. She <u>*'s*</u> only <u>*had*</u> it for a week.

Tom and Sue [1]_____ an old French car. It [2]_____ a very big engine, so it doesn't go very fast. Tom and Sue don't mind though. They love it. In fact, they [3]_____ a name for it – Harold. They [4]_____ the car for eight years, and it's the only car they [5]_____ ever _____ Before that, they were students. They were very poor and they [6]_____ a car. They only [7]_____ bicycles. Now they [8]_____ enough money for a new car, but they don't want to change. They're happy with the car that they [9]_____ , even though it [10]_____ some engine problems in the last few months.

● I think he _____ it since 1989. But it's sad because he _____ much time to go there these days.

4 Write the correct forms of these expressions.

have breakfast, have a chance, have a chat, have coffee, have a game, have a look, have lunch, have a rest, have a run, have a swim, have time

Don and Lyn Blake work hard all week, so at the weekend they like to relax. They <u>*have breakfast*</u> at 9.00 instead of 7.30. Then Don [1]_____ _____ at the newspaper and Lyn often [2]_____ _____ with her mother on the phone. They never [3]_____ to do much shopping in the week, so they go to the supermarket and do the week's food shopping. After that they usually [4]_____ in a café. Then they go to the sports centre together. Lyn usually [5]_____ of tennis with a friend, while Don [6]_____ in the indoor pool. When they go home, they are hungry, so they [7]_____ and then they [8]_____ because they are tired. Later Don often [9]_____ round the park and Lyn [10]_____ to write all her letters.

20 Review: main verb forms

talk, talked, talked, talking, talks

Only use the *s* form with the 3rd person singular of the present simple. (See Unit 2 for the *s/es* difference.)

> He **talks**.   She **crashes**.   It **falls**.

The past and past participle forms of regular verbs are the same.

> *talked, talked   crashed, crashed*

With irregular verbs they are often different. (See Appendix 1 for a list of common irregular verbs.)

> *fell, fallen   took, taken*

Use the verb forms as follows.

Forms	Uses	Examples
1 Infinitive form	Infinitive	*He tried to **stop**.*
	Imperative	***Look** at me!*
	Future with *will*	*He'**ll hurt** himself.*
	Present simple	*Children **make** mistakes.*
2 The *s* form	Present simple (3rd person)	*That boy often **makes** mistakes.*
3 Past form	Past simple	*He **crashed**. He **fell** off.*
4 Past participle	Perfect tenses (present, past, future)	*He'**s damaged** his bike.* *He crashed just after the boy **had warned** him.* *We'**ll have finished** by 3.00.*
5 Present participle (the *ing* form)	Continuous tenses (present, past, present perfect, future)	*The boy **is talking** to an adult.* *He **was going** too fast when he crashed.* *He'**s been crying** ever since he crashed.* *His arm is broken. He **won't be riding** a bike again for a long time!*

We use different forms of the auxiliary verbs *be, do* and *have* with main verbs.

> *be → am, is, are, was, were, been, being*
> *do → do, does, did   have → have, has, had, having*

Together, auxiliary verbs and main verbs form the verb structure of a sentence. Verb structures add extra information to the meaning of the main verbs, including information about the time of the action – present, past or future. (See Unit 21 for more about auxiliary verbs.)

> *I'**m riding** a bike.   **Did** you **know** that boy?*
> ***Have** you **hurt** yourself?*

48

Exercises

1 Write the verbs in the present simple.

Example: ● *Where does Ann* <u>live?</u> *(live)*
○ *She* <u>lives</u> *in New York. (live)*

1 ● *Do you _____ Joe Lee? (know)*
○ *Yes, he _____ a BMW, doesn't he? (drive)*

2 ● *When does the film _____ (start)*
○ *It _____ at 7.45. (begin)*

3 ● *Ann doesn't _____ watching TV in the morning. (like)*
○ *No, but she _____ it a lot in the evening. (watch)*

4 ● *What does Peter _____ for lunch? (have)*
○ *He usually _____ a sandwich. (have)*

2 Write the verbs in the present simple or present continuous.

Examples: *Steve always* <u>comes</u> *at 8.00. (come)*
Look! He <u>'s coming</u> *now. (come)*

1 *Helen _____ work at 5.00 most days. (finish)*

2 *Quiet! I _____ to the news. (listen)*

3 *I _____ I'm not late. (hope)*

4 *What _____ with those bits of wood? (he / make)*

5 *How _____ to school every morning? (she / go)*

6 ● *_____ the film? (you / enjoy)*
○ *No, not really. Let's go home.*

3 Write the infinitive, past form and past participle of these irregular verbs.

cost, cut, earn, get, give, hit, let, make, pay, read, ride, see, take, wear

Infinitive	Past form	Past participle
Verbs with no change		
cost	_____	_____
_____	_____	_____
_____	_____	_____
_____	_____	_____

Infinitive	Past form	Past participle
Verbs with one change		
learn	_____	_____
_____	_____	_____
_____	_____	_____
_____	_____	_____

Infinitive	Past form	Past participle
Verbs with two changes		
ride	_____	_____
_____	_____	_____
_____	_____	_____
_____	_____	_____

4 Write the verbs in the past simple.

Example: ● *Who did you* <u>see</u> *at the party? (see)*
○ *I* <u>saw</u> *Ann and Steve. (see)*

1 ● *Did Mary _____ herself? (cut)*
○ *Yes, she _____ her hand with a knife. (cut)*

2 ● *Did you _____ any cakes? (make)*
○ *Yes, I _____ two. (make)*

3 ● *Did Tom _____ my bike? (ride)*
○ *No, he didn't _____ yours. (ride) He _____ his own. (ride)*

4 ● *Why did you _____ him go? (let)*
○ *I didn't _____ him go. (let) He _____ me and _____ away. (hit) (get)*

5 Write the verbs in the present perfect.

Example: ● *What have they* <u>done?</u> *(do)*
○ *They've* <u>taken</u> *the old car. (take)*

1 ● *What have the children _____ (do)*
○ *They've _____ these models. (make)*

2 ● *Has Bob _____ the report yet? (see)*
○ *No, I haven't _____ it to him yet. (give)*

3 ● *Have you _____ the list of verbs yet? (read)*
○ *Yes, but I haven't _____ them yet. (learn)*

4 ● *Ow! I've _____ myself! (hit)*
○ *Yes, and you've _____ yourself too. (cut)*

21 Review: auxiliary verb forms
be, do, have

The forms of main verbs help to form verb structures. (See Unit 20.)

1	2	3	4	5
look	*looks*	*looked*	*looked*	*looking*
know	*knows*	*knew*	*known*	*knowing*

The auxiliary verbs *be*, *do* and *have* also help to form verb structures.

> *be → am, is, are, was, were, been, being*
> *do → do, does, did*
> *have → have, has, had, having*

Together, auxiliary verbs and main verbs form verb structures. Verb structures add extra information to the meaning of the main verb, including information about the time of the action – present, past or future.

	Auxiliary	Main	
John	**is**	**talking**,	*so please listen.*
Peter	**has**	**found**	*his bag.*
Lyn	**didn't**	**answer**	*the question.*

Use auxiliaries with *not (n't)* to form negative questions. These *Yes/No* question forms show surprise.

> **Isn't** *he winning the match?* (He was champion last year!)
> **Don't** *you like the food?* (Most people love it!)
> **Haven't** *you heard of her before?* (She's famous!)

These *Wh* question forms ask about a non-action. *Why* questions are the most common type of negative *Wh* questions.

> **Why aren't** *you going?* (*You aren't going. Why not?*)
> **What didn't** *we do?* (*We didn't do something. What?*)
> **Who haven't** *we called?* (*We haven't called somebody. Who?*)

Use auxiliaries to form tag questions. Tag questions can check information. (See also Unit 25.) They expect the listener to agree. Use a falling tone (➘).

> *You're coming later,* **aren't** *you?*

> *You live in Liverpool,* **don't** *you?*

> *You* **haven't** *read the book,* **have** *you?*

Tag questions can also be like a real question. The speaker does not know for sure. Use a rising tone (➚).

> *You're coming later,* **aren't** *you?*

The tag question is usually the opposite (positive/negative) of the main verb.

Positive *You've met*	*Harry,*	➤	Negative **haven't** you?
*She **hasn't** done* Negative	*the job,*	➤	**has** she? Positive

Use auxiliary forms in short answers, and do not repeat the main verb.
Use them to reply to ordinary *Yes/No* questions and to tag questions.

- ● **Are** *you **looking** for your bag?*   ○ *Yes, I **am**.*
- ● **Do** *you **know** where it is?*   ○ *No, I **don't**.*
- ● **Have** *you **found** it yet?*   ○ *Yes, I **have**.*
- ● *You're worried,* **aren't** *you.*   ○ *Yes, I **am**.*
- ● *You **haven't** found it,* **have** *you?*   ○ *No, I **haven't**.*

Use auxiliary forms with *So, Nor* and *Neither*. Be very careful – the word order looks like a question. (See also Unit 28.)

- ● *I'm tired.*   ○ **So am** *I.*
- ● *He doesn't work hard.*   ○ **Nor does** *she.*
- ● *We haven't finished.*   ○ **Neither have** *they.*

Use auxiliary forms for special emphasis in reply to another speaker's words.

- ● *Please read it.*   ○ *I **am** reading it.*
- ● *You didn't finish.*   ○ *Actually I **did** finish.*
- ● *We haven't studied Unit 3.*   ○ *We **have** studied it.*

be, do and *have* are not only auxiliary verbs. They can also be main verbs. We can use *be, do* and *have* (auxiliary) with *be, do* and *have* (main) in the same sentence.

Use *be* as an auxiliary with a main verb.

> *We **were writing** letters.*   ***Is** he **eating** lunch?*

Use *be* as a link verb with a noun or adjective.

> ***Is** she **a doctor**.*   *They were **clever**.*

Use *be* as an auxiliary with *be* as a main verb.

> *Why **are** you **being** so stupid?* (behaving stupidly)

Use *do* as an auxiliary with a main verb in questions and negative statements.

> ***Do** you **like** football?*   *She **doesn't want** to leave.*

Use *do* as a main verb.

> *Is he **doing** his homework?*   *I **did** my exercises.*

Use *do* as an auxiliary with *do* as a main verb in questions and negative statements.

> ***Does** he **do** his homework every day?*   *I **didn't do** my exercises.*

Use *have* as an auxiliary with a main verb.

> ***Have** you **finished** yet?*   *When I arrived it **had started**.*

Use *have* as a main verb.

> *When are you **having** lunch?*   *I **had** a rest.*

Use *have* as an auxiliary with *have* as a main verb.

> ***Have** you **had** this car for long?*   *Ann **has had** her lunch.*

Exercises

1 Write the correct forms of *be*.

Example: *Lyn* <u>was</u> *working all day yesterday.*

1 *I* _____ *taking Ann home next week.*

2 *Look! Where* _____ *Ed going with my bike?*

3 *We* _____ *flying to Japan at this time tomorrow.*

4 *Alan* _____ *staying in London since last month.*

5 *What* _____ *you doing at 9.00 last night?*

6 *At last, you're here! I* _____ *waiting for hours.*

7 _____ *you doing anything at the moment?*

8 *I* _____ *phoning Pam when Tom arrived.*

2 Write the correct forms of *do*.

Example: ● <u>Does</u> *Peter Speak German?*
　　　　　 ○ *He* <u>doesn't</u> *speak much, but he can read a little.*

1 ● *How* _____ *you play this game?*
　 ○ *I'm not sure. We* _____ *have any instructions.*

2 ● _____ *you want to go home, Sue?*
　 ○ *No, I* _____ *want to go home just yet.*

3 ● *When* _____ *you get home last night?*
　 ○ *I* _____ *go home. I stayed at a hotel.*

4 ● *Why* _____ *he keep looking at us?*
　 ○ *I* _____ *know. I'll tell him to stop.*

5 ● _____ *you say much at the meeting?*
　 ○ *No, I* _____ *say anything. I kept quiet.*

6 ● _____ *Fred play tennis?*
　 ○ *No, he* _____ *, but he plays football.*

3 Write the correct forms of *have*.

Example: ● *How much* <u>has</u> *Andy written?*
　　　　　 ○ *He* <u>hasn't</u> *written much. Just a page.*

1 ● _____ *the trucks crossed the river yet?*
　 ○ *No, they* _____ *because we* _____ *built a bridge yet.*

2 ● *Why were you so angry with Bob?*
　 ○ *Because he* _____ *done the work.*

3 ● _____ *you found your shoes yet?*
　 ○ *I* _____ *found one, but I* _____ *found the other one. I don't know where it is.*

4 ● *Why did he come late?*
　 ○ *Because he* _____ *noticed the time.*

5 ● *Will their car be ready by 5.00?*
　 ○ *Oh, yes. We* _____ *finished before then.*

6 ● *How long* _____ *Fred lived here now?*
　 ○ *He* _____ *been here for five years.*

7 ● *I need your report by Friday.*
　 ○ *I'm sorry. I* _____ *finished it by then.*

8 ● *Why didn't the boys have any money?*
　 ○ *Because they* _____ *spent it all on sweets.*

4 Re-order the words to make negative questions.

Examples: *(job/didn't/the/finish/you)*
<u>Didn't you finish the job?</u>
(job/didn't/the/finish/you/why)
<u>Why didn't you finish the job?</u>

1 *(Paul/home/hasn't/come/yet)*
_____

2 *(they/the/call/didn't/police/why)*
_____
_____

3 *(enjoying/film/aren't/you/the)*
_____

4 *(you/agree/don't/why/me/with)*
_____

5 *(Rosie/the/isn't/wedding/going/to)*
_____
_____

6 *(questions/they/yet/answered/which/haven't)*
_____
_____

7 *(you/go/have to/home/now/don't)*
_____
_____

8 *(parts/don't/have to/we/which/learn)*
_____
_____

5 Write tag questions.

Examples: *They're going to crash, <u>aren't they?</u>*
You didn't finish, <u>did you?</u>

1 *You haven't understood, _____*

2 *He likes her, _____*

3 *They were angry with you, _____*

4 *You don't know Tony, _____*

5 *He arrived late, _____*

6 *They've done the shopping, _____*

7 *Alan doesn't like travelling, _____*

8 *Ann was studying last night, _____*

9 *You aren't enjoying this, _____*

10 *Nick didn't get home until midnight, _____*

6 Agree with the first speaker.

Examples: ● *I'm hungry. (I)*
○ *<u>So am I.</u>*
● *She didn't like the film. (he)*
○ *<u>Neither/Nor did he.</u>*

1 ● *They don't understand the question. (we)*
○ _____

2 ● *Peter likes the new teacher. (Alan)*
○ _____

3 ● *I've never been to India before. (I)*
○ _____

4 ● *Sam didn't do his homework. (Lisa)*
○ _____

5 ● *Sue has called her parents. (her brothers)*
○ _____

6 ● *We aren't going to buy the book. (she)*
○ _____

7 ● *I'd never seen such a lovely place. (we)*
○ _____

8 ● *The car broke down again yesterday. (the van)*
○ _____

9 ● *You aren't telling the truth. (you)*
○ _____

10 ● *Kate has been to America. (Andy)*
○ _____

7 Write questions and answers with *do, have* and *be* as main verbs. Use a) the present continuous, b) the past simple and c) the present perfect.

Examples: (● *Which question / you / do*)
(○ *we / do / number 2*)
a) ● *<u>Which question are you doing?</u>*
○ *<u>We're doing number 2.</u>*
b) ● *<u>Which question did you do?</u>*
○ *<u>We did number 2.</u>*
c) ● *<u>Which question have you done?</u>*
○ *<u>We've done number 2.</u>*

1 (● *What / you / have / for lunch*)
(○ *we / have / chicken*)
a) ● _____
○ _____
b) ● _____
○ _____
c) ● _____
○ _____

2 (● *How much work / he / do*)
(○ *he / do / ten hours*)
a) ● _____
○ _____
b) ● _____
○ _____
c) ● _____
○ _____

3 (● *Why / they / be / so slow with their work*)
(○ *because they / be / careful*)
a) ● _____
○ _____
b) ● _____
○ _____
c) ● _____
○ _____

22 Short form or full form
I'm angry!   I am angry!

's can mean *is* or *has*, so check the main part of the verb.

    She's coming home. (**'s** = *is*)   *She's come home.* (**'s** = *has*)

Do not confuse *it's* and *its.*

    It's** going to sleep.* (It's** = It is*)
    *The cat is closing **its** eyes.* (**its** = pronoun)

Also, do not confuse the possessive *'s* and *'s* meaning *is.*

    *This is Alan**'s** hat.* (**'s** = possessive)   *Alan**'s** at home.* (**'s** = *is*)

'd can mean *had* or *would*, so check the main part of the verb.

    *They**'d** finished by 12.00.* (**'d** = *had*)
    *They**'d** like to finish by 12.00.* (**'d** = *would*)

CROSSCHECK

Short forms

Use short forms for normal speaking.

    *They**'re** trying to finish early.*

Use short forms for ordinary statements.

    ● *He **isn't** working.*

Use short forms for informal writing, eg a letter to a friend.

    Dear Sally,
    *We**'re** having a great holiday.*

Full forms

Show strong feeling with full forms and stress.

    *I **am** sad you **have** to go away!*

Use full positive forms with stress to correct statements.

    ○ *Oh, yes, he **is** working!*

Use full forms to ask questions and at the end of sentences.

    ● ***Are** they working hard?*
    ○ *Yes, they **are**.*

Use full forms for most writing, eg a business letter or a report.

    Dear Sir,
    *We **are** pleased to inform you …*

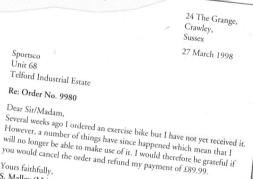

24 The Grange,
Crawley, Sussex
Monday 27th March

Dear Alan,
    It's been a long time since I last saw you. So many things've happened that I don't know where to begin. At the moment I'm looking after my baby niece while her mother's in hospital. That's her crying now. I think I'll give you a ring in a few days.
        Best wishes,

24 The Grange,
Crawley,
Sussex

27 March 1998

Sportsco
Unit 68
Telford Industrial Estate

Re: Order No. 9980

Dear Sir/Madam,
Several weeks ago I ordered an exercise bike but I have not yet received it. However, a number of things have since happened which mean that I will no longer be able to make use of it. I would therefore be grateful if you would cancel the order and refund my payment of £89.99.
Yours faithfully,
S. Malley (Ms)

Exercises

1 Write the short forms.

Example: (I have) _I've_ been here all day.

1 (You are) _____ right.

2 (He has) _____ hurt his leg.

3 (I am) _____ 18 next month.

4 (What is) _____ her name?

5 (We will) _____ be late.

6 If (he is) _____ wrong, (he will) _____ lose all his money.

7 If you were on that plane, (you would) _____ be half-way to India now.

8 If (she had) _____ gone to the interview, (she would) _____ have got the job.

9 (They have) _____ finished their lunch.

10 (I would) _____ like a cup of tea, please.

2 Write the negative short forms.

Example: Mary _hasn't_ eaten since yesterday.

1 I _____ like coffee. I never drink it.

2 She _____ singing at the moment.

3 Peter _____ seen Tom for ages.

4 We _____ be late again tomorrow.

5 _____ watch the film, Sam. I saw it at the cinema and I _____ enjoy it.

6 I _____ going to eat at that restaurant again.

7 This engine _____ much use. It _____ work properly.

8 If you _____ called me yesterday morning, I _____ have woken up in time.

9 Mike and Sue _____ been to Malta before. This is their first time.

10 Joe _____ at school yesterday because he felt sick.

3 Write the positive or negative short forms.

Tom is worried about his friend, Ben.

Tom: *What's wrong, Ben? You _don't_ look well.*

Ben: *I 1_____ feel very well either. I 2_____ ill.*

Tom: *What 3_____ the matter exactly?*

Ben: *Oh, I 4_____ got a headache and I feel bad.*

Tom: *You 5_____ better see the doctor.*

Ben: *I 6_____ like to do that, but I 7_____ got any time. I 8_____ going to an important meeting this morning.*

Tom: *9_____ be stupid. You 10_____ ill, so if you go to the meeting, you 11_____ be able to work properly. Can Roger go instead of you?*

Ben: *He 12_____ really know enough about the project, but perhaps he can. I 13_____ call him and ask him.*

Tom: *Good. I know he 14_____ say yes. And then we 15_____ go to the doctor together.*

Ben: *Thanks. That 16_____ really kind of you.*

4 Write the full forms.

The bank manager has written an unpleasant letter to a customer.

Dear Mr Morton,

(I'm) _I am_ writing to you about your company's latest sales figures, which (we've) 1_____ recently received.

As you say in your letter, the figures (aren't) 2_____ good and they (don't) 3_____ seem to be improving. Your figures have been showing losses for three years, and (I'm) 4_____ very sorry to say that (they're) 5_____ still showing large losses. As a result, you (won't) 6_____ be surprised to know that (we're) 7_____ getting very worried about the business loan which you (haven't) 8_____ yet been able to start repaying.

5 Write the full forms.

The letter from the bank continues.

Until your latest sales report, (we'd) 1_____ hoped (you'd) 2_____ succeed, but (it's) 3_____ clear now that the company will soon have to close. Our accountant is still studying your sales figures, but (he's) 4_____ decided that we must now close your loan account with this bank. (He's) 5_____ sending you a copy of his report in tomorrow's post. (I'd) 6_____ like to suggest that we meet early this week.

23 Question forms 1

Are you from Japan?

Use *Yes/No* questions to check information.
- **Is he from America**?
  ○ *Yes, he is./No, he isn't.*
- **Does the film start at 7.30**?
  ○ *Yes, it does./No, it doesn't.*

Form questions from statements in the following ways.
With one auxiliary verb, do this.
- **They can** *understand.* → **Can they** *understand?*
- **He is** *working.* → **Is he** *working?*
- **They were** *reading.* → **Were they** *reading?*

With two auxiliary verbs (eg *has been, is going to*), do this.
- **He has been** *working hard.* → **Has he been** *working hard?*
- **He is going to** *work hard.* → **Is he going to** *work hard?*

With no auxiliary verbs, add *do* or *does* in the present simple and add *did* in the past simple. In the present and past simple, use only the infinitive form of the verb.
- *I* **know** *her.* → **Do** *I* **know** *her?*
- *He* **knows** *her.* → **Does** *he* **know** *her?*
- *He* **knew** *her.* → **Did** *he* **know** *her?*

Form *Yes/No* questions with *will* and modal auxiliary verbs + infinitive.
- **Will** *he* **win**?
- **Can** *she* **speak** *French?*
- **Must** *you* **go**?

Use auxiliaries with *not (n't)* to form negative questions. These *Yes/No* questions show surprise.
- **Isn't** *he winning the match?* (He was champion last year!)
- **Don't** *you like the food?* (Most people love it!)
- **Haven't** *you heard of her before?* (She's famous!)

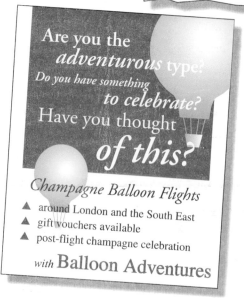

Exercises

1 Write questions from the statements.

Examples: *Ed speaks French. (German)*
Does Ed speak German too?
She's having a piano lesson. (he)
Is he having a piano lesson too?

1 *Bob likes basketball. (football)*

_____

2 *Sally is good at cooking. (Lucy)*

_____

3 *The boys have had dinner. (Dad)*

_____

4 *Jim cooked some vegetables. (meat)*

_____

5 *We're going out tonight. (you)*

_____

2 Write questions from the statements.

Example: *Rob can speak Japanese. (you)*
Can you speak Japanese too?

1 *I have to go now. (he)*

_____

2 *She must finish the report. (letters)*

_____

3 *He can run fast. (swim fast)*

_____

4 *We should train every morning. (evening)*

_____

_____

5 *We'll have to write to all our relatives. (friends)*

_____

_____

3 Re-order the words to make questions.

Examples: *(be/married/Liz and Bill)*
● *Are Liz and Bill married?*
○ *Yes, they are.*
(in London/live/they)
● *Do they live in London?*
○ *No, they don't. They live in Manchester.*

1 *(for long/be/married/they)*
● _____

○ *Yes, they've been married for eight years.*

2 *(move/at that time/to Manchester/they)*
● _____

○ *No, they moved there a year later.*

3 *(they/any children/have got)*
● _____

○ *Yes, they have got one son and one daughter.*

4 *(go/the children/to school)*
● _____

○ *The boy does, but the girl is still too young.*

5 *(soon/she/school/start)*
● _____

○ *Yes, she's starting school in September.*

4 Write negative questions.

Example: ● *I'm tired. I want to stay at home.*
○ *Really? (you/not/want to meet Sue)*
Really? Don't you want to meet Sue?

1 ● *Don't buy that car.*
○ *Why? (it/not/be/a good one)*

_____

2 ● *Let's take the train, not the plane.*
○ *Really? (you/not/like/flying)*

_____

3 ● *Rod is working at the bank.*
○ *Why? (he/not/go/to college yet)*

_____

4 ● *The children are starting another game on the computer.*
○ *Really? (they/not/go/to bed soon)*

_____

5 ● *Pam has just bought a new pen.*
○ *Why? (she/not/buy/one yesterday)*

_____

_____

Use *Wh* questions to get more information.
- ● **Where is he going**?
- ○ *To London.*
- ● **What does he do**?
- ○ *He works for IBM.*

Form questions from statements in the following ways. First use a question word.

> *Where, When, Why, What, Who, Whose, Which, How, How much, How many, How old,* etc

Then change the subject and the auxiliary verb.

> *Where **are we** going?*
> *What **has she** been doing?*
> *How **does he** like the town?*
> *Why **did they** leave?*

Who and *What* can ask about the subject or the object of an action.

> *A car hit the cat.* → ● **What hit** *the cat?* (subject) ○ **The car** *hit the cat.* OR ● **What did** *the car **hit**?* (object) ○ *The car hit* **the cat**.
> *Tim called Ken.* → ● **Who called** *Ken?* (subject) ○ **Tim** *called Ken.* OR **Who did** *Tim **call**?* (object) ○ *Tim called* **Ken**.

Use auxiliaries with *not (n't)* to form negative questions. Use *Wh* questions to ask about a non-action. *Why* questions are the most common.

> **Why aren't** *you going? (You aren't going. Why?)*
> **What didn't** *we do? (We didn't do something. What?)*
> **Who haven't** *we called? (We haven't called somebody. Who?)*

Still looking for Cinderella

We met at Tony's party. Why haven't I seen you again? Why did you leave early without telling me your name? I can't forget you. Can we meet again? I was the one with the yellow suit you said you liked, or were you joking? Contact Phil. PO Box 6790

pop quest

1. What nationality are Aqua?
2. Which band had a 1982 hit with *Down Under*?
3. Who sings the theme song from the James Bond film, *Tomorrow Never Dies*?
4. Which punk band did Rat Scabies sing with?
5. Which Underworld track featured in *Trainspotting*?

What comes at the end of every year?
The letter R.

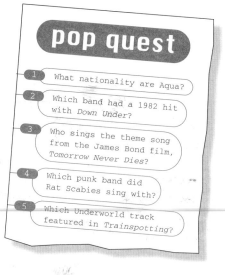

Q How much sunscreen should I take for a two-week holiday?

A *On average, you should allow about 200-250ml per person per week.*

Exercises

1 Write the question words.

Example: ● _When_ did Liz and Bill get married?
○ _Eight years ago._

1 ● _____ do they live?
○ In Manchester.

2 ● _____ parents live with them?
○ Bill's.

3 ● _____ have they lived in Manchester?
○ For seven years.

4 ● _____ children have they got?
○ Two. A son and a daughter.

5 ● _____ one is older?
○ Their son. He's seven.

6 ● _____ is their daughter going to start school?
○ This year.

7 ● _____ do they live in Manchester?
○ Because Bill has got a good job there.

8 ● _____ does he do?
○ He's an engineer.

2 Re-order the words to make questions. Then write true answers about yourself.

Example: (your/what's/name)
● _What's your name?_
○ _My name's_ ...

1 (you/are/how/old)
● _____
○ _____

2 (your/address/what's)
● _____
○ _____

3 (father/do/does/your/what)
● _____
○ _____

4 (got/and/brothers/have/how many/you/sisters)
● _____
  _____
○ _____

5 (you/learning/why/are/English)
● _____
○ _____

3 Write negative questions.

Example: We didn't finish something. (What)
What didn't we finish?

1 Tom hasn't answered my letter. (Why)
_____
_____

2 We haven't done something. (What)
_____

3 They won't be able to go on holiday. (Why)
_____
_____

4 We didn't go somewhere. (Where)
_____

5 Ann isn't going to go out tonight. (Why)
_____
_____

6 I don't like this television programme. (Why)
_____
_____

4 Write questions with *Who* or *What*.

Example: Somebody called the manager.
Who called the manager?
The customer called somebody.
Who did the customer call?

1 Somebody called the police.
_____

2 Something went wrong.
_____

3 Bob found something by the door.
_____

4 Tom phoned somebody.
_____

5 The car ran over something.
_____

6 Somebody saw Peter.
_____

7 Julie ate something.
_____

25 Tag questions

Alan is finishing college soon, isn't he?

Alan is finishing college soon, isn't he?

Yes, he is.

The tag question is usually the opposite (positive/negative) of the main verb.

| **Positive** *You've met* | *Harry,* | **Negative** *haven't you?* |
| **Negative** *She hasn't done* | *the job,* | *has she?* **Positive** |

With one auxiliary verb, use the opposite auxiliary form, eg *is → isn't*.

With two auxiliary verbs, use the opposite of the first auxiliary, eg *will have → won't have*.

With no auxiliary verbs, in the present and past simple, use a form of *do* (main verb → *don't, doesn't* or *didn't*). *have to* and *need to* also work like this.

Tag questions are not ordinary questions. We can use them to check information. They expect the listener to agree. Use a falling tone (↘).

*You're 18, **aren't you**?* *You live in Liverpool, **don't you**?*

We can also use this type of tag question to help a conversation.

● *It's a good film, **isn't it**?* ○ *Yes, it's great. The acting is wonderful.*

Tag questions can be more like ordinary questions – the speaker does not know something for sure. Use a rising tone (↗).

*You're 18, **aren't you**?* *You live in Liverpool, **don't you**?*

Note the negative tag after *I am*.

*I'm late, **aren't I**?*

You were listening to that, weren't you? Because those were our summer competition prize questions and you've got just one more chance to phone in with your answers.

GOLFERS' ULTIMATE AIR SHOT

Two golf balls collided in mid-air when players in separate games teed off at exactly the same moment for the 10th and 11th holes at Sturminster, Dorset. The club secretary said, 'It's amazing, isn't it? When you think how small the balls are and the tees are 150 metres apart. I think it must be a record, don't you?' A local school–teacher, also a member of the club, calculated the odds of such a collision at over a million to one.

Exercises

1 Write tag questions.

Examples: It's hot today, _isn't it?_

He won't be working late, _will he?_

With one auxiliary and most modal verbs

1 You'll be at home tonight, _____

2 The letter hasn't arrived yet, _____

3 They're doing the shopping, _____

4 It rained last night, _____

5 She isn't at home now, _____

6 Peter wasn't working yesterday, _____

7 Barry can't come to the party, _____

8 He should finish by 5.00, _____

9 We needn't pay now, _____

10 She might arrive tomorrow, _____

With two auxiliaries

11 He'll be working all day, _____

12 You haven't been listening to me, _____

13 The boys will have gone by 4.00, _____

14 The window hasn't been mended, _____

15 Your book isn't being printed yet, _____

16 Tony's car was being serviced yesterday, _____

With no auxiliaries and with modal auxiliaries _have to_ and _need to_

17 Bob owns all his land, _____

18 You forgot to post the letters, _____

19 You need to ask the boss, _____

20 Mary had to sell the house, _____

2 Write tag questions.

You're interviewing the famous film star, Rocky Reed.

Example: Mr Reed, you've made nearly 40 films,
haven't you?

1 Your last film earned $30 million, _____

2 Your early films weren't so successful, _____

3 You're going to make your next film in Mexico,

_____

4 You don't like being away from your home and family,

_____

5 Your wife isn't interested in films, _____

6 You've got four children, _____

7 They won't be going into the film industry,

_____

These tag questions check information. Mark the tags with a falling tone (↘).

3 Write tag questions.

You're at a party.

Example: It's a lovely house, _isn't it?_

1 The food is wonderful, _____

2 There aren't many people here yet, _____

3 Bob and Celia aren't coming, _____

4 I haven't seen you since last year, _____

5 You met my wife at the last party, _____

6 We'll be seeing you next week, _____

These tag questions encourage the listener to speak. Mark the tags with a falling tone (↘).

4 Write tag questions.

Lucy and her daughter, Emma, are going to the airport. Emma is very worried, but Lucy is calm.

Emma: _Mum, you didn't forget to bring the passports,_
did you?

Lucy: _Don't worry. I told you I'd brought them,_
1_____

Emma: _Yes, that's right. I forgot. And you've got the_
tickets, 2_____

Lucy: _Yes, don't you remember? They were on the table_
with the passports, 3_____

Emma: _Yes, I suppose so. But Mum, what's the time?_
We're going to be late, 4_____

Lucy: _Calm down, Emma. It's 10.30 now and the_
flight doesn't leave until 12.30,
5_____ _And we only have to go_
another 30 kilometres, 6_____

Emma: _I guess you're right._

Lucy: _Well, then, there's nothing to worry about,_
7_____

Emma is unsure. Mark her tags with a rising tone (↗).

Lucy is sure. Mark her tags with a falling tone (↘).

61

26 Short answers
Yes, I am.   No, I can't.

A short answer can be a *Yes* or a *No* answer. The verb in the answer matches the verb in the question.

● *Is the room* on fire?
○ *Yes, it is.*
● *Can you* see the boy now?
○ *No, I can't.*

We always use full forms in *Yes* answers, when the verb is the last word.

Yes, I am.   Yes, it is.   Yes, I can.

We usually use short forms in *No* answers.

No, it isn't.   No, I can't.   No, they didn't.
(But *No, I'm not.*)

Here are some more examples.

Present
● *Are they* at home?   ○ *Yes, they are./No, they aren't.*
● *Is Ann* going home?   ○ *Yes, she is./No, she isn't.*
● *Do you* like Italian food?   ○ *Yes, I do./No, I don't.*

Perfect
● *Has Peter* posted the letter?   ○ *Yes, he has./No, he hasn't.*
● *Had the film* started by 8.00?   ○ *Yes, it had./No, it hadn't.*

Past
● *Were the children* at home?   ○ *Yes, they were./No, they weren't.*
● *Was the cat* eating?   ○ *Yes, it was./No, it wasn't.*
● *Did you* see Susan last night?   ○ *Yes, I did./No, I didn't.*

Future
● *Are we* going to be late?   ○ *Yes, we are./No, we aren't.*
● *Will Joe* be at home tonight?   ○ *Yes, he will./No, he won't.*

In conversation, we often give extra information after a short answer. This helps the conversation to continue.

● *Do you know Helen?*
○ *Yes, I do. **I've known her for years**.*
● *Have you finished work yet?*
○ *No, I haven't. **I still have to write a report**.*

Will you love and honour her, in sickness and in health?

I will.

'Tom!'
'Well, Becky?'
'They'll miss us and hunt for us!'
'Yes, they will! Certainly they will!'
'When would they miss us, Tom?'
'When they get back to the boat, I rekon.'
'Tom, it might be dark then - would they notice we hadn't come?'
'I don't know. But anyway, your mother would miss you as soon as they got home.'

(*The Adventures of Tom Sawyer*, Mark Twain, 1835–1910)

Exercises

1 Complete the answers.

Some people are talking at a wedding party.

Example: ● *Are you a member of the family?*
○ *No, I'm not. I'm a friend.*

1 ● *Have you met Tony?*
○ *No, _____ Hello.*

2 ● *Do you know Mary?*
○ *Yes, _____ We're old friends.*

3 ● *Are you from London?*
○ *No, _____ . I'm from Liverpool.*

4 ● *Should we go and get some food now?*
○ *Yes, _____ It's in the next room.*

5 ● *Would you like some more wedding cake?*
○ *Yes, _____ It's delicious.*

6 ● *Are there any more sandwiches?*
○ *No, _____ They're all gone.*

7 ● *Have you known Susie for long?*
○ *No, _____ But I know Ian well.*

8 ● *Is Ian going to give a speech?*
○ *Yes, _____ He's standing up now.*

9 ● *Can you hear what Ian is saying?*
○ *No, _____ It's too noisy.*

10 ● *Did you enjoy the wedding?*
○ *Yes, _____ It was lovely.*

11 ● *Must you go already?*
○ *Yes, _____ . I'm sorry.*

2 Complete the answers in the game, *Who am I?*

The answer to 10 is *Yes, I was.*

1 ● *Are you alive?*
○ *No, _____*

2 ● *Have you died recently?*
○ *No, _____*

3 ● *Were you a woman?*
○ *No, _____*

4 ● *Did you come from Britain?*
○ *No, _____*

5 ● *Were you European?*
○ *Yes, _____*

6 ● *Were you a soldier?*
○ *Yes, _____*

7 ● *Did you lead your country?*
○ *Yes, _____*

8 ● *Were you like a king?*
○ *Yes, _____*

9 ● *Did you live about 200 years ago?*
○ *Yes, _____*

10 ● *Were you Emperor Napoleon of France?*
○ *Yes, _____*

3 Write true short answers about yourself.

Example: ● *Are you studying English?*
○ *Yes, I am.*

1 ● *Are you a full-time student?*
○ _____

2 ● *Do you ever speak English outside class?*
○ _____

3 ● *Is English a difficult language to learn?*
○ _____

4 ● *Are you learning any other language?*
○ _____

5 ● *Do most people learn English in your country?*
○ _____

6 ● *Do a lot of people in your country use English in their work?*
○ _____

7 ● *Do you think you will use your English in the next year?*
○ _____

8 ● *Will you travel abroad in the next year?*
○ _____

9 ● *Have you ever been to Britain or the USA?*
○ _____

10 ● *Would you like to visit an English-speaking country?*
○ _____

27 Indirect forms
Could you tell me what time it is?

Indirect questions are a polite form, and we often use them to ask for information or opinions. There are several common ways of starting indirect questions.

> *Could you tell me ...?*   *Do you know ...?*
> *Do you have any idea ...?*   *Can you tell me ...?*

A *Wh* question continues like this.

> *Could you tell me **what** (or **when**, **where**, **why**, **how**, etc) ...?*

A *Yes/No* question continues like this.

> *Do you know **if** (or **whether**) ...?*

The following subjects and verbs are not in question form. They are like subjects and verbs in a statement.

> *Could you tell me what time **it is**?*   *Do you know if **he went**?*

Be careful about *do*, *does* and *did*. We use them in ordinary present simple and past simple questions, but not in indirect questions.

> *What **does** the bank **close**? → Could you tell me what time the bank **closes**?*
> ***Did** the bank **close** at 4.30? → Can you tell me if the bank **closed** at 4.30?*

We can use indirect forms in statements too.

I know/don't know	*what time it is.*
I can/can't tell you	*when the bank closes.*
I've no idea	*if the bank opens late.*
I wonder	*whether it's open now.*

Indirect forms are similar to reported forms. (See Unit 47.)

> ***Where can I get** some stamps? → **Do you know where I can get** some stamps?* OR ***He wants to know where he can get** some stamps.*

We often use the form *Do you think ...?* to ask for an opinion.

> ***Is it** going to rain? → **Do you think it is** going to rain?*

A *Yes/No* question does not take *if* or *whether*.

> ***Do you think she went** home?   **Do you think she was** angry?*

The question word is at the beginning in a *Wh* question.

> ***Where** do you think she went?*
> ***How long** do you think he'll stay?*

Brain Twisters *No.601*

An opinion poll interviewer phones a house and says, 'Can you tell me how many people live there?' He is told that there are three in the household. Then he asks, 'Could you tell me what their ages are?' and he is told that the product of the three ages is 200 and the sum of the three ages is an odd number. The interviewer then thinks for a while and says, 'I cannot figure out the ages from this information. I must ask another question. I wonder if there is someone in the house over 21?' The answer is yes, and now the interviewer knows the three ages.

Do YOU know what they are?

Answer: 25, 2 and 4

In a coastal emergency DIAL 999 and ask for the COASTGUARD.

PLAN YOUR TRIP
Know how long the trip is likely to take, who will keep watch and what safe havens are en route. Leave these details with someone.

BE SAFE AT SEA!

Exercises

1 Write indirect questions with *Wb* forms.

Example: *What time is it? Can you tell me?*
   Can you tell me what time it is?

1   *What date is it today? Do you know?*

_____

_____

2   *When is Ann coming home? Could you tell me?*

_____

_____

3   *Why has Tom gone? Do you have any idea?*

_____

_____

4   *How long will you be away? Can you say?*

_____

_____

5   *Where have they gone? Can you tell me?*

_____

_____

2 Write indirect questions with *Yes/No* forms.

Example: *Is the shop open? Can you tell me?*
   Can you tell me if/whether the shop is open?

1   *Have they had lunch? Do you know?*

_____

_____

2   *Will you be home tonight? Can you say?*

_____

_____

3   *Are the team going to win? Do you have any idea?*

_____

_____

4   *Are we having a test this week? Can you tell us?*

_____

_____

3 Write indirect questions with *do/did* forms.

Example: *Did they leave at 1.00? Do you know?*
   Do you know if/whether they left at 1.00?

1   *Does Tom go to school? Can you tell me?*

_____

_____

2   *Did the ring cost a lot? Can you say?*

_____

_____

3   *Do they play tennis? Do you have any idea?*

_____

_____

4   *When did the bus go? Could you tell us?*

_____

_____

5   *How does the engine work? Do you know?*

_____

_____

6   *Where do they always go? Can you tell me?*

_____

_____

4 Write indirect questions with ... *do/Do you think ... ?*

Examples: *Will it rain?*
   Do you think it'll rain?
   When did he go?
   When do you think he went?

1   *Why does he arrive late?*

_____

_____

2   *Are they going to finish today?*

_____

_____

3   *How far did they walk?*

_____

_____

4   *Have we made a mistake?*

_____

_____

5   *Where will you live when you go to college?*

_____

_____

28 *So and Neither/Nor; so and not*

So am I.   Neither/Nor do I.   I think so.   I'm afraid not.

So and Neither/Nor

So follows a positive statement. *Neither* or *Nor* follow a negative statement.

- ● *I'm hungry.*   ○ *So am I.*
- ● *I'm not hungry.*   ○ *Neither/Nor am I.*

The next word is a verb. It matches the verb in the first statement. It may be a form of *be*, *do* or *have*, or it may be a modal verb, eg *can*, *should*, *ought to*.

- ● *I'm thirsty.*   ○ *So am I.*
- ● *I can't do it.*   ○ *Neither can we.*

do or *does* follow a positive present simple statement. *did* follows a positive past simple statement.

- ● *She likes TV.*   ○ *So does he.*
- ● *He watched the news.*   ○ *So did she.*

The subject comes after the verb.

So am I.   Neither did we.   So will they.

Use these forms to agree with another speaker's statement. Compare the replies.

● *I often go out on Saturday.*	● *He didn't arrive on time.*
○ *I often go out on Saturday too*.	○ *We didn't arrive on time either*.
OR *So do I.*	OR *Neither did we*.

so and not

You can use *so* after *hope*, *think*, *believe*, *expect*, *suppose*, *guess* and *be afraid*. Verb + *so* shows a positive feeling.

- ● *Is this answer right?*   ○ *I hope so*. OR *I think so*.

There are two negative forms – positive + *not* and negative + *so*.

- ● *Perhaps the bus isn't coming.*   ○ *I guess not*. OR *I'm afraid not*.
- ● *Are you going to be rich?*   ○ *I don't imagine so*.

With *believe*, *expect* and *suppose*, we can use either positive + *not* or negative + *so*.

- ● *Is Tom arriving tomorrow?*
- ○ *I believe not*. OR *I don't believe so*.

Exercises

1 Complete the conversation. Use *So ...* or *Neither/Nor ...*

Two people on a train journey are talking.

Examples: Tony: *I'm travelling to Glasgow.*
Nick: <u>*So am I.*</u>
Tony: *I don't like long journeys much.*
Nick: <u>*Neither/Nor do I.*</u>

Tony: *I don't come from Glasgow.*
Nick: ¹_____ . *I'm from London.*
Tony: ²_____ . *I'm going to a meeting.*
Nick: ³_____ *You know, I had to get up at 6.30 this morning to catch this plane.*
Tony: ⁴_____ . *I didn't enjoy that at all.*
Nick: ⁵_____ . *I wanted to have the meeting in London.*
Tony: ⁶_____ . *I couldn't understand why they didn't want a meeting in London?*
Nick: ⁷_____ . *I was told I had to go to the Head Office in Glasgow.*
Tony: ⁸_____ *Where's your meeting?*
Nick: *It's at Northern Technical.*
Tony: ⁹_____ *That's amazing. What time does your meeting start? Mine starts at 10.00.*
Nick: ¹⁰_____ *That's even more strange! My meeting is about their new steel pipe project.*
Tony: ¹¹_____ *Tell me, who are you meeting?*
Nick: *Dr Tony Blair.*
Tony: *That's me!*

2 Look at the table. Then complete the statements.

	Ken	Sally	Ted	Claire
Tennis	✗	✗		
Judo	✗			✗
Swimming		✗	✗	
Computer games			✗	✗

Examples: *Ken does judo, and* <u>*so does Sally.*</u>
Ted can't play tennis, and <u>*neither/nor can Claire.*</u>

1 *Sally isn't interested in judo, and* _____ _____

2 *Ken is very good at tennis, and* _____ _____

3 *Ted loves playing computer games, and* _____ _____

4 *Sally hates computer games, and* _____ _____

5 *Sally can swim very well, and* _____ _____

6 *Ken can't swim at all, and* _____ _____

3 Complete the answers.

Examples: ● *Does the bank open on Saturday morning?*
○ <u>*I think so.*</u> *(think) Most big banks do.*
● *I think it's going to snow.*
○ <u>*I hope not.*</u> *(hope) I haven't got a coat.*

1 ● *Will Tessa get home late again tonight?*
○ _____ *(expect) She usually gets home late.*

2 ● *I think they're going to build the new road.*
○ _____ *(suppose) Everybody says they are.*

3 ● *Are you going to wear the blue shirt?*
○ _____ *(not/think) I don't like it any more.*

4 ● *Do you think Alex passed her exam?*
○ _____ *(be afraid) She didn't do any work.*

5 ● *I don't think Tom is coming.*
○ _____ *(guess) He should be here by now.*

6 ● *I wonder if we'll get to the shop in time.*
○ _____ *(think) It doesn't close until 6.00.*

29 Modal auxiliary verbs 1

can, could, be able to   can't have, could have, couldn't have

Help! I can't swim!

can

Use *can* to express ability and possibility in the present and future.
The negative form is one word – *cannot*. The short form is *can't*.

> She **can swim** very well.   It's warm, so we **can go** swimming.
> The boy **cannot swim**.   Help! I **can't swim**.

could

Use *could* to express ability and possibility in the past.

> She **could swim** when she was five.
> It was warm, so we **could go** swimming.

Use *could not (couldn't)* for an impossible action in the past.

> He was underwater. He **couldn't breathe**.

Use *could* for an action in the past with these verbs: *feel, hear, see, smell, taste, remember, understand*. (For most other verbs see below.)

> I **could hear** his call for help.   I **could see** that he needed help.

be able to

You can use *be able to* for ability and possibility in the present and past, but it is more formal than *can* and less common.

> She**'s able to swim** ten kilometres.

Use *be able to* instead of *can* in the present perfect.

> I've had some free time, so I**'ve been able to write** some letters.

Use *be able to* instead of *could* for a past action with most verbs.

> We had some free time, so we **were able to look** round town.

can't have, could have and couldn't have

Use *can't have* or *couldn't have* when something was impossible in the past. (See also Unit 34.)

> He **can't/couldn't have been** in Tokyo yesterday. I saw him in London.

Use *could have* to talk about a missed opportunity in the past.

> You **could have visited** Ann in hospital. Why didn't you?

We often use *could have* when something was possible in the past.

> The thief **could have entered** through the door or the kitchen window. We don't know which.

As round as a butter bowl, as deep as a cup.
All of the Mississippi river, can't fill it up.

(Answer: **a sieve**)

As light as a feather, as round as a ball.
Yet all the king's men cannot carry it at all.

(Answer: **a bubble**)

ANNE

Well, Michael, your father's gone. Now we're on our own. Just you and me. Now we can stop holding our breath.

MICHAEL

I'm glad he's gone. If it hadn't been for him, I could've done well. I could've stayed on at school. I could've got a good job. Instead of following in his footsteps.

They can't play any instruments, have never had a Top 10 hit and prefer a good laugh to a serious discussion of their art. But, says Charlie Porter, *that's all part of Saint Etienne's charm, and the secret of their long life* ...

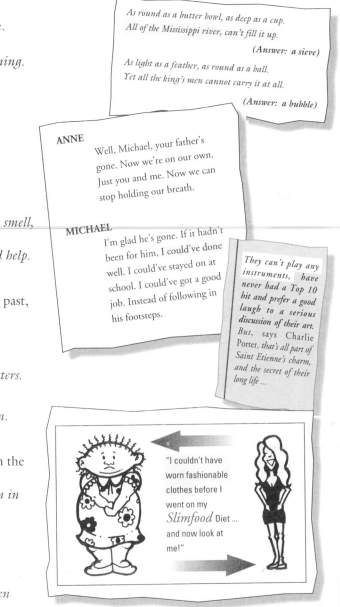

"I couldn't have worn fashionable clothes before I went on my *Slimfood* Diet ... and now look at me!"

Exercises

1 Complete the statements. Use *can* or *can't* and these verbs.

catch, go, hear, see, walk

Example: *Please speak up. I* <u>can't hear</u> *very well.*

1 *I* _____ *Lucy now. Look!*

2 *I've finished, so I* _____ *home.*

3 *Tim is only a baby. He* _____ *yet.*

4 *You* _____ *me! I'm too fast for you.*

2 Complete the statements. Use *can/can't* or *could/couldn't*.

Example: *I* <u>can</u> *speak French well now, but I* <u>couldn't</u> *speak it at all five years ago.*

1 *Poor old Mr Black* _____ *play football now, but he* _____ *play well when he was young.*

2 *Sally* _____ *read now, but she* _____ *read at all when she was five.*

3 *I* _____ *understand the game last time, and I still* _____ *understand now. It's very difficult.*

4 *Fifty years ago, you* _____ *buy a house for £500, but you certainly* _____ *do that now.*

3 Complete the statements. Use *could* and choose from these verbs.

feel, hear, remember, see, smell, taste, understand

Example: *I woke up suddenly. I* <u>could smell</u> *something burning downstairs.*

1 *The waterfall was huge. You* _____ _____ *the noise a kilometre away.*

2 *I thought about the girl. I* _____ _____ *her face, but not her name.*

3 *Ann* _____ *the words, but she still wasn't sure what the French girl wanted.*

4 *I* _____ *the rain running down my neck. It was horrible.*

4 Complete the statements. Use *could* or *be able to*. Use *could* where possible.

Example: *The door was open, so we* <u>were able to</u> *go straight in.*

1 *Lucy* _____ *hear somebody outside.*

2 *Lisa* _____ *read when she was four.*

3 *The police* _____ *stop the two men.*

4 *The plane crashed, but the pilot* _____ *get out.*

5 *Dan* _____ *see the mountains 20 kilometres away.*

5 Complete the story. Use *can/can't* or *could/couldn't* or *be able to*.

Luckily, we <u>were able to</u> *hire a four-wheel drive vehicle quite easily. Next day we started early, and we* ¹_____ *travel fast across the open country. Later we climbed into the hills and stopped for a rest. From there, we* ²_____ *look back across the flat land to the city. Maria pointed. 'Look, Rod,' she said. 'You* ³_____ *still see the castle.' Rod looked, but he wasn't wearing his glasses and he* ⁴_____ *see it. 'Let's go,' I said. 'If we hurry, we may* ⁵_____ *reach the valley by 6.00. Later we ran into some deep mud. 'It's no good,' I said. 'We* ⁶_____ *go forward or back.' Then we got out and pushed. In the end we* ⁷_____ *move the vehicle, but we were covered in mud. Rod and I looked at ourselves and laughed, but Maria was upset. She* ⁸_____ *see what was funny at all.*

6 Complete the statements. Use *can't have* or *could have*.

Example: *Peter* <u>can't have</u> *bought a car. He hasn't got any money.*

1 *You* _____ *finished already. Nobody can work as fast as that.*

2 *Lucy* _____ *gone to the party, but she decided to stay at home.*

3 *Ed* _____ *been at the restaurant because I was there and I didn't see him.*

4 *We don't know how Steve went, but he* _____ *by train or bus.*

30 Modal auxiliary verbs 2

can, could, would, may

> Could you be quiet, please?

Can/Could/Would you ...?

Use these verbs for requesting + 2nd or 3rd person.

Can you help me for a moment? (informal)
Could you give me your name, please, Sir? (polite/formal)
Would guests kindly leave their rooms by midday? (more formal)

Can/Could/May I ...?

Use these verbs for requesting + 1st person.

Can I borrow your pen for a second? (informal)
Could I have your phone number, Sir? (polite/formal)
Ladies and gentlemen, **may I have** your attention, please? (more formal)

Yes, you can/may.

Use these verbs for permission.

- Could I borrow some money, Sam?
- **Yes**, of course **you can**. How much? (informal/formal)
- Could I talk to the King, please?   ○ **Yes. You may see** him at 10.00 tomorrow. (very formal/old-fashioned)

When we refuse permission, we do not usually use the negative of *can* or *may*.

- Can I borrow your jacket tonight?
- **No, I'm sorry**. I need it tonight.

If we use *cannot (can't)* or *may not*, it shows very strong feeling.

- Dad, could I have this week off school?
- No, **you certainly can't**! OR No, **you most certainly may not**!

can/may

Use these verbs for offering.

You can ride my bike if you want. (informal)
Can I help you, Mr Hill? (informal)
Good morning, Barclays Bank. How **may we help** you? (more formal)
Regular customers may open a monthly account if they wish. (more formal)

WESSEX electricity

I called today to read your electricity meter, but received no reply.

I will call back AM/PM between ....

If this is not convenient, or if you do not want to be disturbed, could you please leave the reading on the reverse of this card, tear off at the perforation and display it where I can read it?

Thank you.

To *Sophie*

From *Uncle Tony xxx*

This voucher may be exchanged for goods at any of our 150 branches. It cannot be exchanged for cash or replaced if lost.

Could YOU spare a couple of hours one day a week to work in your local **RESPONSE** charity shop?

We are looking for volunteers to sort donations and serve in the shop. No shop experience needed. Perhaps you could ask a friend to volunteer with you.

Exercises

1 Complete the requests with suitable modal verbs.

Example: You're speaking to an old friend.
Ed, _can_ you pass the dictionary?

1 You're speaking to an old friend.
Ed, _____ you tell me what this means?

2 You're speaking to a foreign visitor at your firm.
_____ you come with me, Mr Hoffman?

3 A stewardess is speaking to the passengers.
_____ all passengers kindly return to their seats?

4 You're speaking to an old friend.
Jim, _____ I use your bike for ten minutes?

5 You're speaking to a foreign visitor at your firm.
_____ I have your name, Sir?

6 A stewardess is speaking to a passenger.
_____ I take your cup, if you've finished?

2 Complete the requests with suitable modal verbs.

Example: A stewardess wants all passengers to fasten their seat belts.
Would all passengers kindly fasten their seat belts?

1 You want to borrow your friend's book.
_____

2 You want your friend to lend you his pen.
_____

3 You want to know the company visitor's address.
_____

4 You want the company visitor to take a seat for a moment.
_____

5 A stewardess wants to put a passenger's bag away.
_____

6 A stewardess wants all passengers to remain in their seats until the plane stops.
_____
_____

3 Write the answers. Use *Yes, you can ...* or *No, you can't ...*

Example: ● *Can I turn right here?*
○ _No, you can't turn right here._ It says NO ENTRY.

1 ● *Can I go now?*
○ _____ The lights are green.

2 ● *Can I park here?*
○ _____ It says NO PARKING.

3 ● *Can I pass this bus?*
○ _____ There are no cars coming.

4 ● *Can I turn round here?*
○ _____ It's dangerous.

4 Complete the conversation. Use suitable modal forms for requesting, permitting and offering.

Simon Bell has brought a German businessman, Franz Hoffman, home for dinner.

Simon: *Come in, Franz. _Can_ I take your coat for you?*

Franz: *Thanks very much.*

Simon: *Now, ¹_____ you like to meet the family?*

Franz: *Please.*

Simon: *This is my wife, Carol, and these are the children– Luke and Lisa.*

Carol: *It's nice to meet you Mr Hoffman.*

Franz: *And it's very good to meet you too. But one thing. ²_____ you just call me Franz?*

Carol: *Yes, of course. Now ³_____ you all come and eat? Dinner's getting cold.*

Ten minutes later

Simon: *⁴_____ you pass the salt, please?*

Carol: *Yes, of course. Here you are.*

Lisa: *Dad, ⁵_____ you help me with my German homework after dinner?*

Simon: *No, I ⁶_____ My German isn't very good.*

You look really tired! I think you should stop now. You ought to go to bed.

should and *ought to*

These are nearly the same, but *ought to* is a little stronger and more formal. Use *should* and *ought to* for advising the right thing to do in a particular situation.

> That hat looks terrible, Tom! You **should try** this one.
> You look very ill, Mr Jones. I think you **ought to see** the doctor.

Also use *should not (shouldn't)* and *ought not to (oughtn't to)* for advising what not to do.

> You **shouldn't wear** those shoes, Tom. They're not very nice.
> You **oughtn't to work** today. Really! Please go and see the doctor.

Use *should* and *ought to* for saying what is always the right or wrong thing to do.

> Parents **should teach** their children to be polite.
> People **oughtn't to play** loud music at night.

Use *should* and *ought to* for saying what is wrong and what is necessary.

> Excuse me. The bill **shouldn't be** £5.50. It **ought to be** £3.70.

had better

had better ('d better) is like *should* and *ought to* (first use) for advising the right thing to do in a particular situation.

> That hat looks terrible, Tom! You**'d better try** this one.
> You look very ill, Mr Jones. I think you**'d better see** a doctor.

Also use *had better not ('d better not)* for advising what not to do.

> You**'d better not wear** those shoes.   You**'d better not work** today.

You cannot use *had better* for the other uses of *should* and *ought to*. But *had better* can be much stronger than *should* or *ought to*. It can be a threat.

> You**'d better work** a lot harder, or you're going to lose your job!
> You**'d better not say** that again, or I'll be angry!

should (not) have and *ought (not) to have*

Use these past forms when somebody did the wrong thing.

> Tom crashed the car. He **shouldn't have driven** so fast. OR *He* **should have driven** more slowly.
> Susie has broken all the plates. She **ought to have been** more careful. OR *She* **oughtn't to have carried** so many.

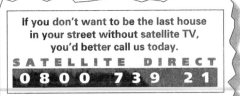

Confucius (551–479 BC) was a wise teacher. His ideas greatly influenced the Chinese. He taught that people should be courteous, loyal and unselfish.

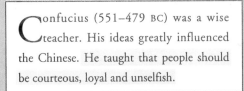
After the match Exmouth captain Nick Waters said, 'We should have dominated this league this season; we've got the players to do it, but we haven't produced our top form as often as we should have.'

23 *Ask a Vet*

Q   Last summer my two rabbits died after I gave them lettuce to eat. I thought I was giving them a treat, but a neighbour told me I ought to have known better. Was it my fault? Is lettuce dangerous?

A   Lettuce is not dangerous in itself, but too much too suddenly can be fatal, so in that sense you should have been more careful. However,

Exercises

1 Complete the conversation. Use *should* or *ought*.

Eve and Sam are getting ready for a party.

Eve: *What time __should__ we go?*

Sam: *We __ought__ to leave here at 7.30. And it's 6.30 now, so we ¹_____ to hurry now. What do you think I ²_____ wear?*

Eve: *I think you ³_____ to wear a jacket and tie. Do you think I ⁴_____ wear my red dress?*

Sam: *Yes, you ⁵_____ It looks very good.*

2 Complete the conversation. Use *should/shouldn't* or *ought/oughtn't*.

Tina and Steve are going to visit his parents.

Tina: *Do you think we __should__ go by train?*

Steve: *No, we __oughtn't__ to do that. We'll have too much to carry. We ¹_____ to go by car.*

Tina: *Well, OK, but we ²_____ to take too much. We're only going for two days.*

Steve: *All right, but I think we ³_____ take some warm clothes. The weather may be cold. And ⁴_____ we to take some toys for the children? They may be bored.*

Tina: *No, we ⁵_____ do that. I think we ⁶_____ just take one or two books for them to read. Now what time do you think we ⁷_____ leave?*

Steve: *Well, it takes five hours by car, so we ⁸_____ to leave here after 2.00.*

3 Complete the statements. Use *had better* or *had better not*.

Example: You *'d better not* play with those matches. They're dangerous.

1 You look ill. You _____ see a doctor.

2 Ed has got a lot of homework to do. He _____ _____ go out this evening.

3 We've only got a little food. We _____ _____ waste it.

4 The children are tired. They _____ go to bed.

4 Give advice.

Example: ● *I'm overweight. (should / not / eat / so much)*
○ *You shouldn't eat so much.*

1 ● *I'm unfit. (ought / do / more exercise)*
○ _____

2 ● *I've got a bad toothache. (better / see / a dentist)*
○ _____

3 ● *I've got a lot of work to do. (should / not / watch / TV / so much)*
○ _____
_____

4 ● *I've got a huge phone bill. (ought / not / use / the phone / so much)*
○ _____
_____

5 ● *It's still raining. (better / not / go out / yet)*
○ _____

6 ● *It's nice and sunny now. (should / go / to the beach)*
○ _____

5 Write the replies.

Example: ● *Andy felt really ill this morning. (ought / not / go / to work)*
○ *He oughtn't to have gone to work.*

1 ● *Tim was ill this morning. (should / go / to the doctor)*
○ _____
_____

2 ● *The boys got wet in the rain. (should / not / play / outside)*
○ _____
_____

3 ● *We're on the wrong road. (ought / turn / left / the traffic lights)*
○ _____
_____

4 ● *Maria doesn't like her new jacket. (ought / not / buy / it)*
○ _____
_____

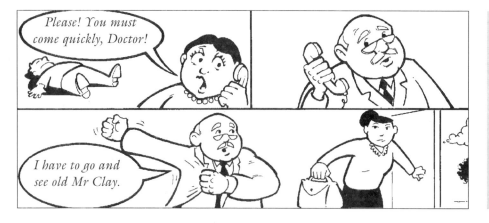

We use *must* and *have to* for saying something is necessary now or very soon.

*It's late. You **must stop** work and **go** to bed now, Tom.*

● ***Must** you **drive** so fast?*

○ *Yes, or we'll miss the plane.*

*He **has to start** work at 8.00 tomorrow.*

*I **have to go**. My boss is calling me.*

Use *have to* for other times. (*have to* has tenses, but *must* does not.)

● *Did you **have to work** late?*   ○ *Yes, we **had to stay** until midnight!*

● *Has Ann **had to go** to hospital?*   ○ *Yes, she has. She's very ill.*

*We can't finish now. We'**ll have to come back** next week.*

We often use *have got to* instead of *have to*. Use *have got to* in conversation. Use it for saying something is necessary now or very soon.

*I'**ve got to go** or Dad will be angry.*

● ***Have** we **got to do** all this?*

○ *Yes, you **have**. It's part of the job.*

The law is changing.

Keep on the right side of the law.

From next year, when you receive a vehicle licence reminder you must take action whether you use or keep your vehicle on the public roads or not. If you intend to use or keep your car on the road, you must apply for a licence by completing the form in the usual manner. This must be done quickly. But, if you do not use or keep your vehicle on the public road, you must complete the new declaration on the VII form and take it to a post office or send it to us.

Driver and Vehicle Licensing Agency (DVLA)

CROSSCHECK

must

Use *must* when the speaker feels a strong need inside.

*Quick! We **must run** for the bus!*
*You **must come** quickly, Doctor!*

have to

Use *have to* when the speaker expresses a need from outside, eg from a boss or teacher or parent.

*I **have to go** and **see** old Mr Clay.*
*I **have to do** some Maths for Mr Davis.*

must not

Use *must not* for necessity not to do something. Use the short form *mustn't* in conversation. (Do not pronounce the *t* in the middle.)

*Stop! You **mustn't drink** that! It'll make you ill.*

We often use *can't* like *mustn't*.

*You **can't hold** the ball. It's against the rules.*

not have to

Use *not have to* for no necessity to do something. (See Unit 33 for information on *didn't need to* and *didn't have to*.)

*You **don't have to take** the exam if you don't want to.*

Hidden Salts, Fats and Sugars

Experts estimate that in the UK alone over 60,000 people die prematurely each year from diet-related diseases (eating too much fat/salt and too few fruits and vegetables), yet nutrition panels on food packaging do not have to tell us how much fat, salt or sugar there is in a product.

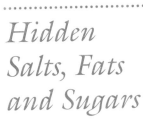

At all times dogs must not be allowed to foul footpaths or other areas.

Maximum Penalty £100

Exercises

1 Complete the questions with *have to*.

Example: *Paul has had to buy a car.*
         Why <u>has Paul had to buy a car?</u>

1 *Paul has had to pay a lot of money for it.*
   How much _____
   _____

2 *Emma will have to go to London soon.*
   When _____
   _____

3 *The Smith family had to go last week.*
   Where _____
   _____

4 *Ann has to change all her plans.*
   Why _____
   _____

5 *Ed and Sue have had to live in the flat for years.*
   How long _____
   _____

2 Complete the statements. Use *must* or *have to*.

Examples: *He said, 'You must finish by 5.00, Ann.'*
         So Ann <u>has to finish by 5.00.</u>
         The children have to go to bed now.
         Mum said, 'You <u>must go to bed now,</u>
         <u>children.'</u>

1 *Old Mr Robbins has to rest for a week.*
   The doctor said, 'You _____
   _____

2 *The bill says they must pay immediately.*
   So they _____

3 *We have to check in one hour before the flight.*
   The air tickets say: 'Passengers _____
   _____

4 *The hotel sign says: 'All guests must complete a registration form.'*
   So all guests _____
   _____

5 *Jimmy has to be home by 6.00.*
   His mother said, 'You _____

6 *The policeman said, 'You must go to the police station, Mr Reece.'*
   So Mr Reece _____
   _____

3 Complete the statements. Use *must* or *have to*.

Examples: *We* <u>had to</u> *work all day yesterday.*
         The fireman said, 'Quick! You <u>must</u> *leave the building immediately.'*

1 *I* _____ *read Ian York's new book. I love his writing.*

2 *Alan* _____ *go to the shop for some milk. Do you want anything?*

3 *You* _____ *listen to what I tell you. It's very important.*

4 *Last week we* _____ *wait for hours at the airport because of bad weather.*

5 *We really* _____ *buy a new TV. This old one is terrible.*

6 *Our new trainer is tough. We* _____ *run ten kilometres every morning.*

7 *This job looks interesting. I* _____ *ask for an application form.*

4 Complete the statements. Use *mustn't* or *not have to*.

Examples: *You* <u>don't have to</u> *buy a new pen. You can use mine.*
         Bob <u>mustn't</u> *go out. He's ill.*

1 *You* _____ *be late or you won't get into the cinema.*

2 *Students* _____ *wear a uniform at this school.*

3 *You* _____ *talk like that. It's rude.*

4 *I* _____ *be late home. I've got a lot of homework to do.*

5 *Ruth* _____ *go to work tomorrow. She's on holiday.*

6 *I* _____ *eat it if I don't want to.*

33 Modal auxiliary verbs 5
needn't, mustn't, didn't need to, needn't have

You needn't run. The bus isn't here yet.

You mustn't cross the road. The lights are red.

CROSSCHECK

needn't

Use *need to* (or *have to*) for saying something is necessary.

> *Come on! We **need to hurry**.*

Use *need not* (or *not need to/not have to*) for no necessity to do something.

> *We **needn't go** to the cinema to see it. We can get the video.
> We **don't need to buy** the video. We can rent it.
> We **don't have to rent** it. We can borrow it from Peter.*

mustn't

Use *must* for saying something is necessary.

> *We **must get** there by 11.00.*

Use *mustn't* for necessity not to do something.

> *You **mustn't play** with that knife. You'll cut yourself.
> You **mustn't cross** the road when the lights are red.*

didn't need to

Use *didn't need to* (or *didn't have to*) + infinitive when something was not necessary.

> *She's very clever, so she **didn't need to work** for the test.*

didn't need to (or *didn't have to*) usually means that an action was not necessary, so it did not happen.

> *Tom **didn't need to arrive** until 8.00, but he was there at 7.00. He likes being early.*

But we can use it when an action was not necessary, but it still happened – like *needn't have*.

> *You **didn't have to pay** him any money. He was happy to work for nothing.*

needn't have

Use *needn't have* + past participle when something happened, but it was not necessary.

> *Poor Sam **needn't have worked** so hard for the test. It was cancelled!*

Back to school with RIGHT PRICE

Kids! School uniforms needn't be ugly!
Parents! Good quality needn't be expensive!

Check out our fashionable ranges at a **RIGHT PRICE** clothes store near you.

Players must not wear shoes with coloured soles on court.

You mustn't miss our latest bargains!

Come in and look around.

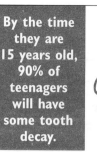

By the time they are 15 years old, 90% of teenagers will have some tooth decay.

This needn't happen if parents start thinking about the effects of sugar on teeth from the very beginning.

Exercises

1 Complete the statements. Use *needn't* or *mustn't*.

Examples: We _needn't_ hurry. We've got lots of time.
We _mustn't_ swim here. It's dangerous.

1 Don't you like it? Well, you _____ drink it if you don't want to.

2 Listen! You _____ be late again or you'll be in bad trouble.

3 You _____ make so much noise. This is a library.

4 You _____ finish the report today, but please can I have it tomorrow?

5 Children _____ play with knives. They're dangerous things.

6 Ann _____ stay. Carol can do everything.

2 Re-order the words to make positive and negative statements and questions.

Examples: (there / he / go / to / have / doesn't)
He doesn't have to go there.
(need / what / buy / we / do / to)
What do we need to buy?

1 (work / to / I / late / have)

_____

2 (they / go / to / where / have / do)

_____

3 (she / need / go / does / to / so soon)

_____

4 (tomorrow / you / do / to / have / work)

_____

5 (need / I / homework / don't / do / my / to)

_____

6 (learn / why / to / they / French / do / need)

_____

3 Complete the conversation. Use *need to*, *needn't* or *mustn't*.

Neil is telling his parents about his school trip to France.

Neil: On the day we go I _need to_ be at school at 7.45. The bus goes at 8.00.

Mum: What clothes do you _need to_ take with you? [1]_____ wear your school uniform? (you)

Neil: No, we [2]_____ do that. We can wear our ordinary clothes. We also [3]_____ take clothes for outdoor activities – jeans, boots and anoraks. You [4]_____ look at this list of clothes and equipment and this letter from school.

Dad: How much is it going to cost?

Neil: It's £200, but you [5]_____ pay it all yet. The letter says you only [6]_____ pay half now.

Dad: Good. We [7]_____ spend too much now because we haven't got much money this month. How soon [8]_____ give the school the first £100? (we)

Neil: I [9]_____ take it by next weekend.

Mum: It sounds great fun.

Neil: Yes, but they've made a special rule. As soon as we get on the bus we [10]_____ speak English any more. We can only speak French for a whole week!

4 Complete the statements. Use *didn't need to* or *needn't have*.

Examples: I _needn't have_ gone to the meeting. Nobody else was there.
Yesterday was a holiday, so I _didn't need to_ go to work.

1 At my school we _____ wear a uniform. People just wore their ordinary clothes.

2 They _____ worked so hard. Nobody even noticed all the work they did.

3 We _____ hurried. Everybody else was late too.

4 Sally _____ buy a coat. Her brother gave her a very nice one.

5 I _____ send the money. Mr Brant came for it.

6 You _____ written to them. I'd already told them your answer.

34 Modal auxiliary verbs 6

may, might, could, may be, must be, can't be, may have, must have, can't have

may, might and could

Use *may* or *might* to say something is possible in the future.
> The score is 3-3, so either side **may/might win**.

Use *could* to say something is possible, but not likely.
> The score is 3-1 against City. They **could win**, but I don't think so.

may not and *might not* mean something negative is possible.
> I'm very busy, so I **may not/might not have** time to go to the match.

cannot (can't) and *could not (couldn't)* mean something negative is impossible.
> City **can't/couldn't win** against Rangers. Rangers are too good.

may be, might be, must be and can't be

Use *may be* or *might be* when something is not certain in the present.
> Bill isn't in his office. He **may be** in Room 303, or he **might be seeing** Mr Bell.

must be and *can't be* are opposites. Use them when something is certain in the present. *must be* means certain (negative).
> Look at that car! It **must be doing** 250 kph. The driver **must be** crazy.
> This boy says he's 16, but he looks so young. He **can't be telling** the truth. He **can't be** more than 14.

may have, must have and can't have

Use these (and *might have* or *could have*) when something is certain or uncertain in the past.
> Jerry **must have left** his bag somewhere because he hasn't got it now.
> He **can't have left** it at school because he's checked and it isn't there.
> He **may have left** it somewhere on the way home.

Exercises

1 Complete the statements. Use *may (not) / might (not)*.

Example: We're very late for the plane. We <u>may/might</u> miss it.

1 I _____ be late home tonight, so don't worry if I'm not back at the usual time.

2 Dr Jones _____ have time to see you, but I don't think so. Ask his secretary.

3 If we go on playing this badly, we _____ win the game.

4 I _____ catch the 9.00 train, but I'll probably get the one at 9.30.

5 We _____ have enough milk. Could you buy some, please?

6 I'll try and get a green sweater in town, but I _____ be able to find one.

2 Write statements. Use *may (not) be/might (not) be, must be* or *can't be*.

Examples: ● Do you know where Paul is?
    ○ (It's late, so he isn't at school.)
      <u>He can't be at school.</u>
    ● (Perhaps he's at home.)
      <u>He may/might be at home.</u>
    ○ (He's always with his friends in the evening.)
      <u>He must be with his friends.</u>

1 ● How old do you think Mr Lee is?
  ○ (I'm sure he isn't under 60.)
  _____

  ● (Perhaps he's about 64 or 65.)
  _____

  ○ (I know he's 65 because he's just retired from work.)
  _____
  _____

2 ● Is that Rod coming across the beach.
  ○ (I'm sure it's Julian because that looks like his jacket.)
  _____
  _____

● (Perhaps it isn't him. He's walking towards some other people.)
_____
_____

○ (I'm sure it isn't Rod. Rod is taller.)
_____

3 Complete the conversation. Use *may be/ might be, must be* or *can't be* + present participle.

? = *may be/might be*, ✓ = *must be*, ✗ = *can't be*

Tina: Do you know what Dave is doing?
Nick: I'm not sure. He <u>may/might be riding</u> his bike. (? ride)
Tina: No, he [1]_____ that. (✗ do) His bike is still in the garage.
Nick: Well, he [2]_____ upstairs. (✗ play) The house is too quiet.
Tina: Oh, look. His baseball bat has gone. He [3]_____ baseball in the park. (✓ practise)

4 Complete the conversation. Use *may have/ might have, must have* or *can't have* + past participle.

? = *may have/might have*, ✓ = *must have*, ✗ = *can't have*

Dave: Mum, have you seen my wallet in the dining-room?
Tina: No, you <u>can't have put</u> it there. (✗ put) I've just tidied the dining-room and I didn't see it.
Dave: And I [1]_____ it in the park because I didn't take my money. (✗ drop)
Tina: You [2]_____ it upstairs in your bedroom. (? leave)
Dave: I'm not sure.
Nick: Wasn't your wallet in your jeans pocket yesterday?
Tina: And didn't you throw your jeans in the washing machine this morning?
Dave: Oh, so I [3]_____ my wallet in the washing machine too. (✓ put) I'll have to hang my money out to dry!

35 Modal auxiliary verbs 7: past forms
could, had to, needed to, may have, must have, can't have, could have, etc

FORMS

Grandad: *I could run 100 metres in ten seconds
           when I was young.*

Grandson: *Wow! You must have been the fastest
           in the country.*

Grandad: *Yes, I should have been in the Olympic
           team, but I was ill. I couldn't go.*

could, had to and needed to

Use *had to* and *needed to* to talk about past necessity and need. (*must* has no past form.) (See Units 32/33 for more information.)

> *I was late for the meeting. I **had to run**.*
> *We **needed to get** some milk, so I went to the shop.*

Use *could* and *could not* to talk about ability and possibility in the past.

> *I **could run** 30 kilometres when I was 20.*
> *He **couldn't swim** when he was five.*

Use *could not* for an action that did not happen.

> *I was so tired that I **couldn't walk** any more.*

We usually use *be able to* instead of *could* for a past action. But you can use *could* with verbs of feeling (*see, hear*, etc) and thinking (*remember, forget*, etc). (See Unit 29.)

> *After a long sleep, I **was able to get up** and **start** walking again.*
> *After a long while I **could see** a farm ahead of me.*

may have, must have and can't have

Use these (and *might have* or *could have*) when something seems certain or uncertain in the past. (See Unit 34 for more information.)

> ● *There's nobody at home. They **must have gone out**.*
> ○ *They **may have gone** to the beach.*
> ● *No. They **can't have done** that. Their car is still here.*

could have, should have and would have

Use these (and *ought to have* or *might have*) when somebody did something wrongly or differently.

> *You **could have called** earlier. Why didn't you?*
> *I'm sorry. I can't pay. I **should have brought** more money.*

would have is the same form as in Type 3 conditionals. (See Unit 45.)
Use these negative forms in the same way: *should not have, ought not to have, would not have, need not have.* (See Units 31/33.)

> *We **would have visited** you, but we didn't know you were at home.*
> *He **shouldn't have shouted** at her. Look! She's crying now!*
> *You **needn't have gone** to town for a newspaper. You can get them near here.*

Compare *needn't have* and *didn't need to.*

> *I **didn't need to go** to work, so I stayed in bed.*

Everyday Etiquette

Q   My previous employer and I had a difference of opinion over certain pronunciations, particularly with frequently used words such as 'integral'. When asked to read back his dictation, should I have used his version or mine?

Margaret Hills, Manchester

A   Yours. Modern good manners do not require one person to imitate the mistakes of another!

Scientists believe there may have been life on Mars three billion years ago!

'A wonderful play set in British India brought to life by director, Peter Wells.'

The actors create situations and places that until now you could only have imagined. This extraordinary production has received critical and popular acclaim for its tour of the north.

THE TIGER

Did you know that at the beginning of the 20th century there may have been 100,000 tigers living in the forests and on the plains of Asia? Today there are less than 6,000 and their numbers are still falling.

Exercises

1 Complete the story. Use past forms of *can, be able to, have to, need* or *need to*.

When Larry's boat hit a rock, he *didn't need to* look below. He 1_____ hear the water rushing in, and he knew the boat was going down. He also knew he 2_____ get off the boat in two or three minutes. He 3_____ pull out the orange life-raft and he threw it quickly into the water, where it filled with air. Next, he ran to the cabin. He 4_____ collect as many things as possible – food, water medicine, a map, and so on. The only thing he 5_____ take was petrol – the life-raft had no motor. Soon water was coming into the cabin, and he 6_____ get out quickly. He looked round for the raft. He 7_____ see it! Then he did. It was ten metres away. Larry dropped his supplies on top of the cabin and jumped into the sea. He 8_____ get that raft! He reached it, climbed in and started rowing back for his supplies. As he rowed, he 9_____ see the boat sinking. He rowed harder. He 10_____ those supplies as much as the life-raft itself. He 11_____ let those supplies go down with his boat.

Complete these possible endings.

But he 12_____ get there in time. He lost everything. OR
He got there just in time, and he 13_____ save everything.

2 Complete the conversation. Use *may have* (or *might have/could have*), *must have* or *can't have*.

Bob and Lucy are looking for their son, Joe, at the beach.

Bob: *He can't have gone into the water. He's still wearing his T-shirt and shorts.*

Lucy: *And he 1_____ gone to the ice-cream van or the beach shop because he hasn't got any money.*

Bob: *He 2_____ gone to the beach shop just to look around.*

Lucy: *Yes, he 3_____ done that. He was asking me to buy a ball before. He's crazy about volleyball.*

Bob: *Talking about volleyball, there are some people playing volleyball over there, and there are some people watching. He 4_____ gone to watch the game. What do you think?*

Lucy: *You're wrong. He isn't watching. He's playing. He 5_____ gone and asked to join the game.*

3 Complete the conversation. Use *could have, would have ('d have), shouldn't have, should have, wouldn't have* or *needn't have*.

The Green family are coming back from a terrible holiday in the south of France. It rained all the time and it was very cold.

Mum: *Well, nobody could have guessed the weather would be so bad.*

Dad: *Yes, if we'd known about the weather, we certainly 1_____ gone there.*

Tim: *We 2_____ taken our raincoats, rubber boots, hats, gloves and scarves.*

Jo: *And I 3_____ bought that new summer dress. I didn't wear it once. I'm so disappointed.*

Dad: *We 4_____ chosen a holiday in Greece as easily as the one in France. It 5_____ been the same price. In fact, I 6_____ chosen Greece except that we can all speak French, but not Greek.*

Mum: *We 7_____ listened to the travel agent. She said the weather was always wonderful in the south of France.*

Dad: *We 8_____ done better to stay at home and save our money.*

Mum: *Well, next year we'll go somewhere else – somewhere warm and dry.*

36 Review: modal auxiliary verbs

can, could, would, be able to, should, ought to, must, have to, etc

Ability (See Unit 29.)

*Most birds **can fly**.*
*Some people **can't swim**.*
*Ann **could write** when she was three.*
*I **was able to finish** the test in an hour.*

Requests, offers and permission (See Unit 30.)

***May I speak** to Mr Hill, please?*
***Could you keep** the noise down, please?*
***Would you post** this for me, please?*
***Would you like** a part-time job?*
● ***May I go** home early today?*
○ ***Yes**, of course **you can**.*

Advice (See Unit 31.)

*You **shouldn't eat** so much.*
*You **oughtn't to play** computer games so much.*
*You look tired. You**'d better go** home.*

Obligation and necessity (See Unit 32.)

*You **mustn't copy** his work. That's wrong.*
*At my new job I **have to start** at 9.00.*
*I**'ve got to go** now, or my parents will be angry.*
*You **can't walk** on the grass. Look! The notice says: 'Keep off the grass.'*
*If you want a licence, you **need to fill in** this form.*

Non-obligation (See Unit 33.)

You **needn't do** this work now. You can finish it tomorrow.
We **didn't have to work** at the weekend, but we wanted to help as much as we could.

Certainty and uncertainty (See Unit 34.)

He **might come**, but I don't think so.
She **definitely will/won't be** at the wedding.
They **could arrive** this evening, but I don't think so.
He **can't be** at the office. He never works this late.
He **must be visiting** a friend.

Past forms of modals (See Unit 35.)

We **should have gone** to school, but we went to the football match.
You **oughtn't to have used** the money. Now we haven't got any to buy food.
They **couldn't stay**. They **had to go** home.
Nobody answered the phone, so they **can't have been** at home. They **must have been** out.

Exercises

1 Complete the statements and questions. Use *can*, *can't*, *could*, *couldn't* or *be able to*.

Examples: *I'm tired. I __can't__ go on any longer.*
At last, we __were able to__ escape.

1 I _____ understand the problem. _____
you?

2 Alex _____ already swim when he was three.

3 I tried to move, but I _____

4 You were near the accident, Mr Jones. _____
you see what happened?

5 In the end, we _____ save enough
money to buy a car last year.

6 What happened when he got lost? _____
_____ find his way of the woods? (he)

2 Write requests. (You can often give more than one answer.)

Example: A business caller wants to talk to the manager.
● *May I speak to the manager, please?*

1 A girl wants to borrow her friend's book.
● _____

2 A shop assistant offers to help a customer.
● _____

3 A manager asks his assistant to get the red file.
● _____

4 Somebody offers a friend a cup of tea.
● _____

5 A receptionist asks a business visitor his name.
● _____

6 Somebody asks a friend to lend him some money.
● _____

7 An office worker asks her boss for a day off next week.
● _____

8 A visitor asks if he can park his car outside the entrance.
● _____
_____

3 Give advice. (You can often give more than one answer.)

Examples: ● *I feel ill. (see the doctor)* OR *(not go to work today)*
○ *You'd better see the doctor.* OR
You oughtn't to go to work today.

1 ● *I've got a terrible toothache. (go to the dentist)*
○ _____

2 ● *The boys have got a lot of work tonight. (not watch TV)*
○ _____

3 ● *I can't see very well. (get some glasses)*
○ _____

4 ● *My brother wants to make more money. (find a better job)*
○ _____

5 ● *Tom wants a good grade in Maths. (not miss the next test)*
○ _____

6 ● *Sam wants to play outside, but it's still raining. (not go out yet)*
○ _____

4 Complete the statements. Use *must, mustn't, have to* or *can't*.

Examples: Mary's new contract: *Employees __must__ work 38 hours a week*
Mary to her parents: *I __have to__ work 38 hours a week.*

1 Teacher to a new student: *Tony, you _____ come late again. You _____ always be here on time.*

2 Friend to Tony: *We _____ come to school late. If we do, we _____ stay behind for an hour after school.*

3 Notice on a beach: *DANGER! Visitors _____'_____ remain close to the beach at all times. When the red flag is up, swimmers _____ leave the water.*

4 Swimmer to friend: *Look! The red flag is up. That means we _____ stay in the water. We _____ get out.*

5 Complete the statements. Use the present form *needn't* and the present and past forms of *(not) need to* or *(not) have to*.

Example: *There is a holiday next week, so we <u>don't have to</u> come to work.*

1 *You _____ go shopping. I've been already.*

2 *I _____ write a report last month. There was nothing to write about.*

3 *We _____ wear a uniform at work, but the boss always says we _____ dress smartly.*

4 *When I was at school, we _____ wear the school uniform until the last year, but in the last year, we _____ wear the uniform any more.*

5 *I _____ use the car again this week, so you can have it. But I _____ have it again by Monday morning.*

6 ● *How many questions did you _____ answer in the exam?*
   ○ *We _____ answer five questions.*

6 Complete the conversation. Choose from *will, won't, could, may (not)* or *might (not)*.

Two friends are waiting at the station for another friend, Ted, and for a train.

Tony: *I hope Ted isn't going to be late. The train <u>will</u> be here in a minute.*

Lisa: *Don't worry. Ted ¹_____ be here in a minute. He promised.*

Tony: *I don't know. He's often late. He ²_____ get here, but he ³_____ Look! The train is coming. It ⁴_____ be here in a minute.*

Lisa: *You ⁵_____ be right. But he still ⁶_____ come. There's still a chance.*

Tony: *No. He ⁷_____ get here in time now. It's too late. The train is here.*

Ted: *Hi, Tony. Hi, Lisa. I'm here.*

7 Read Ann Green's diary for today. Then answer her colleague's questions. Use *can't be, may be* or *must be*.

9.00 – 10.30	visit GLA
10.30 – 12.00	travel to Birmingham
12.00 – 1.00	meet Stephen Fisher
1.00 – 2.00	have lunch with Eric Ross at the City Hotel or the Ritz Grill
2.00 – 3.30	travel to Liverpool or Manchester

Examples: ● *What's she doing at the moment?* (It's 9.30.)
   ○ *She <u>must be visiting GLA.</u>*
   ● *Is she in Birmingham now?* (It's 11.15.)
   ○ *No, she <u>can't be in Birmingham.</u> She <u>must be travelling there.</u>*

1 ● *What's she doing now?* (It's 12.30.)
   ○ *She _____*

2 ● *Where's she having lunch?* (It's 1.15.)
   ○ *She _____*
      or she _____

3 ● *Is she in Birmingham now?* (It's 2.45.)
   ○ *No, she _____*
      She _____
      _____

8 Complete the statements with past forms. Choose from these modals.

could have, should have, ought to have, would have ('d have), can't have, couldn't have, shouldn't have, oughtn't to have, needn't have.

Examples: *Jean <u>needn't have</u> cooked so much. Nobody was very hungry.*

1 *I _____ said thank you, but I forgot.*

2 *They _____ crossed the desert. They had no water.*

3 *You _____ made your little brother cry.*

4 *We _____ taken our coats. It was warm.*

5 *I _____ given you the money if I'd known you needed it.*

37 Passive verb forms 1
Every bike is checked.

Every bike is checked before it leaves the factory.

Statements			Yes/No questions		
I	*am* *am not*	*checked.*	*Am*	*I*	*checked?*
He *She* *It*	*is* *is not*	*checked.*	*Is*	*he* *she* *it*	*checked?*
We *You* *They*	*are* *are not*	*checked.*	*Are*	*we* *you* *they*	*checked?*

Wh questions

Where are they checked?
When is it done?

Full answers

They are checked at the factory.
It is done all the time.

Short forms: *I am = I'm   he is = he's   we are = we're*
I am not = I'm not   he is not = he isn't, he's not
we are not = we aren't, we're not   was not = wasn't
were not = weren't

Form the present simple passive with *am, is, are* + past participle, eg *am checked, is checked* and *are checked*. (See Appendix 1 for a list of common irregular participle forms.)
> **Active:** *Our workers* **check** *all the bikes.*
> **Passive:** *All the bikes* **are checked** *by our workers.*

Form the past simple passive with *was, were* + past participle eg *was made*, and *were made.*
> *The first bike* **was made** *100 years ago.*
> *The first bikes* **were made** *100 years ago.*

Form negative passives and passive questions like active sentences.
> ● **Are** *all these cars* **sold** *in Europe?*
> ○ *No, they* **aren't**. *Some cars* **are sold** *in America.*
> ● *How many* **are sent** *to America?*   ○ *About 500 a month.*

Use the passive to focus on the object of an active sentence, eg we are more interested in the cars than who built them – the agent.
> *The first plane* **was built** *by somebody nearly 100 years ago.*

You can leave out the agent if it is not important.
> *The first planes* **were built** *nearly 100 years ago.*

Sometimes, we use the passive because we do not know the agent.
> *The wheel* **was invented** *thousands of years ago.*

We often use the passive in technical English to explain how we do something. (Who does it is not important.)
> *The engines* **are put** *together in 85 separate steps.*

We often use the passive in formal English, eg in business agreements.
> *Under this agreement it* **is understood** *that both parties* **are committed** *to completing the project by 31st December, 1999.*

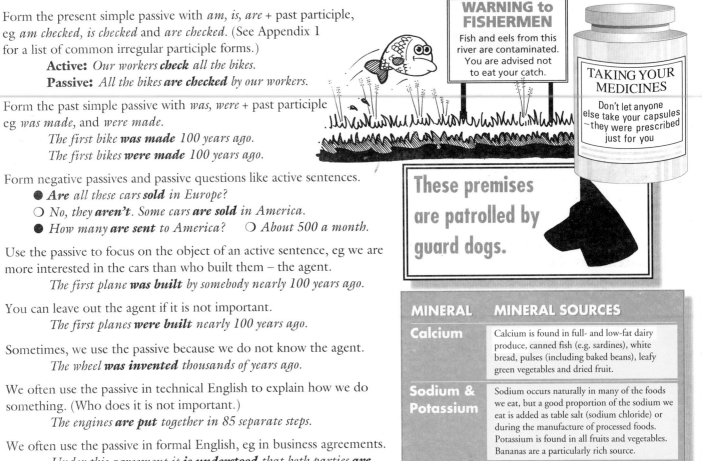

WARNING to FISHERMEN
Fish and eels from this river are contaminated. You are advised not to eat your catch.

TAKING YOUR MEDICINES
Don't let anyone else take your capsules – they were prescribed just for you

These premises are patrolled by guard dogs.

MINERAL	MINERAL SOURCES
Calcium	Calcium is found in full- and low-fat dairy produce, canned fish (e.g. sardines), white bread, pulses (including baked beans), leafy green vegetables and dried fruit.
Sodium & Potassium	Sodium occurs naturally in many of the foods we eat, but a good proportion of the sodium we eat is added as table salt (sodium chloride) or during the manufacture of processed foods. Potassium is found in all fruits and vegetables. Bananas are a particularly rich source.

Exercises

1 Write the verbs in the present simple passive.

The European Airbus A320 _is built_ by a group of European aeroplane makers. (build) The nose of the plane [1]_____ by the French. (make) The body of the plane [2]_____ by the Germans. (produce) The wings [3]_____ by the British. (provide) Then of all the parts [4]_____ to one factory in France where the plane [5]_____ together. (brought) (put) The finished A320 planes [6]_____ to their customers. (deliver)

2 Write the verbs in the past simple passive.

One of the first flying machines _was designed_ by Leonardo da Vinci. (design) The first real plane [1]_____ by the Wright brothers in 1903. (build) Planes soon became more common, and they [2]_____ in World War 1. (use) In 1919 letters [3]_____ across the Atlantic for the first time. (fly) Other ways of using planes [4]_____ too. (find) Passengers [5]_____ on regular flights, also in 1919. (carry) In the same year, the first international passenger flights [6]_____ between London and Paris. (begin) Airline services developed fast. In 1925 the first hot meals for passengers [7]_____ by a French airline. (provide) The first stewardess [8]_____ by an American airline in 1937. (employ)

3 Change the active statements into passive statements. Leave out the agents.

Example: They didn't tell people about the plan.
       People weren't told about the plan.

1 First the company built the new factory.

_____

2 Then the engineers designed the new Superbike 2,000.

_____
_____

3 They didn't show the design to anyone.

_____

4 People bought 1,000 in the first year.

_____

4 Read. Then write questions and answers.

Examples: (What/oil/need/for today)
● _What is oil needed for today?_
○ _It's needed for modern transport and industry._
(oil/know/in ancient times)
● _Was oil known in ancient times?_
○ _Yes, it was._

Our modern world needs large amounts of oil for industry and modern forms of transport. But oil was first known and used thousands of years ago. In ancient times, it was burned in oil lamps for light at night. Boats were also covered with it to keep water out. It was also used as a surface for roads by the Chinese.

About 100 years ago, far more oil was suddenly needed as modern transport and industry developed. Oil wells were drilled and large amounts of oil were found in many parts of the world, including the Middle East and the USA.

Today, oil is less easy to find, but new supplies are still discovered. Nearly 50 million barrels of oil are pumped from the ground every day.

1 (When/oil first/use)
● _____
○ _____
_____

2 (it/burn/for light)
● _____
○ _____

3 (When/far more oil/need)
● _____
○ _____

4 (more oil/find/at that time)
● _____
_____
○ _____

5 (How many barrels/oil/pump/every day now)
● _____
_____
○ _____
_____

38 Passive verb forms 2

It's being checked.   It's been checked.   It can be checked.   Get it checked.

> The roof was finished last week.

> I want to have the building finished this month.

Tense forms

Form the different passive tenses like this.

Active	Passive
*They **check** everything.*	*Everything **is checked**.*
*They **checked** everything.*	*Everything **was checked**.*
*They **are checking** everything.*	*Everything **is being checked**.*
*They **were checking** everything.*	*Everything **was being checked**.*
*They **have checked** everything.*	*Everything **has been checked**.*
*They **had checked** everything.*	*Everything **had been checked**.*
*They **will have checked** everything.*	*Everything **will have been checked**.*

Compare the different forms of *be* in continuous tenses and perfect tenses.

> *It **is being** finished.   They **are being** finished.*
> *It has **been** finished.   They have **been** finished.*

Future and modal passive forms

Use the following with *be* + past participle: *will, would, going to, can, could, may, might, must, should, have to, ought to*, etc.

Form the different future and modal passives like this.

Active	Passive
*They **will finish** everything.*	*Everything **will be finished**.*
*They **are going to finish** everything.*	*Everything **is going to be finished**.*
*They **must finish** everything.*	*Everything **must be finished**.*
*They **have to finish** everything.*	*Everything **has to be finished**.*

have/get something done

Use this form when you give somebody else some work to do for you.
Form it with *have* or *get* + object + past participle.

> *I**'m going to have the car checked** by a mechanic.*
> *They **got the work done** for £10,000.*

Use *had*, not *got*, in the present perfect.

> *We've **had the room decorated** and we've **had new curtains made** too.*

CUSTOMER CARE

DELIVERY IN 14 DAYS, GUARANTEED

On receipt, we will confirm your order details. Your order will be delivered direct to your door WITHIN 14 DAYS.

Delivery UK only (excluding Channel Isles).
All items are subject to availability.

BOYS' PE NEWS
Cricket

David Culshaw has been selected to attend the 2nd round of trials on Monday, 6th April, for the Devon Under-16 Cricket Squad for the coming season.

SALCOMBE REGIS CHURCH
Salcombe

Open daily during daylight hours.
Parties welcome.

Guided tours can be arranged.

Forthcoming events:
SUMMER FUNCTION

An informal function is being arranged for

Saturday 18th July in Cottrill Hall.

5-piece band, refreshments, bar

Time: 8.00 pm-12.00 midnight
Cost: £10 per head

Tickets will be available sometime in May, from Miss Parsons in the School Office.

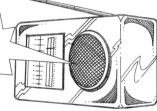

Some business news now ...
Techno, one of Britain's biggest electronic retail chains, has been bought by a Canadian consortium ...

Exercises

1 Write statements with verbs in continuous passive tenses.

Example: *The boy shouted for help. (he/carry/out to sea)*
<u>*He was being carried out to sea.*</u>

1 *We heard a noise and turned. (we/call/by somebody)*

2 *The towers are dangerous. (they/pull/down/next week)*

3 *The boss was angry. (the work/not/do/efficiently)*

4 *I didn't see little Ann yesterday. (she/look after/by Sue)*

5 *I haven't got my car. (it/service/at the garage)*

2 Write statements with verbs in perfect passive tenses.

Example: *I couldn't open the door. (it/lock/on the inside)*
<u>*It had been locked on the inside.*</u>

1 *The village is different now. (many new houses/build)*

2 *I managed to start the old car. (it/not/drive/for 20 years)*

3 *The bus has gone. (we/leave/behind)*

4 *We were angry about the plan. (we/not/tell/about it)*

3 Write the official rules.

Example: *Read this. It says we must pay bills within 30 days.*
<u>*Bills must be paid within 30 days.*</u>

At the library

1 *It says we can borrow up to five books.*

2 *It says we should return books on time.*

At work

3 *It says you must wear protective clothing at all times.*

4 *It says we mustn't eat food in the office.*

4 Write statements. Use *have/get* + object + past participle.

Example: *The door needs painting soon.*
Let's <u>*get the door painted soon.*</u>

1 *The window needs mending now.*
Let's _____

2 *These films need printing soon.*
Let's _____

3 *This wall needs rebuilding tomorrow.*
Let's _____

5 Change the active statements into passive statements. Leave out the agent if it is not important.

Examples: *The police are checking the house.*
<u>*The house is being checked by the police.*</u>
They haven't cleaned this room.
<u>*This room hasn't been cleaned.*</u>

1 *They built this castle in 1760.*

2 *Somebody was pulling Tony along the road.*

3 *Alan won't win the match. Jim will win it.*

4 *People should always read contracts before they sign them.*

5 *Bob has written a memo and the staff are reading it.*

I want to go.   I love going on the rides.

CROSSCHECK

Verb + *to* + infinitive

Some verbs take this form. These are the most common.

> *agree, aim, appear, arrange, ask, attempt, can't afford, can't wait, choose, decide, expect, fail, happen, hesitate, hope, learn, manage, offer, plan, prepare, pretend, promise, refuse, seem, tend, threaten, train, want, wish*

> I **agreed to go** with the others.
> We **aim to get** home by 9.00.
> Has Ed **promised not to spend** any more money?

Verb + *ing* form

Some verbs take this form. These are the most common.

> *admit, avoid, can't face, can't help, can't stand, carry on, consider, delay, deny, detest, dislike, enjoy, fancy, finish, give up, imagine, involve, keep, keep on, mention, mind, miss, postpone, practise, put off, quit, regret, risk, suggest*

> Steve **avoided seeing** Bob for months.
> Have you **finished writing** that letter?
> I **enjoy not getting up** early at the weekend.

Some verbs take either a *to* + infinitive or an *ing* form, eg *continue, love* and *start*. (See Unit 40.)

> It **continued to rain** all day.   It **continued raining** all day.
> Tom always **loves to win**.   Tom always **loves winning**.
> She **started to run**.   She **started running**.

Some verbs take an object + *to* + infinitive, eg *ask, persuade* and *remind*. (See Unit 41.)

> The manager **asked us to wait**.
> Tom **persuaded me to go**.
> Could you **remind me to call** Mr Hill at 4.00?

Some verbs take a preposition + *ing* form, eg *think of* and *blame ... for*. (See Unit 42.)

> We're **thinking of buying** a new car.
> I can't **blame her for leaving** that boring job.

Exercises

1 Write these verbs in the correct forms.

climb, finish, get, give, learn, move, play, see, win

Example: I've managed _to finish_ the report in time.

1 Tom agreed _____ for our team.

2 Sandra refused _____ her son any more money.

3 I can't wait _____ my cousins again. They've been away for a long time.

4 Bob promised _____ here on time. He's late.

5 She's hoping _____ the competition.

6 My parents have decided _____ to a house in the country.

7 We're preparing _____ the mountain.

8 I've chosen _____ German this term.

2 Write these verbs in the correct forms.

buy, crash, eat, lose, say, smoke, wait, walk, watch

Example: Drive slowly. We don't want to risk _crashing_ Dad's new car.

1 I can't stand _____ that TV programme.

2 They can't deny _____ the money. It's gone.

3 We've delayed _____ a car. We're short of money.

4 I enjoy _____ breakfast in the garden.

5 Don keeps on _____ he's clever, but he seems stupid to me.

6 Do you mind _____ here? Mr Price will be here soon.

7 I've given up _____ . I feel fitter already.

8 We'll have to carry on _____ We can't stop here.

3 Write the verbs in the correct forms.

Jean: I hate all these bills – gas, electricity, phone, the garage.

Joe: I detest _dealing with_ them too. (deal with) But we can't afford _to pay_ them any longer. (pay)

Jean: We seem [1]_____ all our money as fast as it comes in. (spend)

Joe: That's right. The bills keep on [2]_____ (arrive)

Jean: Do you think we can afford [3]_____ a holiday this summer? (have)

Joe: Maybe. If we try hard, I think we'll manage [4]_____ enough. (save)

Jean: We should give up [5]_____ (smoke) That would save a lot of money.

Joe: You're right. Anyway, where do you fancy [6]_____ (go)

Jean: I've always wanted [7]_____ Italy. (see) Would you mind [8]_____ that? (do)

Joe: No, that's a good idea. And I suggest [9]_____ in June. (go) I can get some free time then.

Jean: Fine. Let's plan [10]_____ then. (go) I can imagine [11]_____ around the streets of Venice and Rome already! (walk)

4 Complete the statements with negative forms.

Examples: Are you sorry that you didn't pass the exam?
Do you regret _not passing the exam?_
Please don't break the contract.
Please agree _not to break the contract._

1 Jean looks as if she doesn't mind what he said.
Jean seems _____

_____

2 Please don't make so much noise.
Would you mind _____

_____

3 'It's true. I don't have the money to repay Sam,' Tom said.
Tom admitted _____

_____

4 'I'm not going to go out with the others,' Suzie said.
Suzie decided _____

_____

5 'I'm not going to talk to Bill any more,' Ann said angrily.
Ann threatened _____

_____

When did you start racing, Tony?

Verb + *to* + infinitive or verb + *ing* form (no change of meaning)

Some verbs can take either form with no change of meaning, eg *begin, start, continue, intend, propose* and *bother*.

> It **began raining** at 10.00.   It **began to rain** at 10.00.
> I **intend visiting** my mother this weekend.
> I **intend to visit** my mother this weekend.
> Only 20 people **bothered coming** to the garden party.
> Only 20 people **bothered to come** to the garden party.

Do not put two *ing* forms together.

> People **were starting to leave** when the sun suddenly came out.
> (not *leaving*)

These verbs also take the *ing* or the *to* + infinitive form: *like, love, hate, prefer*.

> Tony **loves driving** fast.   Tony **loves to drive** fast.
> I **prefer drinking** tea.   I **prefer to drink** tea.

Note the difference between *like* + *ing* and *like* + *to* + infinitive.

> He **likes driving** classic racing cars. (He enjoys this.)
> He **likes to check** the oil and tyres before he drives anywhere.
> (He thinks this is the right thing to do.)

Note the differences between *hate/would hate, like/would like, love/would love* and *prefer/would prefer*.

> I **love** my mother and father very much.
> I'm really thirsty. I'**d love** a cup of tea.
> I always **prefer driving to going** by bus.
> I'**d prefer to drive** there tonight. The bus might be late.

Some verbs can take either verb + *ing* form or object + *to* + infinitive with no change of meaning, eg *advise, allow, encourage, permit* and *recommend*.

> Bill **advised doing** some exercise.
> Bill **advised me to do** some exercise.
> I **don't allow smoking** in my house.
> I **don't allow people to smoke** in my house.

Verb + *to* + infinitive or verb + *ing* form (change of meaning)

Some verbs can take either verb + *to* + infinitive or verb + *ing* form, but with a change of meaning.

CROSSCHECK

Verb + *to* + infinitive

remember/forget + *to* + infinitive (for necessary actions)

> Please **remember to buy** a newspaper.
> Please **don't forget to buy** some milk.

stop + *to* + infinitive (stop one thing and do something else for a short time)

> On our way home we **stopped to buy** some stamps.

try + *to* + infinitive (make a strong effort, do your best)

> We **tried to mend** the engine all night, but we failed.

mean + *to* + infinitive (1 plan to do something, 2 be required to do something)

> 1) I **meant to call** you, but I was busy.
> 1) I'm very sorry! I **didn't mean to hit** you.
> 2) You're **meant to sign** the papers here. Then they'll give you your money.

regret + *to* + infinitive (for showing you are sorry about what you are saying)

> We **regret to tell** you that Mr Briggs has died.

need + *to* + infinitive (has to do)

> Harry **needs to fly** to Cairo tonight as he has a meeting there tomorrow.

go on + *to* + infinitive (do something new after finishing another thing)

> She **went on to become** a famous artist.

Verb + *ing* form

remember/forget + verb *ing* (for memories of the past)

> I **remember climbing** that mountain in 1985.
> I'll never **forget reaching** the top. It was great!

stop + verb *ing* (end an action)

> Let's **stop fighting** and start talking.

try + verb *ing* (do something in a new way)

> I don't like the table here. Let's **try putting** it over there.

mean + verb + *ing* (one thing makes another thing necessary)

> I want to go to college, but that **means working** really hard.
> The bus has broken down. That **means waiting** for an hour for the next one.

regret + verb *ing* (for showing you are sorry about doing something)

> I **regretted leaving** my money at home. I needed it in town.

need + verb *ing* (for something that is necessary)

> Look at that dirty floor. It really **needs cleaning**.

go on + verb *ing* (continue doing)

> Sally **went on working** hard, even after her terrible accident.

Exercises

1 Write these verbs in the correct forms.

ask, be, come, form, provide, take

Someone is making a speech.

Ladies and gentlemen,

Thank you for bothering to come to this meeting on a cold, wet December evening. I know most of us would prefer ¹_____ at home. I don't intend ²_____ much of your time, but I have an important proposal to make. I'm proposing ³_____ a group of us to collect money for our local hospital. For many years, the hospital has continued ⁴_____ us all with a great service. Recently, though, the hospital has not been getting enough money for things such as children's toys. That's why the staff have started ⁵_____ for help from us, the local community.

2 Write the verbs in the correct forms.

Example: *Ed loves going on holiday. (go)*

Ed would love to go away this year. (go)

1   *Alan hates _____ early in the morning. (get up)*

2   *Would you like _____ out to the cinema this evening? (go)*

3   *I like _____ that all the windows and doors are shut at night. (check)*

4   *We always prefer _____ in the sea to _____ in a pool. (swim)*

5   *Ben doesn't like _____ very much. (read)*

6   *Which would you prefer _____ tomorrow – stay at home or go out? (do)*

7   *I'd love _____ London and see Buckingham Palace. (visit)*

8   *When Emma was small, she loved _____ with her doll's house. (play)*

9   *Ann always likes _____ exactly where her children are. (know)*

10 *I'd hate _____ alone. (live)*

3 Write the verbs in the correct forms.

Tina: *Did you remember to post the letters and buy the new TV licence? (post)*

Bob: *Well, I remembered ¹_____ the letters. (post) But I didn't get the licence.*

Tina: *Oh, no. You really forgot ²_____ the licence? (buy) I clearly remember ³_____ you to do that when you went out this morning. (ask)*

Bob: *Well, I don't remember ⁴_____ you. (hear) Perhaps I was too far away.*

Tina: *That's wrong. I remember you ⁵_____ , 'I'll get it on the way home.' (say)*

Bob: *Don't be silly. People don't forget ⁶_____ things like that. (say)*

Tina: *Well, you did. Anyway, please don't forget ⁷_____ it tomorrow. (get)*

Bob: *All right. I'll remember ⁸_____ that. (do) I promise.*

4 Write the verbs in the correct forms.

1   At a cleaners

Customer: *Can you try to clean this jacket for me, please? (clean) I've tried _____ these marks out, but I can't. (get)*

Assistant: *Have you tried _____ Vanish? (use) It's very good.*

2   At a hotel

Clerk: *Excuse me, Sir. Could you complete this form, please? It just means _____ your home address and _____ at the bottom. (write) (sign)*

Guest: *Oh, yes, of course. I meant _____ it when I arrived, but I had to make a quick phone call. (do)*

3   In an office

Manager: *This report needs _____ (correct)*

Secretary: *When would you like me to do it?*

Manager: *Oh, you don't need _____ it now. (do) Tomorrow is all right.*

5 Join each pair of statements to make one statement.

Example: Bob didn't get the licence. He forgot.
Bob forgot _to get the licence._

1 Ian said some terrible things to Emma. He didn't mean it.
Ian didn't _____
_____
_____

2 I thought I could develop a new kind of engine. I tried for years.
For years I tried _____
_____
_____

3 They say I had fights with other children. I don't remember them.
I don't _____
_____
_____

4 They shouldn't make so much noise late at night. They should stop.
They should _____
_____
_____

5 I hate telling you this, but your son has done badly in his exams. I regret that.
I regret _____
_____
_____

6 What about buying some things for dinner? Let's stop at this supermaerket.
Let's _____
_____
_____

7 Throw your work away and start again. That's what this mistake means.
This mistake means _____
_____
_____

8 I'm sorry. I didn't telephone you this morning. I meant to.
I'm sorry. I meant _____
_____
_____

9 We should paint the dining-room. It really needs it.
The dining-room really _____`_____
_____

6 Write the verbs in the correct forms.

Alan Jones is talking to a careers adviser about starting a new career.

Adviser: *We need _to work out_ a plan for your future. (work out) What have you done up to now?*

Alan: *Well, I tried _working_ in a shop. (work) I also tried [1]_____ as an office worker. (train) But I've stopped now. I need [2]_____ something more interesting. (find)*

Adviser: *How long did you go on [3]_____ those jobs? (do)*

Alan: *For two years. Now what I need [4]_____ is to change completely. (do) I want to become a doctor.*

Adviser: *That's a very big change. It needs [5]_____ about. (think) First of all, it means [6]_____ a lot of exams. (pass) It's a pity you left school early. You must really regret [7]_____ without doing your final school examinations. (leave)*

Alan: *Yes, I do. I meant [8]_____ them. (take) But my dad suddenly got very ill, I regret [9]_____ (say) And I had to leave school and get a job to help support the family. Anyway, now I'm studying hard and I'm trying [10]_____ (catch up) If I do well enough in my exams next summer, I'll go on [11]_____ at medical college after that. (study)*

Adviser: *Well, I certainly hope you succeed.*

Verb + object + *to* + infinitive

Dad has invited us to stay.   He wants us to go.

Verb + object + *to* + infinitive

Dad has invited us to stay with him.
He has asked me to phone you.

Verb (+ object) + *to* + infinitive

He wants us to go on Saturday.
He wants to go to the theatre with us.

Verb + object + *to* + infinitive

Some verbs take an object + *to* + infinitive, eg *cause, enable, force, get* (*persuade*), *instruct, invite, let, make, order, permit, persuade, remind, teach, tell* and *warn*.

> The officer **ordered his men to start**.
> I **told the children not to play** with matches.

After *let* and *make* use an infinitive without *to*.

> We **let students go** home at 4.00.   The boss **made us work** late.

Verb (+ object) + *to* + infinitive

Some verbs work with, and also without, an object, eg *ask, beg, expect, help, intend, mean* (intend), *want, (would) hate, (would) like, (would) love* and *(would) prefer*.

> She **asked to meet** the President.
> She **asked us to meet** the President.
> Steve **expects to pass** his driving test.
> Ann **expects everybody else to do** the work for her.

After *help* use either a *to* + infinitive or an infinitive without *to*.

> I **helped** (them) **to make** dinner.   I **helped** (them) **make** dinner.

The verbs *hate, like, love* and *prefer* can take all these forms.

> I **hate going**.   I **hate you going**.
> I **hate to go**.   I **hate you to go**.

Note the difference in meaning between forms of *like*.

> He **likes us visiting** him. (He enjoys this.)
> He **likes to call** him first. (He feels this is the right thing to do.)

These verbs can take an object + *to* + infinitive or the *ing* form: *advise, allow, encourage, permit, recommend.*

> We **don't allow people to smoke**.   We **don't allow smoking**.

After *suggest* do not use an infinitive or an object + infinitive. Use one of these forms.

> I **suggest going** to the park.   I **suggest (that) we go** to the park.

After *offer* and *promise* do not use an object + infinitive. Use one of these forms.

> I **promised Tim** a new book. (verb + object only)
> I **promised to buy Tim** a new book. (verb + *to* + infinitive only)
> I **promised (that) I would buy Tim** a book. (verb (+ *that*) + will/would)

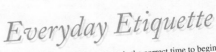

Police in France have ordered their forces to stop and search all cars leaving Paris in the hunt for a suspected terrorist.

Everyday Etiquette

Q   During a dinner party, when is the correct time to begin eating?

A   Some people expect everyone to wait until all the guests have been served. This is quite unnecessary and it is acceptable to begin eating as soon as you receive your food. However, the sophisticated guest expects to wait a few moments before tucking in.

This cinema is surrounded by residences.

We would be grateful for your co-operation and we ask you to leave quietly at the end of the film.

Exercises

1 Complete the statements.

Example: 'Be careful, Steve!' John said.
John warned <u>Steve to be careful.</u>

1 'Be quiet, Alan,' the teacher said.
The teacher told _____

2 The weather was bad and Ann said, 'Rob, don't drive so fast.'
Ann warned _____
_____

3 'Don't take photos,' the soldier said to me.
The soldier ordered _____
_____

4 Lucy always says to her son, 'Take your medicine after lunch.'
Lucy always reminds _____
_____

5 Nick said, 'Try this cake, everybody.'
Nick invited _____
_____

6 'Stop!' the policeman said to the man.
The policeman instructed _____

2 Join each pair of statements to make one statement.

Example: I went out last night. Bill persuaded me.
Bill persuaded <u>me to go out last night.</u>

1 Tina didn't buy the dress. Suzie persuaded her.
Suzie persuaded _____
_____

2 The climbers turned back. The bad weather forced them.
The bad weather forced _____
_____

3 Our boat rolled over. A wave caused it.
A wave caused _____
_____

Be careful these are different!

4 You can buy now and pay later. This credit card lets you.
This credit card lets _____
_____

5 The boys ran five kilometres. The new trainer made them.
The new trainer made _____
_____

6 We didn't go out. Dad didn't let us.
Dad didn't let _____.

3 Complete the statements.

Example: 'Can I listen, please?' Julie said.
Julie wanted <u>to listen.</u>
'Listen, everybody,' Julie said.
Julie wanted <u>everybody to listen.</u>

1 It would be great to buy that car.
I'd love _____

2 I'll be very angry if Tom gets the job.
I would hate _____

3 'Could you leave your cases there, Mrs Jones?' he said.
He asked _____
_____

4 Tony said, 'Can I see the contract, please?'
Tony asked _____

5 Our friends cut down a tree. We helped.
We helped _____
_____

6 You saw your present. We didn't want that yet.
We didn't mean _____
_____

4 Write the verbs in the correct forms.

Examples: I suggest <u>going</u> home. (go)
I suggest we <u>go</u> home. (go)

1 He doesn't allow people _____ in the river. (swim)

2 Our dentist likes everybody _____ a check-up every six months. (have)

3 The taxi driver offered _____ Lucy with her luggage. (help)

4 The doctor advised Bob _____ more exercise. (get)

5 I don't recommend you _____ that car. (buy)

6 I suggest you _____ to your teacher about the problem. (talk)

42 Verb/adjective + preposition + *ing* form

I dream of winning.   *I'm bored with television.*

Verb/adjective + preposition (+ *ing* form)

Some verbs and adjectives can take a preposition. If there is a verb after the preposition, it takes an *ing* form.

> *I'm thinking about the race.*
> *I'm bored with television.*
> *I don't feel like doing any more.*
> *I'm tired of working all the time.*

Verb + preposition + *ing* form

Some verbs can take this form. These are the most common: *apologize for, approve/disapprove of, believe in, decide against, dream of, feel like, insist on, object to, rely on, think of, succeed in.*

> *I apologized for arriving late.*   *They don't approve of smoking.*
> *I decided against buying the car.*   *We can't rely on winning.*

We can also use *about + ing* with these verbs: *ask, complain, dream, speak, talk, think, wonder.*

> *I thought about going.*   *We talked about buying a car.*

Be careful about the different meanings of *think about* and *think of.*

> *I'm thinking about the problem.* (ideas going through your mind) *I'm thinking of going to Spain, but I'm not sure yet.* (ideas going through your mind about a future action)

Verb + object + preposition + *ing* form

Some verbs can take this form. These are the most common: *accuse ... of, blame ... for, congratulate ... on, discourage ... from, forgive ... for, prevent ... from, stop ... from, punish ... for, suspect ... of, thank ... for, warn ... against.*

> *I blame Tom for causing the crash.*   *I thanked her for coming.*

Adjective + preposition + *ing* form

Some adjectives can take this form. These are the most common: *annoyed at, bored with, capable of, enthusiastic about, excited about, fed up with, fond of, good/bad at, grateful for, guilty of, interested in, keen on, pleased about, tired of.*

> *Rick was annoyed at losing.*   *I'm good at dancing.*

No, but I often think of changing him.

Do you think a lot about your boyfriend?

Greenpeace Accuses Government of Neglecting Inner Cities

A spokesperson for Greenpeace yesterday criticized the government for doing nothing to halt the decay of inner city areas. Bill Story told the press at a news conference called to discuss the latest figures on housing development that

Your holiday questions answered

Q | Will a suntan lotion with a high sun protection factor prevent me getting a tan?

A | No, but it will stop your skin from burning when it is first exposed to the sun and allow it to acclimatize gradually.

Exercises

1 Write the verbs in the correct forms and use these prepositions.

about, for, in, like, of, on, to

Example: *Tom tried nine times, but he never succeeded*
__in winning.__ (win)

1 *Mike apologized _____ the vase.*
(break)

2 *He insisted _____ for a new one.*
(pay)

3 *We often wonder _____ house.*
(move) Is it a good idea?

4 *I object _____ out in this terrible*
weather. (go)

5 *What do you feel _____ today? (do)*

6 *We're thinking _____ a sports club*
next year. (join)

2 Join each pair of statements to make one statement.

Example: *She got the job. Her brother congratulated*
her.
__Her brother congratulated her on__
__getting the job.__

1 *I'm going to win. You can't prevent me.*

_____

_____

2 *Ben broke the window. His father punished him.*

_____

_____

3 *Don't go sailing in this wind. I must warn you.*

_____

_____

4 *She hit my child. I can't forgive her.*

_____

_____

5 *He's left that terrible job. You can't blame him.*

_____

_____

6 *The dogs are fighting. We can't stop them.*

_____

3 Write the adjectives and verbs in the correct forms.

Example: *The ship was __capable of crossing__ the*
Atlantic in three days. (capable/cross)

1 *She's very kind. She isn't _____*
anybody. (capable/hurt)

2 *Are you _____ on*
holiday? (excited/go) It's very soon.

3 *I'm very _____ this village.*
(fond/visit) I love the old place.

4 *Which are you _____*
next year – Art or Music? (interested/study)

5 *Is Sam _____*
his exams? (pleased/pass) He got very good marks.

6 *We're _____*
the same music all the time. (fed up/hear)

7 *Tom is _____ (bad/cook) He*
always burns things.

4 Write the verbs in the correct forms.

Mary: *Do you remember the other night? We*
__talked about going__ away for a week. (talk/go)
And we [1] _____
_____ *to Scotland for a week. (think/go)*

Bill: *Yes, but we* [2] _____
_____ *that in the end. (decide/do) You*
[3] _____
_____ *Scotland as it's cold at this time*
of year. (discourage/us/choose)

Mary: *That's right, but I mentioned the idea when I*
called Sheena in Edinburgh this evening. She's
[4] _____ *us*
again. (enthusiastic/see) She says we must come,
and she's really [5] _____
_____ *us Edinburgh.*
(look forward/show)

Bill: *That's really nice of her. I must say I'm*
[6] _____ *all the*
time. Let's go. (tired/work)

Mary: *OK, I'll phone her and* [7] _____
_____ *us. (thank/her/ask) She'll*
be very pleased.

43 Conditional forms: type 0 and type 1

If the wind is strong, the waves are dangerous.

Type 0 conditionals

These express things which always happen. If one thing happens, then another thing always happens. This is similar to *When* + present simple, present simple.

> *If the wind **is** strong, the waves **are** dangerous.*
> *If you **shout** at her, she always **cries**.*
> ***When** the wind **is** strong, the waves **are** dangerous.*
> ***When** you **shout**, she always **cries**.*

We can also use *If* with instructions.

> *If Ann **phones**, please **take** a message.*
> *If your son still **feels** ill tomorrow, **call** me again.*

Type 1 conditionals

We also use *If* sentences to talk about a probable future action or condition. Both parts of the sentence are about the future, but the *If* part is in the present simple, not the future.

> *If it's sunny tomorrow, we'll go to the beach.*
> *If we **hurry**, we'll **catch** the bus.*   *If we **don't hurry**, we'll **miss** it.*

The *If* part of the sentence is about something which may or may not happen. The result – the other part of the sentence – follows from the *If* part.

'If part	The result
If it's sunny, ...	... we'll go to the beach.
If it rains, ...	... we'll stay at home.
If we hurry, ...	... we'll catch the bus.
If we don't hurry, ...	... we'll miss the bus.

unless means *if not*.

> *I'll fail the test **unless I learn** these words. (if I don't learn)*

as long as and *provided (that)* mean *If* with a special emphasis.

> *You can borrow the car **as long as/provided (that) you bring** it back this evening. (if, and only if, you bring it back)*

Three reasons why cigarettes *are bad for your social life.*

If you smoke
- your breath smells.
- your teeth turn yellow.
- your skin becomes wrinkled.

(And if you stop smoking, you live longer.)

Litter – the new law and you

If you drop litter and refuse to pick it up, you will be fined £10.

If you don't pay, you will be taken to court and will face a fine of £1,000.

LEAVING LITTER DOES NOT PAY

10% off voucher

If you present this voucher at any one of the Sparrow Group of stores, you will receive a 10% discount on your next purchase.

If we don't have any item you want in stock, our staff will happily order it for you.

Exercises

1 Complete the Type 0 conditionals. Use these endings.

it becomes ice.   it soon goes bad.
the machinery soon breaks down.   the oil light comes on.
the lights come on.   you get orange.

Example: *If you mix red and yellow, <u>you get</u>*
          <u>*orange.*</u>

1 *If the car needs oil, _____*

2 *If you cool water to 0⁰C, _____*

3 *If you don't keep food cool, _____*

4 *If you press this switch, _____*

5 *If the engineers don't check every month, _____*
   _____

2 Choose the correct form of the verbs.

Example: *If Ann <u>doesn't call</u> me, I'll call her.*
          (doesn't call/won't call)

1 *If the money _____ I'll put it in the bank.*
   (arrives/will arrive)

2 *Peter _____ us if he hears any news.*
   (tells/will tell)

3 *If you don't finish your homework, I _____*
   you watch TV. (don't let/won't let)

4 *You won't know what it tastes like if you*
   _____ it. (don't try/won't try)

5 *If the neighbours don't stop that noise, I*
   _____ the police. (call/'ll call)

6 *I'm sure Tom _____ you some money if you*
   ask him. (lends/will lend)

7 *If you shout like that again, Helen _____*
   to you. (doesn't listen/won't listen)

8 *If the climbers _____ down before the storm,*
   they'll be in great danger. (don't come/won't come)

3 Join each pair of statements to make one statement.

Example: *Tom may call. If so, I'll talk to him.*
          <u>*If Tom calls, I'll talk to him.*</u>

1 *The police may come. If so, they'll ask about Tom.*
   _____
   _____

2 *Enter the race. You'll probably win.*
   _____
   _____

3 *The party may go on till late. If so, we'll go home early.*
   _____
   _____

4 *Call the office at 2.00. Tony will be there.*
   _____
   _____

5 *Ann may not call. I'll be worried.*
   _____
   _____

6 *Finish the job today. Then you won't have to come*
   tomorrow.
   _____
   _____

4 Write the verbs in the correct forms.

Bob is reading the college newspaper.

Bob: *Look. Here's an advert for a water-ski weekend. If*
      we <u>have</u> a group of ten, we <u>'ll get</u> a special
      price. (have) (get)

Steve: *It sounds good. But I ¹_____ to go*
       if it ²_____ in May. (not/be able) (be)

Bob: *No, the offer starts in June. We can go just after*
      the exams.

Steve: *Yes, if we ³_____ to go then, everybody*
       ⁴_____ (decide) (come) Let's ask
       some people. Ask Alan.

Bob: *Alan, ⁵_____ us if we*
      ⁶_____ a water-ski weekend in June?
      (you/join) (organize)

Steve: *If we ⁷_____ just after the exams, we*
       ⁸_____ a great time. (go) (have)

Alan: *OK, I ⁹_____ if it ¹⁰_____ too*
       expensive. (come) (be/not)

Steve: *There's a special group rate.*

Bob: *If we ¹¹_____ another seven people, it*
      ¹²_____ just £30 each. (find) (cost)

Steve: *We'd better hurry. If we ¹³_____ fast,*
       somebody else ¹⁴_____ the offer and
       we ¹⁵_____ the chance. (not/act) (take)
       (miss)

44 Conditional forms: type 2

If someone found him, he would have a huge meal.

Type 2 conditionals express future conditions which are not probable and present conditions which are not true.

> **If** he **won** the prize, he **'d buy** some new clothes. (But he probably won't win.)
> **If** they **had** some money, they**'d stay** at a hotel. (But they don't have any money.)

We use the past simple in the *If* part of the sentence. In the other part we usually use *would* (from *will*) + verb.

> **If** he **won** £10,000, he **would visit** Rome. (sure)

We also use *could* (from *can*) and *might* (from *may*).

> ... he **could visit** Rome. (able to)   ... he **might visit** Rome. (unsure)

We can make statements with *would, could* and *might*, but without the *If* part. The words *would, could* and *might* show that the statement is about something unlikely or impossible.

> ● *Let's invite Bill and Luke.*
> ○ *No, they hate each other. They***'d fight***. (... if we invited them.)*
> ● *I dream of going to Paris.*
> ○ *We* **could have** *a wonderful time there. (... but it's only a dream.)*
> ● *It's a pity Sally and Helen hardly ever meet.*
> ○ *Yes, they* **might become** *friends. (... but they don't meet.)*

We often give advice with Type 2 conditionals, and we can use these special expressions. Note the special form of *be* in Type 2 conditionals.

> **If I were you, I'd get** a new job.
> **If I were in your position, I'd tell** the police what happened.

wish and If only

We use the forms *wish + would/could* and *If only + would/could* to show that we want a change in the future (but we do not really expect the change to happen).

> I **wish** that boy **would do** his work properly!
> I **wish** I **could take** a holiday, but I'm very busy.
> **If only** he**'d answer** the phone, but it just keeps ringing!
> **If only** the neighbours **wouldn't make** so much noise!

We use the forms *wish + past* and *if only + past* to show that we want a change in the present (but we know it is impossible).

> I **wish** things **didn't cost** so much.
> **If only** that man **did** his work properly, we **wouldn't have to do** the work all over again now.

Train Pain

Everyone says there are too many cars, but maybe if public transport was more reliable more people would use it! Train services are appalling. My dad started taking the train to work instead of the car but stopped after a month. The train only ran on time 20 per cent of the time and sometimes it didn't come at all! Get your act together, train companies!

**J Gadd, 12,
Weston-Super-Mare**

A FEW OF MY FAVOURITE THINGS

Our regular interview column with a star who shares his favourite things – past, present and imaginary! This week, Jamie Beaven.

Q What would be your perfect day?

JB It would be a bright summer's day with no work, a group of friends and a trek into the countryside.

Q Who would be your ideal dinner partner?

JB Nelson Mandela. It would be a great privilege to have dinner with him.

Q If you were only allowed to have two books, what would they be?

JB Now, this is a very difficult question.

Exercises

1 Write the verbs in the correct forms.

Examples: If I _had_ enough money, I'd buy that car. (have)

You _'d have_ enough money if you got a better job. (have)

1 If we _____ a bigger house, we could invite people to stay. (have)

2 I _____ out of business if we cut our prices. (go)

3 If I _____ my job, I wouldn't know what to do. (lose)

4 If we _____ the plan exactly, we'd never finish the job. (follow)

5 I think she _____ angry if I didn't invite her this evening. (be)

6 You _____ me if I told you the whole story. (not/believe)

7 If we decided to go to London, we _____ with my brother. (stay)

8 He's so good that I'd be very surprised if he _____ into the team. (not/get)

2 Write Type 2 conditionals.

Examples: (we/be/surprised/Ann/come)

We'd be surprised if Ann came.

(Tom/have/time/he/be/here)

If Tom had time, he'd be here.

1 (Ann/be/pleased/Tom/call)

_____

_____

2 (you/not/visit/us again/we/be/very sad)

_____

_____

3 (I/get/fit quite fast/I/work out/at the gym)

_____

_____

4 (Barry/not/argue/so much/he/have/more friends)

_____

_____

5 (the team/win/more games/they train/harder)

_____

_____

3 Write the verbs in the correct forms to complete the answers without *if*.

Example: ● It'd be great if we had a million pounds.
○ Yes, we _could do_ anything. (can/do)

1 ● Let's give Larry some money.
○ No, he _____ it all. (waste)

2 ● If you could change jobs, what would you do?
○ I _____ a film star. (become)

3 ● I don't want to go out tonight.
○ Why not? You _____ yourself. (enjoy)

4 ● If I could, I'd love to travel through time.
○ But you _____ your friends and family again. (may/never/see)

4 Write questions and answer them without *if*.

Example: You might lose your money. (What/you/do) (go/to the police)

● _What would you do if you lost your money?_
○ _I'd go to the police._

1 They might visit Turkey. (Where/they/stay) (stay/in cheap hotels)
● _____
_____
○ _____

2 We could complain at the Head Office. (Who/we/see) (talk/to the Sales Manager)
● _____
_____
○ _____

3 I might visit Scotland. (How/you/travel) (go/by car)
● _____
_____
○ _____

4 They could leave school now. (What/they/do) (get/jobs)
● _____
_____
○ _____

45 Conditional forms: type 3

If he'd bought a present, she'd have been happy.

Yesterday was Mr and Mrs Carter's wedding anniversary. She remembered it, but he didn't. If he'd bought a present, she'd have been happy!

Type 3 conditionals express something past which was not true.
> *If he'd got a present, she'd have been happy.*
> (... but he didn't!)   (... and she was angry!)

Form Type 3 conditionals like this.
> *If he hadn't forgotten the present, she wouldn't have been angry.*
> (... but he did!)   (... and she was angry!)

In the *If* part of the sentence we use the past perfect. In the other part we usually use *would have* + past participle.
> *If he'd remembered to buy a present, ...*
> *... she'd have been very pleased.* (sure)

But we also use *could have* and *might have*.
> *... he could have got it on the way home.* (possible)
> *... he might have decided to get some flowers.* (unsure)

We can make statements with *would have, could have* and *might have,* but without the *If* part. The words *would have, could have* and *might have* show that the statement is about something past and impossible.
> *I'm sorry that you didn't visit Harry. He'd have loved to see you.*
> (... if you'd visited him.)
> *I wanted to go to New York. We could have seen Manhattan.*
> (... if we'd gone to New York.)
> *He was stupid not to work. He might have passed his exams.*
> (... if he'd worked harder.)

wish and *If only*

We use the forms *wish* + past perfect and *If only* + past perfect to show that we would have liked a change in the past (but we know that it did not happen).
> *Most people wish they'd done a few things differently when they were younger.*
> *I wish I hadn't wasted so much time yesterday.*
> *If only they'd called the doctor immediately, they could have saved his life.*
> *If only we hadn't spent our money, we could have gone out last night.*

NEW ON VIDEO

Dante's Peak
CIC, 12, 1997

A beautiful town in the Pacific Northwest is threatened by the dangers of a volcano and, sadly, characters which appear made out of cardboard. The special effects are very convincing but if the director had paid the same attention to the script, it would have been a much better film. Pierce Brosnan as the volcanologist and Linda Hamilton as the mayor could have tried harder. Our verdict? Don't rush out to rent it!

Awful food? Noisy hotel? Miles from the beach?

If only they'd heard about Paradise Packages ... the holidays where everything works out for the best.

Traffic news now. Serious congestion on the M25 in both directions. I expect all you drivers wish you had stayed at home. Better news for those on the M4 – traffic there is flowing again after this morning's accident.

Exercises

1 Write the verbs in the correct forms.

Examples: *If I 'd driven faster, I'd have arrived in*
time. (drive)
We wouldn't have gone to the show if
Alan hadn't recommended it. (not/go)

1 *If you'd seen the film, you _____*
it. (love)

2 *If she _____ earlier, she'd have seen Pat. (go)*

3 *We wouldn't have noticed the house if you*
_____ it to us. (not/show)

4 *If the weather _____ better yesterday, we'd*
have gone out. (be)

5 *If she _____ some money, she _____*
_____ enough for those shoes. (save) (have)

6 *We _____ for help*
that night if we _____ desperate.
(not/ask) (not/be)

2 Write Type 3 conditionals.

Examples: *(you/come/to the party/you/enjoy/it)*
If you'd come to the party, you'd
have enjoyed it.
(we/be/very sad/John/not/marry/Suzie)
We'd have been very sad if John
hadn't married Suzie.

1 *(Jim/ask/us/we/lend/him our car)*
_____
_____

2 *(I/not/write down/her phone number/I/forget)*
_____
_____

3 *(the car/not/crash/Tom/keep/to the speed limit)*
_____
_____
_____

4 *(I/forget/to buy/Ann's present/you/not/remind/me)*
_____
_____
_____

3 Write Type 3 conditionals.

Example: *The plane didn't crash because the pilot*
landed on a road.
If the pilot hadn't landed on the
road, the plane would have crashed.

1 *We didn't find the house as we didn't have a map.*
_____
_____

2 *The bus arrived late, so we didn't miss it.*
_____
_____

3 *They found the books when they opened the last box.*
_____
_____

4 *The tree didn't fall on the car, so the driver wasn't hurt.*
_____
_____
_____

5 *I got lost on the mountain because I didn't turn back.*
_____
_____

4 Write answers without *if*.

Example: ● *I wanted to go to New York. (we/can/see/*
the Manhattan skyline)
○ *Yes, we could have seen the*
Manhattan skyline.

1 ● *It's a pity Tom's car broke down. (he/might/win/*
the race)
○ *Yes, _____*
_____

2 ● *Why didn't she call the police? (they/can/catch/*
the thieves)
○ *Yes, _____*
_____

3 ● *I should have taken the other road. (we/get/home an*
hour ago)
○ *Yes, _____*
_____

46 Reported speech 1: statements
He said (that) he was late.

You can report a person's exact words in quotation marks (' ... '). This is common in stories.

> *He said, **'I'm late.'** 'What time is it?' he asked.*

In conversation we usually express the speaker's idea in reported speech after a reporting verb such as *say, tell, shout* and *whisper*.

> *He **said** (that) he was late. He **told** us (that) he would call us.*
> *He **shouted** (that) ... She **whispered** (that) ...*

The reporting verb *say* is usually in the past. But it is sometimes in the present, eg when we report a telephone conversation as we listen.

> *He **says** (that) he's in New York now.*

After *say*, we do not usually mention the listener. After *tell* we always mention the listener.

> *He **said** he was working late.*
> *He **told me** he was working late.*

that after the reporting verb is formal. You can leave it out.

> *He **said that** he was tired.* OR *He **said** he was tired.*

There are word changes to show changes of person and place.

> *... call **you** from New York. → ... call **us** from New York.*
> *... **here** at **my** hotel. → ... **there** at **his** hotel.*

There are word changes to show time changes between the statement and reporting the statement.

> *He said, 'I'm flying **tomorrow**.' → He said he **was** flying the **next day**.*

A main verb in the present simple, eg *call* or *calls*, changes to the past simple, *called*. Remember these other common verb changes.

> *am/is → was, are → were, have/has → had, have/has got → had, do/does → did, will → would, can → could, may → might*

Unlike *can* and *may*, these modal verbs do not change.

> *must, might, could, would, should, ought*

Remember these other common ways of showing time changes.

> *tomorrow → the next day/the day after*
> *yesterday → the previous day/the day before*
> *this Saturday → last Saturday/the following Saturday*

PASSING *comment ...*

Lennox Lewis on Frank Bruno
'He didn't make a stand on anything until he said he'd leave Britain if the Tories lost the election.'

The Communist Manifesto

Karl Marx
Friedrich Engels

Karl Marx said that all history was a struggle between the rich rulers and the poor workers and that eventually the workers would overthrow their rulers in a revolution.

Hundreds Witness Meteor

Police and coastguards in the South West received hundreds of calls on Thursday night after a bright light flashed across the sky. The object appears to have been a very bright meteor. Mr John Milton, an astronomer who lives in Bodmin, Cornwall, said that from reports he had received, he believed it was a single fireball. One witness told reporters that there was a large explosion followed by the meteor breaking up into several pieces. Mr Richard Bater, a meteorologist from Newton Abbott, who also saw the meteor, said he believed it was about a metre across and perhaps 40 kilometres up. He said he couldn't say whether anything reached the ground but that it was 'not unlikely', in which case the proper description would be a meteor.

Exercises

1 Report the telephone conversation.

Nick is in Australia and Alan is in Britain.

Nick: *It's hot here, and I'm sitting by our new pool.*
Alan: *It's really cold here, and we're sitting by our fire.*

They're telling their wives about the conversation.

Nick to Suzie: *Alan says <u>it's really cold there, and</u>*
_____

Alan to Celia: *Nick says* _____
_____
_____

2 Write the statements in reported speech. Use *He said …* and *He told me …*

You met an old school friend, Jim, last year

Examples: '*I've got a flat in London.*'

<u>He said he had a flat in London.</u>
'*I'm visiting my parents this weekend.*'
<u>He told me he was visiting his parents that weekend.</u>

1 '*I'm working outside London this month.*'
_____
_____

2 '*I finished my college course a year ago.*'
_____
_____

3 '*I haven't been to see my parents for ages.*'
_____
_____

4 '*I arrived home with my family yesterday.*'
_____
_____

5 '*We're going to go back to London tomorrow.*'
_____
_____

6 '*We can't stay for long as I have to get back to work.*'
_____
_____

7 '*We may come back next year. I don't know.*'
_____
_____
_____

8 '*I'll write soon and send you a photo of the family.*'
_____
_____

9 '*You should stay with us when you have time.*'
_____
_____

3 Write replies to the comments. Use *But you said …* and *But you told me …*

Example: ● *I'm going home. (stay/here)*

○ *<u>But you said you were staying here.</u>*

1 ● *I don't like this music. (love)*
○ _____
_____

2 ● *Tom has sold his bike. (not/sell)*
○ _____
_____

3 ● *I'm not going to call her. (call)*
○ _____
_____

4 ● *The film is on tomorrow. (today)*
○ _____
_____

5 ● *They won the match. (lose)*
○ _____
_____

6 ● *Lisa will be at home tomorrow. (tonight)*
○ _____
_____

7 ● *They have sent me a present. (not/send/anything)*
○ _____
_____

8 ● *The children can swim very well. (cannot/swim/at all)*
○ _____

Reported speech 2: questions

They asked if I was staying long.

FORMS

'Are you staying long?' → They asked if I was staying long.

'Did you have a good journey?' → They wanted to know if I had had a good journey.

'How are your parents?' → They wanted to know how you were.

'When will you go?' → They asked when I would go.

Reported questions usually start with *ask* or *want to know*.

> They **asked** how long I was staying.
> They **wanted to know** how you were.

Reported *Yes/No* questions need *if* or *whether*.

> They asked **if** I had had a good journey.
> They wanted to know **whether** I liked London.

Reported *Wh* questions need a question word, eg *how, when, what*, etc.

> They wanted to know **how** you were.
> They asked **what** I wanted to do.

The verb after *if* or *whether* or question word is not in question form. It is like a verb in a statement.

> They asked **if** I **was** hungry.
> They asked **what** I **wanted** to do.

Be careful about *do, does* and *did*. We use them in ordinary present and past simple questions, but not in reported questions.

> Where **do** you **want** to go? → They asked me where I **wanted** to go.
> How long **did** the journey **take**? → They asked me how the journey **had taken**.

The reported question form is similar to the form of indirect questions. (See Unit 22.)

> Why **does** he like London? → They wanted to know **why he likes London**. OR *Could you tell me* **why he likes London**?

The rules for word changes for change of person, place and time are the same as for reported statements. (See Unit 46.)

> 'How **are you**?' → They asked how **I was**. (change of person)
> 'When will you get **here**?' → They asked when I would get **there**. (change of place)
> 'Did you call **yesterday**?' → They asked if I had called **the previous day**. (change of time)

LINE RESTORED

from Mrs Rita Secombe

Sir,
Our phone having been out of order for seven days, despite numerous calls to British Telecom, I asked again when it would be reconnected. I was told to 'cross my fingers' and it could be within 24 hours. I did – and it was!

Is this the latest advance in digital technology?

Yours faithfully,
Rita Secombe

Reading, Berkshire

So who really needs $8.5m?

An 83-year-old New York woman has given $8.5m, her entire winnings from a lottery jackpot, to her New Jersey council. When reporters asked why she wanted to dispose of her money in such a way, Mrs Helen Barker said, 'I have my pension. I have everything I need.' She in turn asked the journalists whether they thought she was unusual. The replies varied.

She asked me if I could
She asked me if I would
Love her again …

Exercises

1 Report the telephone conversation.

Nick is in Australia and Alan is in Britain.

Nick: *What are you and Celia doing this winter? Are you taking a skiing holiday again?*

Alan: *No, we're staying at home this year. Where are you and Suzie going for your holiday? Are you going to visit us again?*

They're telling their wives about the conversation.

Nick to Suzie: *Alan is asking where* _____

_____

_____ *He wants to know*

_____

_____

Alan to Celia: *Nick is asking what* _____

_____ *He wants to know*

_____

_____

2 Write the *Yes/No* questions in reported speech.

You met your old school friend, Jim, last year.

Examples: Jim: *Are you still at college?*

Jim asked me whether I was still at college.

You: *Do you remember Joe?*

I asked him if he remembered Joe.

1 Jim: *Have you sold your terrible old car?*

_____

_____

2 Jim: *Do you still live with your parents?*

_____

_____

3 Jim: *Are you going to visit London soon?*

_____

_____

4 You: *Is there room for me to stay with you?*

_____

_____

5 You: *Can I have your phone number?*

_____

6 You: *Did you meet your wife at college?*

_____

_____

3 Write the *Wh* questions in reported speech.

Some students are talking to a new French student.

Example: '*What subjects are you going to do?*'

They asked him what subjects he was going to do.

1 '*Where do you come from?*'

_____

_____

2 '*How long have you been in Britain?*'

_____

_____

3 '*Why did you decide to come here?*'

_____

_____

4 '*How long are you going to stay?*'

_____

_____

5 '*Where are you living?*'

_____

_____

4 Write the questions in reported speech.

At a language school

Example: A German student: *How can I renew my my passport?*

A German student asked me how he could renew his passport.

1 A Swedish student: *Do you know the way to the station?*

_____

_____

2 A Turkish student: *Can you help me find a flat?*

_____

_____

3 A Lebanese student: *Which is the best travel agency?*

_____

_____

They told him to be quiet.

Reported orders, invitations, etc

tell, invite, remind, warn and *use* take *to* + infinitive after the object.
In the negative form add *not* before the *to* + infinitive.

Subject	Verb	Object	to + Infinitive
They	**told**	*him*	**to be** quiet.
They	**warned**	*her*	**not to do** it again.

Reported promises, offers, etc

promise, offer, refuse, agree and *threaten* do not take an object before the *to* + infinitive. In the negative form add *not* before the *to* + infinitive.

Subject	Verb	to + Infinitive
He	**promised**	**to turn** it **down**.
They	**agreed**	**not to make** so much noise.

Reported suggestions, apologies, etc

suggest, apologize for, admit and *insist on* take an *ing* form.

Subject	Verb	*ing* form
Nick	**suggested**	**turning** it **down**.
They	**apologized**	**for making** so much noise.

With *suggest* it is possible to use this form.

> *Nick **suggested that they turn** it **down**.*

Other reporting verbs

Reporting verbs like *invite, promise, suggest, warn*, etc, tell us much more than the basic reporting verbs *say, tell* and *ask*. They express the speaker's aim – the type of communication that the speaker produced. In fact, the reporting verb can summarize some or all of the actual words that the speaker used. Similar reporting verbs include *accuse, complain, correct, deny* and *recommend*.

> The police to Mr Saunders: *'We have reason to believe that you took the car, Mr Saunders.'* → The police **accused** *Mr Saunders of taking the car.*
> A neighbour to a teenager: *'Do you have to make that terrible noise?'* → The neighbour **complained** *to the teenager about the terrible noise.*
> Mr MacLaren to a reporter: *'I'm sorry, but you've got my name wrong. It's M-a-c, not M-c.'* → Mr MacLaren **corrected** *the spelling of his name.*
> Mr Saunders to the police: *'I certainly didn't take the car.'* → Mr Saunders **denied** *taking the car.*

In the third century BC, Greek scientists suggested that the Earth and planets move around the sun. The telescope, first used to observe the heavens by Galileo, proved this to be true.

Reality Bites

A restaurant owner has been forced to live on pasta and soup for four months because his dentist removed his teeth after discovering that the patient couldn't pay his bill. Dentist Anders Wick warned John Wilby to pay up or risk having his dental implants taken back. The unfortunate restaurateur had agreed to pay the $500 cost of treatment but by the time he came to settle his bill, his restaurant had run into difficulties and he could not find the money.

Mr Wilby offered to follow a payment plan but the dentist refused, saying he would not be able to afford the payments. Mr Wick apologized to his client for having to take such drastic action when he took Mr Wilby's teeth back.

Mr Wilby meanwhile has accused the dental clinic of cruelty and threatened to take the matter to court.

Exercises

1 Put the direct speech into reported speech.

Example: *'Give me your books,' the teacher told us.*
<u>The teacher told us to give him/her our books.</u>

1 *'Could you open the door?' the girl asked me.*

_____

2 *'Don't use this photocopier,' Carol instructed the new assistant.*

_____

_____

3 *'Come for dinner on Saturday,' Tom invited us.*

_____

_____

4 *'Don't be late for the party,' Celia reminded me.*

_____

_____

5 *'Could you please not make so much noise?' Ann asked everybody.*

_____

_____

6 *'Give your name to the receptionist,' Mrs Davis told Tony.*

_____

_____

7 *'Don't touch the red button,' Bob warned Emma.*

_____

_____

8 *'Remember to post the letters,' the manager reminded her assistant.*

_____

_____

2 Report the conversation. Use these reporting verbs.

agree, offer, promise, threaten

Bill is always late for appointments. His sister, Jean, is tired of it.

Example: *'Can we meet outside the cinema?' Bill said.*
'All right. Outside the cinema,' Jean agreed.
<u>They agreed to meet outside the cinema.</u>

1 *'And can we meet at 7.30?' he said.*
'Fine. 7.30,' she agreed.

_____

2 *'This time I'll be there on time,' he promised.*

_____

3 *'I'm not going to wait for you if you're late,' she threatened.*

_____

4 *'Look, if you like, I'll get there an hour early!' he offered.*

_____

5 *'You don't need to do anything silly like that, but I'll leave if you aren't there at 7.30,' she threatened again.*

_____

_____

6 *'I won't be late. Believe me,' he promised.*

_____

3 Report the statements and questions. Use these reporting verbs.

admit, apologize for, insist on, suggest

Example: *'Let's do something exciting,' Bob suggested.*
<u>Bob suggested doing something exciting.</u>

1 *'Why don't we go parachuting?' Maria suggested.*

_____

2 *'Good idea, but it's getting late. If we're going to go parachuting, we must go right now,' Barry insisted.*

_____

_____

Later, 3,000 metres up in the sky …

3 *'I feel scared,' Barry admitted.*

_____

4 *'I don't want to jump either. I'm sorry, Barry. I was stupid to suggest parachuting,' Maria apologized.*

_____

_____

5 *'Look we can't go back now. Even if you aren't going to jump, I am!' Barry insisted. 'Bye!'*

_____

49 Singular and plural

a girl, an apple, two boys, some chairs

All the things in the picture are countable nouns – we can count them, eg *two boys, three chairs* and *five books*.

They have a singular form (for one), eg *boy*, and a plural form (for more than one), eg *boys*.

We can use *a/an* before the singular form. Use *a* before a hard sound (consonant), eg *a girl, a desk* and *a table* (but *an old table*).

Use *an* before a soft sound (vowel), eg *an apple, an orange* and *an olive* (but *a green olive*).

Compare *a hat* and *an hour*. Use *an* when the *h* is silent.

Compare *an umbrella* and *a university*. Use *a* when the *u* sounds like *you*.

Do not use a singular countable noun by itself. It needs a determiner. (See Unit 52 for more information about *a, an* and *the*.)

> I want **a book**.   I want **my book**.
> I want **that book**.   I want **the book** over there.

We use *a/an* to say what a thing or a person is.
- ● *What's that?*   ○ *It's **a map**.*
- ● *What's her job?*   ○ *She's **an actress**.*

If we talk about more than one thing or more than one person in this way, use the noun alone.
- ● *What are those?*   ○ *They're **maps**.*
- ● *What are their jobs?*   ○ *They're **actresses**.*

We can use the singular or the plural form to make general statements. In both these examples we mean 'all horses'.

> **A horse** is an animal with four legs.
> **Horses** are animals with four legs.

We often want to talk about more than one thing, but we do not know exactly how many. For this use *some*. (See Unit 55 for more information about *some* and *any*.)

> *I'd like a beefburger and **some fries**, please.*

Be careful. *fries* and *some fries*, etc, have different meanings.

> *I love **fries**.* (all fries, at any time, anywhere)
> *I'd like **some fries**.* (a number of fries now)

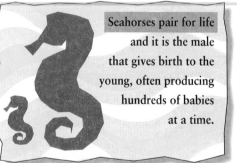

Seahorses pair for life and it is the male that gives birth to the young, often producing hundreds of babies at a time.

At *Peak Park* we run an informal and friendly campsite.

Dogs are welcome but must be kept under strict control.

Peak Park

Exercises

1 Write *a* or *an*.

Examples: *a* girl   *an* apple

1. _____ orange
2. _____ exercise
3. _____ newspaper
4. _____ aeroplane
5. _____ letter
6. _____ easy test
7. _____ magazine
8. _____ old car
9. _____ Italian
10. _____ good book
11. _____ united team
12. _____ unfriendly man

2 Write *a*, *an* or *some* and choose from these words.

book / books, desk / desks, egg / eggs, glass / glasses,
letter / letters, paint / paints, taxi / taxis,
umbrella / umbrellas

Examples: I'm reading *a book* about Japan.
Let's put *some desks* in that classroom.

1. Did you write _____ to Ann?
2. It's going to rain. Take _____ with you.
3. Get _____ and we'll start a picture.
4. The children want a drink, so can you get _____ , please?
5. I usually have _____ , toast and coffee for breakfast.
6. We're late. Let's take _____ to the airport.

3 Write the correct present forms of *be* or *do*.

Examples: Look. Some boys *are* coming.
Does a lesson take 45 or 50 minutes?

1. _____ some students live in college?
2. _____ a new car very expensive?
3. Two girls _____ helping the teacher.
4. _____ a computer disk take long to copy?
5. A secretary _____ typing the report.
6. A good dictionary _____ really useful.
7. _____ the children in bed?
8. The students _____ having lunch.

4 Write *some* or nothing (✗).

Examples: Liz and Joe are ✗ teachers.
We've got *some* new CDs. Look.

1. Could you get _____ oranges, please?
2. I love _____ apples. I eat about five a day.
3. I'm going to buy _____ shoes in the sale.
4. Everybody studies _____ languages at school.
5. You look hungry. Have _____ biscuits.
6. We found _____ old gold coins under a rock.

5 Write alternative general statements.

Example: A tractor is a farm vehicle.
Tractors are farm vehicles.

1. A college is a place to study.
   _____

2. Large planes can carry very heavy loads.
   _____
   _____

3. Nowadays, a student needs to learn to use a computer.
   _____
   _____

4. Cars use more energy per person than trains or buses.
   _____
   _____

6 Write *a*, *an*, *some* or nothing (✗).

At a jeweller's

- ● Hello. Could I look at *some* rings, please? I want to buy *a* ring for my sister.
- ○ Certainly, Madam. Here are [1]_____ rings for ladies.
- ● These are all [2]_____ diamond rings, aren't they?
- ○ Yes, and they're [3]_____ top quality pieces. Look at this one. It's [4]_____ really lovely ring.
- ● Yes, but it's [5]_____ expensive one too.
- ○ Ah, but Madam, [6]_____ things are never cheap.
- ● Perhaps you're right. But could I look at [7]_____ other rings too? Could I see [8]_____ different types of stone?
- ○ Of course. Here's [9]_____ very nice one. This green stone is [10]_____ emerald.

A few countable nouns are usually plural, so they take a plural verb. Learn these: *clothes, contents, thanks.*

> My **clothes** are in the cupboard.
> He opened the bag and poured the **contents** on the floor.
> I want to thank you. Many, many **thanks**!

Some countable nouns are always plural because they have two parts. Learn these: *scissors, jeans, trousers, shorts, glasses, binoculars.* We can make them singular by using *a pair of.*

> Where are my **scissors**?   Those are nice **jeans**!
> There's **a pair of glasses** on the table.

A few countable nouns look singular because they have no *s*, but they are always plural and have no singular form. Learn these: *the police, cattle.* (Use these countable nouns for a singular form: *police officer, cow* or *bull.*)

> **The police** are looking for three men.
> Mr Giles has 200 **cattle** on his farm.

A few nouns look plural, but are not. Learn these: *athletics, news, mathematics, physics, gymnastics, the United States.*

> Here is the 9.00 **news**.
> **Mathematics** was the most difficult subject for me at school.
> **The United States** is 5,000 kilometres from east to west.

Group nouns are singular, but we often think of members of the group and use a plural verb. Learn these: *family, team, club, class, school, staff, committee, government.*

> My **family** are all angry with me.
> The **team** are very happy with the result of the match.
> The **club** are looking for young members to join the team.

A few words are the same in the singular and the plural. Learn these: *sheep, fish, series, crossroads, species, headquarters, aircraft.*

> Mr Giles has 1,000 **sheep** on his farm.
> You only caught one **fish**, but I caught three **fish**!
> I saw three **aircraft** in five minutes.

A few plurals are irregular. (See Appendix 2 for special spelling rules.) Learn these: *child → children, man → men, woman → women, person → people, foot → feet, tooth → teeth.*

> I've got one **child**. My brother has got two **children**.
> One **man** was by the door, and there were three more **men** inside.
> My dentist filled one **tooth** and took two **teeth** out.

What do you call two sheep that live together?

Pen friends.

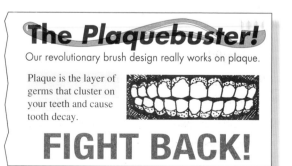

Exercises

1 Complete the statements and questions with plural nouns.

Example: Many _thanks_ for all your help.

1 Somebody has taken all Mrs Bell's money.
The _____ are on their way here now.

2 In the Old West in America, cowboys used to look after thousands of _____

3 Open the can and empty the _____ into a large bowl.

4 I'll cut your hair for you. Where are your _____

5 It's very cold in the mountains, so take some warm _____ with you.

6 Where are my _____ ? I can't see without them!

7 You can't play for our football in jeans. You need some proper _____

8 We get meat, milk and wool from _____

2 Choose singular or plural present forms of *be* or *do*.

Examples: Physics _is_ my best subject.
_Do_ fish feel anything when we catch them?

1 The news _____ very bad. Three people have died and hundreds have been injured.

2 _____ this pair of glasses belong to you?

3 Sheep _____ really stupid animals!

4 _____ mathematics interesting?

5 Your trousers _____ too long. I'd better shorten the legs.

6 ● Which _____ the biggest fish?
○ This one, I think.

7 The new science series on TV _____ very good.

8 Gymnastics _____ dangerous if you don't train carefully.

9 _____ the United States have a prime minister or a president?

10 Aircraft today _____ often able to fly 10,000 miles or more.

3 Complete the statements with singular or plural irregular nouns.

Examples: Two _men_ with beards came to the door.
One _man_ spoke. The other said nothing.

1 We've got two _____ . Pip is five and Lucy is four.

2 There's room for one more _____ in the taxi.

3 My left _____ hurts. I can't walk very well.

4 A normal adult human mouth contains 32 _____

5 This _____ really hurts. The dentist will have to take it out.

6 This bus can carry 70 _____

7 In some countries _____ do the same jobs as men.

8 That _____ mustn't play in the road. It's dangerous. Let's stop her.

4 Complete the statements with the plural forms of these nouns. (Before you start, study Appendix 2.)

battery, knife, life, loaf, match, photo, potato, roof, shelf, wife

Example: Could you put the _shelves_ up here, please?

1 The children shouldn't play with _____ They might cut themselves.

2 The children shouldn't play with _____ either. They might burn themselves.

3 We eat _____ with every meal.

4 I've bought three _____ of bread.

5 Look. These are our holiday _____ This one shows our hotel.

6 The men played golf and their _____ played a game of tennis.

7 This radio runs on four 1.5 volt _____

8 When the ship sank, more than 1,500 people lost their _____

9 The wind blew the _____ off several houses last night.

51 Countable and uncountable nouns

I'd like some olives.   I'd like some olive oil.

CROSSCHECK

Countable nouns	Uncountable nouns
We can count a thing like *an olive* or *three olives*. It has a singular and a plural form and goes with singular and plural verb forms. *These **olives are** very expensive.*	We cannot count a thing like *olive oil*. We do NOT say *an olive oil* or *three olive oils*. We use a singular verb with an uncountable noun. *This **olive oil is** very good.*
Countable nouns can go with other words, eg *some, any, the, this/these, my, many* and *a few*. *I'd like **some oranges**.* *Are there **any bottles**?* ***The glasses** are in the cupboard.* *Could I borrow **a few eggs**?*	Uncountable nouns can go with other words, eg *some, any, the, this, my, much* and *a little*. *I'd like **some orange juice**.* *Is there **any water**?* ***The salt** is in the cupboard.* *Could I borrow **a little milk**?*
We can count amounts of uncountable things by using expressions such as *a litre of/kilo of/can of/loaf of/carton of/bag of/bottle of/box of/ packet of/piece of/roll of.* ***Three cans of** Pepsi, please.* ***Two loaves of** bread, please.*	These nouns are usually uncountable in English: *accommodation, advice, baggage, furniture, hair, health, information, knowledge, luggage, music, news, travel, trouble, work.* *Excuse me. I need **some advice**.* *I'd like to listen to **some music**.*

Some nouns can be countable or uncountable. The countable form is an example or a part. The uncountable form means something in general or a material. Compare the following.

*Football is a great **sport**!* (example) *It's made of large and small **stones**.* (parts of the wall)	*I like **sport**.* (all sports) *The wall is made of **stone**.* (material)

Some nouns can be countable or uncountable, but the meaning is different. Compare the following.

*Do you want a large **glass**?* (for drinking) OR *She wears **glasses**.* (for seeing) *Rob has a small **business**.* (a small company)	*Windows are made of **glass**.* (material) *They want to do **business**.* (work together)

Special Offer!
Sweet apples
2 kilos for the price of 1

I bought these apples from you this morning. They're sour!

Sagittarius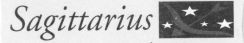

November 23 – December 22

It's a difficult week for Sagittarians and you could get tired and fed up. Some of the best advice you will get involves staying at home with your family. Take it easy – your health is very precious!

Exercises

1 Write the kitchen things in two lists – countable and uncountable. Write the countable nouns in the plural.

apple	cheese	pea
apple juice	cooking oil	potato
banana	egg	rice
bean	milk	salt
biscuit	mineral water	soup
bread	olive	sugar
butter	onion	tea
carrot	orange	tomato

Countable nouns

1 _apples_
2 _____
3 _____
4 _____
5 _____
6 _____
7 _____
8 _____
9 _____
10 _____
11 _____
12 _____

Uncountable nouns

13 _apple juice_
14 _____
15 _____
16 _____
17 _____
18 _____
19 _____
20 _____
21 _____
22 _____
23 _____
24 _____

2 Write the nouns with or without *s*.

● We need some _things_ for dinner. (thing) For example, we haven't got any ¹_____ (meat)

○ Yes, and we've only got a few ²_____ (vegetable)

● You're right. We'd better get some ³_____ and ⁴_____ (bean) (onion)

○ How much ⁵_____ have we got? (rice)

● Only a little. And look, this ⁶_____ is old. (bread) We should buy some more. And I'd like to get a few ⁷_____ too. (bread roll)

○ These ⁸_____ are going bad too. (tomato)

● Yes, and we must remember to buy a bottle of ⁹_____ too. (olive oil)

○ OK. Now I'm going to write a ¹⁰_____ , so we don't forget anything. (list)

3 Choose the correct words.

Examples: *I love this _music_. (music/musics)*
I want to buy _a_ newspaper. (a/some)

1 *My father gave me _____ good advice. (a/some)*

2 *Can you give me some _____ about your company? (information/informations)*

3 *I've got some _____ for a new book. (idea/ideas)*

4 *Here _____ the 9.00 o'clock news. (is/are)*

5 *Put all the _____ in the corner, so we can clean the floor. (furniture/furnitures)*

6 *I must go. I have to do _____ work now. (a/some)*

7 *I've got _____ job to do at home tonight. (a/some)*

8 *Where did you leave your _____ (luggage/luggages)*

9 *Helen has got long, dark _____ (hair/hairs)*

10 *Have you got _____ writing paper, please? (a/any)*

4 Match the two halves.

1 a packet of   a kitchen paper
2 a carton of   b cheese
3 a five-litre bottle of c matches
4 a roll of   d cooking oil
5 three loaves of   e tea
6 four cans of   f bread
7 a box of   g potatoes
8 a two-kilo bag of   h Pepsi
9 a piece of   i milk

1 _e_   I'd like _a packet of tea._
2 ___   I need _____
3 ___   I'd like _____
      _____
4 ___   I need _____
5 ___   I'd like _____
6 ___   I need _____
7 ___   I'd like _____
8 ___   I need _____
      _____
9 ___   I'd like _____

52 Articles 1: *a*, *an*, *the* and *some*

Larry saw an old woman.   The woman smiled.

Yesterday, Larry saw *an* old woman in *the* park next to *the* bus station. She had *an* umbrella and *a* packet of sandwiches with her. *The* sun suddenly came out and *the* woman smiled. She sat down on *a* bench by *the* pond, and she put *the* umbrella on *the* bench beside her. She started to eat *the* sandwiches, and she threw *some* pieces of bread to *the* birds on the water. Half *an* hour later, she went, but she forgot *the* umbrella. Larry picked it up and went after her. He found her in *the* bus station. She was getting on *the* Number 26 bus to Old Town. She was really pleased. 'Stupid me!' she said. 'I nearly went home without it. Thank you for being such *an* honest person!'

a or *an*

Use *a* before a hard sound (consonant).
> *a bench, a packet, a sandwich, a woman*

Use *an* before a soft sound (vowel).
> *an old woman, an umbrella, an ice-cream, an egg, an apple*

But compare the following.
> *an umbrella*   BUT   *a university* (Use *a* when the *u* sounds like *you*.)
> *a hat, a house* BUT   *an hour, an honest person* (Use *an* when the *h* is silent.)

a, an, some or *the*

Use *a* or *an* when you first mention something, eg *an old woman, an umbrella* and *a packet of sandwiches.*
> *Larry saw **an old woman**. She had **a packet of sandwiches**.*

Use *some* for plural and uncountable nouns.
> *She threw **some pieces of bread**.   She threw **some bread**.*

Use *the* when you mention something (singular, plural or uncountable) again. It is now old information. You already know, for example, about *the woman* and *the packet.*
> *The old woman smiled.   She opened **the packet**.*

We do not always use *a* or *an* when we mention something new. We use *the* when we all know the thing, eg *the sun* and *the sky.*
> ***The sun** suddenly came out.   **The sky** was blue.*

More examples from nature: *the earth, the moon, the country(side), the air, the ground.*

More examples when you talk about a particular thing in a particular country: *the capital, the government, the army, the police.*

More examples when local people talk about particular local places.
> *... in **the park** next to **the bus station**.* (the only bus station in the local town)

Annual membership is £3.

Please ask at the box office for an application form and a programme of this term's activities.

If you lose your cheque book:

Contact your branch immediately or call 01426 330300.

You should also tell the police.

The French historian, Edouard de Laboulaye, proposed the Statue of Liberty in 1885 as a gift from France to commemorate the friendship between France and the United States of America. The famous statue in New York harbour was designed by engineer Alexandre Gustave Eiffel, who later built the Eiffel Tower which dominates the Paris skyline.

More examples when family members and friends talk about their things.

> *Let's do some work in **the garden** today.* (our particular garden)
> *Did you hear **the phone** ring?* (the only phone in our house)
> *I think **the boss** has gone home.* (our boss, the boss that we both work for)
> *You should see **the doctor**.* (your family doctor)

The speaker can point to something and use *the*. Compare the following.

> *She had **an umbrella**.*
> *Look. Whose is **the umbrella** on **the bench** over there?*

The speaker can give extra information to show which thing and use *the*.

> *She was getting on **the Number 26 bus**.*
> *She was getting on **the bus to London**.*
> *She was getting on **the bus outside the ticket office**.*

Special uses of *a, an* and *the*

Numbers: We usually use *a* with these numbers.

> *a hundred, a hundred and ninety-nine*
> *(I've got about **a hundred**.* BUT *I've got exactly **one hundred**.)*
> *a thousand, a thousand and ninety-nine*
> *(one thousand one hundred* BUT *one thousand nine hundred and ninety-nine)*
> *a million, a billion, a trillion*

Other quantities: We use *a* with other quantities such as *a month, a kilo, a litre, a dollar* and *a kilometre*.

Rates: We can use *per* or *a/an* in the following.

> *100 kilometres per hour* OR *100 kilometres an hour*
> *three dollars per kilo* OR *three dollars a kilo*

We use *the* to help talk about the position of things.

> *We live **in the middle of London/on the edge of town**.*
> *The house is **on the right/left**.*

Superlatives: A superlative adjective + noun needs *the* because there is only one (like *the sun* and *the moon*, etc).

> *It's **the fastest car** in the world.*
> *Question three was **the most difficult** in the whole exam.*
> *Leaving school early was **the worst mistake** he has ever made.*

We also use *the* to talk about correct information.

> *What's **the time**, please?* (the correct time now)
> *Can you tell me **the way** to the cinema?* (the correct road)
> ***The right answer** to Question 3 is ...* (We also say *the wrong answer*.)

Exercises

1 Write *a* or *an*.

Example: *I only had <u>an</u> apple for lunch.*

1 *Would you like _____ orange?*

2 *We planted about _____ hundred trees.*

3 *The car was travelling at 160 kilometres _____ hour.*

4 *Are we going to stop for _____ rest soon?*

5 *Slow down or we'll have _____ accident!*

6 *I've got _____ young son. He's only four.*

7 *When you work for _____ airline, you have to wear _____ uniform.*

8 *Alan was _____ honest person. He never told _____ lie in his life.*

2 Write *a, an* or *the*.

Example: At a leather goods shop
● *I want to buy <u>a</u> red, leather bag. Can you help me?*
○ *Yes, Madam. I think this is exactly <u>the</u> right bag for you.*

1 At a restaurant
● *I'd like ¹_____ table for three people, please.*
○ *Yes, of course. Please take ²_____ table over there by the window.*

2 After shopping
● *I've bought ¹_____ book and ²_____ magazine.*
○ *Is ³_____ magazine for me?*
● *No. ⁴_____ book is for you, but ⁵_____ magazine is for me.*

3 On the local radio news
● *Here's another piece of local news. There was ¹_____ bank robbery in central Oxford this afternoon. Police Inspector Ross, have you caught ²_____ robbers yet?*
○ *No. We're looking for two men in ³_____ orange BMW. ⁴_____ driver of ⁵_____ car is wearing ⁶_____ green anorak. ⁷_____ passenger is wearing ⁸_____ old leather jacket.*

4 In a garden near home
● *Excuse me. I'm looking for ¹_____ small, black cat. It's run away from home.*
○ *Ah, yes. Look over there. Is that ²_____ cat you mean?*
● *Yes, that's ³_____ one. Thanks very much.*

5 In a street
● *Can you tell me ¹_____ way to Stanford Office Equipment?*
○ *Go along Charles Street for ²_____ kilometre, and you'll come to ³_____ big crossroads. Turn left there, and you'll see three big buildings on ⁴_____ left. Stanford Office Equipment is ⁵_____ building in ⁶_____ middle.*

3 Write *a, an* or *the*.

1 A holiday postcard
I wrote a postcard to my friends at work when I was on holiday last month. It was only ¹_____ picture of ²_____ hotel where I stayed, so it wasn't ³_____ very special card, but I was angry. You see, ⁴_____ card didn't reach ⁵_____ office until ⁶_____ week after I got back.

2 Two accidents in one day
Harry has got ¹_____ broken leg and ²_____ broken arm. He got ³_____ broken arm in ⁴_____ car accident, but he got ⁵_____ broken leg later. He was sitting in ⁶_____ wheelchair and he was waiting for ⁷_____ X-ray of ⁸_____ broken bone. Unfortunately, he was waiting very near some stairs, and he moved ⁹_____ wheelchair a little bit. One wheel went over ¹⁰_____ edge of ¹¹_____ stairs, and that was how Harry's second accident happened. ¹²_____ chair ran all ¹³_____ way down ¹⁴_____ stairs; Harry fell out of ¹⁵_____ chair and into ¹⁶_____ wall at ¹⁷_____ bottom of ¹⁸_____ stairs. ¹⁹_____ doctors say Harry will have to stay in hospital for ²⁰_____ month!

4 Complete the paragraph with *the* and these words.

beach, birds, fields, hill, sand, sea, sky, sun, trees, waves, wind, world

I remember a wonderful day when I was very young. We left our holiday home early, and we walked down <u>the hill</u> for a swim at ¹_____ It was a beautiful summer morning. ²_____ was shining, and ³_____ was blue. ⁴_____ were singing up in ⁵_____ tall, green ⁶_____ In ⁷_____ wide, green ⁸_____ to our left and right

there were millions of flowers. They were all moving in
9_____ gentle 10_____ Ahead of us, we could see
11_____ blue and silver 12_____ and 13_____
fast, white 14_____ as they crashed onto 15_____
golden 16_____ For us, 17_____
was a perfect place that day.

5 Write *a* or *the*.

Examples: a) *The boys always stop at <u>the</u> park on their way home from school.*

b) *The Town Council are thinking of building <u>a</u> new park.*

1 a) *John, _____ phone is ringing. Could you answer it, please?*

b) *My brother has got _____ phone in every room.*

2 a) *We used to visit our grandparents every summer. We loved _____ old house.*

b) *Mr Brook is rich. He's got _____ very big house.*

3 a) *It's warm now. Let's eat lunch in _____ garden.*

b) *We're going to move house. We want somewhere with _____ big garden.*

4 a) *Susan is training to be _____ doctor.*

b) *Jimmy is feeling very ill. Quick. Call _____ doctor.*

5 a) *Is Mr Bradley _____ good boss?*

b) *Where's _____ manager, please? I need to see her.*

6 a) *I'm going to pay this money in at _____ bank today.*

b) *Excuse me. Is there _____ bank near here?*

7 a) *Your train is at 1.00, so I'll take you to _____ station now.*

b) *Our town used to have _____ station, but it's closed now.*

8 a) *I go to _____ dentist every six months.*

b) *I wouldn't like to be _____ dentist. I think it's a horrible job!*

9 a) *Every old town in England has _____ town square.*

b) *I'll meet you in _____ town square at midday.*

10 a) *Could you get some stamps at _____ post office for me, please?*

b) *There's _____ post office in King Street.*

6 Write *a* or *the* and these words instead of the underlined words.

long letter, mountain, phone, police officer, postman, present, reporter, ship, vase

Examples: *He brings our post every morning.*
<u>The postman brings our post every morning.</u>

The plane crashed into <u>something</u>.
<u>The plane crashed into a mountain.</u>

1 *<u>Somebody</u> answered when I phoned the newspaper.*

_____

_____

_____

2 *Joe fell and knocked <u>something</u> over.*

_____

_____

_____

3 *<u>He</u> stopped me for driving too fast.*

_____

_____

_____

4 *<u>It</u> can travel from Britain to the USA in four days.*

_____

_____

_____

5 *When I was away, I bought <u>something</u> for my parents.*

_____

_____

_____

6 *I picked <u>it</u> up and called my sister.*

_____

_____

_____

7 *Sarah wrote <u>something</u> to her father.*

_____

_____

_____

53 Articles 2: general and specific
A plane is a beautiful thing.

FORMS

John is a pilot, and for him *a plane* is a beautiful thing – a man-made bird. '*The plane* has changed our world,' he says. '*Planes* allow us to travel anywhere in less than a day.' He flies a small jet, and he carries *people by air* from London to France, Germany and *the Netherlands*. But to John, flying is not just a job from *Monday to Friday*. *At home at the weekend*, he does not watch *TV* or read *the newspaper*. After *breakfast* on *Saturday morning*, he always goes straight to *the garage* and takes out his other plane – *a microlite*!

General statements – singular

We can use a singular noun to make a general statement. *A plane* means 'any plane'. *The plane* means the type of thing called 'plane'.

> **A plane** *is a beautiful thing.*   **The plane** *has changed our world.*

We can make general statements with plural nouns, eg *people*, and uncountable nouns, eg *life*. Compare the general statements (without *the*) and the specific statements (with *the*).

	General	**Specific**
Plural:	**People** *fly every day.*	**The people** *here are Dutch.*
	Students *are usually poor.*	*Meet* **the new students**.
Uncountable:	*I like strong* **curry**.	*I enjoyed* **the curry** *last night.*
	We need **water** *to live.*	**The water** *is hot now.*

Special expressions – *the* + things in groups

Groups in society: We often use *the* + adjective for groups in society, eg *the poor*, *the rich*, *the sick*, *the old* and *the young*.

> *The gap between* **the rich** *and* **the poor** *is getting wider.*

National groups: We use *the* with national and regional groups of people, eg *the Japanese*, *the French*, *the Germans*, *the Arabs* and *the Europeans*.

> **The Japanese** *and* **the Germans** *have worked hard to become rich.*

Geographical groups: Most country names do not take *the*, eg *Japan*, *France* and *Egypt*. But *the* is necessary for countries that are a group of smaller parts, eg *the Netherlands*, *the United Arab Emirates* and *the United States of America*.

Other groups of places also take *the* – islands, eg *the West Indies* and *the Seychelles*, but not single islands, eg *Madagascar*. Also mountains, eg *the Alps* and *the Himalayas*, but not single mountains, eg *Mount Everest*.

Regions: We talk about regions in different ways. Some are names with *the*, eg *the Far East*, *the Middle East*, *the Rift Valley*, *the Sahara Desert* and *the Nile Delta*. But names with direction + noun do not take *the*, eg *North America* and *South Korea*.

We can also talk about regions in this way.

> *northern/southern/eastern/western Australia* OR *the north/the south/the east/the west of Australia*

A woman without a man is like a fish without a bicycle

BAN THE BOMB

Last year's Cézanne exhibition at the Tate Gallery broke all records. Demand for tickets was huge, and the press called it 'a gorgeous experience … a revelation', 'quite simply an unmissable event'.

Now you can book for its successor: Bonnard, at the Tate from 12 February to 17 May 1998.

Bonnard at the Tate
12 February – 17 May

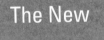

The New

National Marine Aquarium

where truth is stranger than fiction

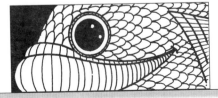

Rivers, etc: Rivers, canals, seas, gulfs, oceans and deserts all need *the*.

> *The (River) Mississippi flows into the Gulf of Mexico.*
> *The Panama Canal connects the Caribbean (Sea) and the Pacific (Ocean).*

Special expressions without and with articles

Places: We do not use *the* when we talk about normal activities that happen *at/to school, at/to work, at/to home,* and *in town, in bed, in hospital,* etc.

> *Ann is at school.*   *Bob's gone to bed.*

We use *the* when we talk about a specific building or place.

> *The school is opposite the hospital.*   *Tom was on the bed.*

Time: We do not usually use *a, an* or *the* with most time words and phrases. But we use an article when we add something extra about these times. Compare the following.

> *New Year was on a Sunday.*   *We had a fantastic New Year.*
> *I came last week.*   *I came the week Tom was born.*

Remember these special expressions: *at night, during the night, on Saturday and Sunday, at the weekend, on Monday morning, in the morning.*

> *I woke up during the night.*
> *I was away on Saturday and Sunday.*
> *I was away at the weekend.*
> *I went out on Monday morning.*

Meals: We do not usually use *a, an* or *the* with *breakfast, lunch, dinner* and *supper.* But we use an article when we add something extra about these meals. Compare the following.

> *I have breakfast at 8.00.*
> *I woke up at 9.00 and had a late breakfast.*
> *We had steak for dinner.*   *That was the best meal of my life!*

Transport: We do not use *a/an* or *the* when we talk about the method of transport. But we use an article when we talk about a specific plane, car, etc. Compare the following.

> *I came by plane.*   *I came on the 5.00 plane from Paris.*
> *She likes travelling by car.*   *It's a very comfortable car.*

Entertainment: Note the use of articles in the following.

> *I watch TV a lot, but I never listen to the radio.*
> *We like going to the cinema, and we often go to the theatre too.*

Musical instruments: We use *the* to talk about playing instruments.

> *He plays the piano/the guitar/the drums.*

Exercises

1 Match the objects and their uses.

1	A camera		a	picking up food.
2	A pen		b	holding papers.
3	A fork	is for	c	taking phone messages.
4	A file		d	taking pictures.
5	A diary		e	writing.
6	A fridge		f	keeping food cold.
7	An answering machine		g	noting dates of meetings, etc.

1 _d_ _A camera is for taking pictures._
2 __ _____
3 __ _____
4 __ _____
5 __ _____
6 __ _____
7 __ _____

2 Match the people and their inventions.

1	Bell		a	the electric lamp.
2	Otis		b	the radio.
3	Marconi	invented	c	the modern car tyre.
4	Biro		d	the lift (or *elevator).
5	Edison		e	the sewing machine.
6	Dunlop		f	the ballpoint pen.
7	Singer		g	the telephone.

*American English

1 _g_ _Bell invented the telephone._
2 __ _____
3 __ _____
4 __ _____
5 __ _____

6 __ _____
7 __ _____

3 Write true statements about these things. Use *I like*, *I don't like* or *I don't mind*.

black coffee, chocolate, fast cars, homework, long journeys, loud rock music, swimming, tennis

Examples: *I like chocolate.*
I don't like long journeys.

1 _____
2 _____
3 _____
4 _____
5 _____
6 _____

4 Choose the correct words.

Examples: *All children like ice-cream.*
(ice-cream/the ice-cream)
Did you enjoy the film last night?
(film/the film)

1 Peter is riding _____ which was ill last week. (horse/the horse)

2 My brother visits _____ all over the world. (companies/the companies)

3 Could you pass _____ , please? (salt/the salt)

4 _____ aren't here. Where are they? (Books/The books)

5 _____ isn't the most important thing in the world. (Money/The money)

6 People can't live for long without _____ (water/the water)

7 _____ live in Africa and India. (Elephants/The elephants)

8 _____ is ringing. Could you answer it, please? (Phone/The phone)

5 Complete the statements with *the* and these words.

old, poor, rich, unemployed, young

Example: <u>The rich</u> have to pay high taxes.

1 In the old days the government did very little to help _____

2 These days _____ receive payments while they are unable to work.

3 Today, _____ are living for longer than ever before.

4 _____ have to learn from their parents and their teachers.

5 _____ often use a dog or a stick to help them find their way.

6 Write the names of the people.

Country	People
1 Australia	the Australians
2 Britain	_____
3 China	_____
4 Denmark	_____
5 Egypt	_____
6 France	_____
7 Indonesia	_____
8 Japan	_____
9 Kuwait	_____
10 Netherlands	_____
11 Portugal	_____
12 Spain	_____
13 Russia	_____
14 Turkey	_____
15 the United States	_____
16 Venezuela	_____

Now write the names of your country and your people.

_____

_____

7 Write *the* or nothing (✗).

Example: <u>The</u> Netherlands is a small country in
<u>✗</u> Europe.

1 _____ Mississippi is the longest river in _____ United States.

2 _____ Lake Victoria is a beautiful lake in _____ east Africa.

3 _____ Mount Everest is the highest mountain in _____ Himalayan Mountains to _____ north of India.

4 _____ Jamaica is a beautiful island in _____ West Indies, which are in _____ Caribbean Sea.

5 _____ Suez Canal lies along _____ western edge of _____ Sinai Desert in _____ Egypt. It connects _____ Mediterranean and _____ Red Sea.

8 Write *the* or nothing (✗).

Paul Ross is an international rock star now, but life was not always so good. He grew up in <u>the</u> north of England and went to <u>✗</u> school there. He did not enjoy his schooldays very much, but there was a very good music teacher at [1]_____ school, and she helped him a lot. He learned to sing well there, and he started to play [2]_____ guitar when he was 12. At the age of 18, he went to [3]_____ music college, and there he studied other instruments, including [4]_____ drums.

When he left [5]_____ college, he could not find [6]_____ work, so he started the rock band Magic Machine with some friends. Soon they were doing well and they went south to London. They went on [7]_____ TV for the first time on [8]_____ day Paul was 22.

When they went to London, they drove there in Paul's old car, but now they travel everywhere by [9]_____ air.

Paul and the others work hard, but at the moment, they are on holiday. Paul wakes up late in [10]_____ morning, and he eats [11]_____ breakfast late. He usually stays at [12]_____ home for most of the day, and he listens to new music on CDs or [13]_____ radio. Then in [14]_____ evening, he often goes to [15]_____ cinema.

54 Demonstratives
this, that, these, those

one and *ones*
one, ones

this, that, these and *those* as demonstrative adjectives

Use *this* and *these* for things which are near in place or time. Use *that* and *those* for things which are not near in place or time.

> *... on **that** bookcase ...*
> *... over there on **those** tables ...*

Use *this* or *that* with a singular or uncountable noun.
> ***This wallet** is mine.*   ***That purse** is Sally's.*

Use *these* or *those* with a plural noun.
> ***These shoes** are cheap.*   ***Those boots** are really nice!*

Use expressions with *that* to say something is right or wrong.
> ***That**'s right.*   *No, **that**'s wrong.*

this, that, these and *those* as demonstrative pronouns

When the meaning is clear, we can leave out the noun and *one* or *ones*.
> ***This** is boring. Let's change channels.* (this programme)
> *Look at **these**! They're my size.* (these shoes or clothes)

one and *ones*

We use the pronouns *one* and *ones* instead of a noun. Use *one* or *ones* instead of repeating a noun.

> *Which **vase**? → Which **one**?*
> *Which **plants**? → Which **ones**?*

Use *one* or *ones* when you can show what you are talking about.

- *Which is your jacket? Is it this **one**?* (pointing)
- *No, it's that **one** over there. Look!* (pointing)
  *It's the green **one** with red buttons.* (describing)
  *It's the **one** on the chair.* (saying where it is)

Use *ones* just like *one* – for plural countable nouns.

- *What colour shirts would you like?*
- *A white **one**, please, and two red **ones**.*

Do not use *one* or *ones* with uncountable nouns. Use *some* instead.
> *I'd like **some** white cloth, please, and **some** red cloth.*

No stamp needed, but using one will save WorldAid money.

This car park is for residents only.

cult classics
The first in an essential guide to cult films
Tuesday 20 January

APOCALYPSE NOW (18)
Director: Francis Ford Coppola
Starring: Martin Sheen and Marlon Brando

This is Coppola's epic exploration of America's heart of darkness – Vietnam.

Who can become a blood donor?
Anyone between 18 and 60 who is healthy and not subject to certain medical conditions.

What types of blood are needed?
All types – especially the most common ones because they are the ones that are most in demand.

Odd One Out
Which one of these is the odd one out and why?
a) ostrich   b) seagull   c) eagle   d) pigeon

Answer: a) It can't fly.

Exercises

1 Write *this, that, these* or *those*.

Example: *I can't see. What are <u>those</u> things over there?*

1 *Could you put the bookcase over there between _____ two windows?*

2 *_____ curry last night was very good.*

3 *Look how _____ diamonds shine when I turn them in the light.*

4 *Look, you have to press _____ button here to start the machine.*

5 ● *Do you remember _____ people from Canada? We met them at _____ party in London last November.*
 ○ *Do you mean _____ teachers – Bob and Lisa?*
 ● *Yes. Well, they're coming for dinner _____ evening.*
 ○ *Great!*

2 Write *this, that, these* or *those*.

Example: ● *Is <u>this</u> your car here?*
 ○ *No, mine is blue, not red. <u>That</u>'s it over there.*

1 ● *Alice, _____ is Tom Barnes, our new salesperson. Tom, _____ is Alice Parker, our Finance Director.*
 ○ *Nice to meet you.*
 ● *Good to meet you too.*

2 ● *Could you look at my book, please Miss. Is _____ the right answer?*
 ○ *Yes, _____'s right. Well done!*

3 ● *Excuse me. Is _____ Hill Farm here?*
 ○ *No, _____ is Lower Farm. Just keep going up the hill. _____'s it, up there at the top.*

4 ● *Here you are, Susan. _____ is your desk, and _____ are your files. Enjoy your new job!*
 ○ *Thanks very much. _____ is a nice office.*

5 ● *No, Tom. You've brought me the wrong books. I don't want _____*
 ○ *Oh, so do you want _____ over there?*
 ● *Yes, _____ are the ones.*

3 Write *this/that (one)* or *these/those (ones)*.

Example: ● *Look, <u>this</u> must be your bag.*
 ○ *No, <u>this one</u> isn't my bag. Mine is <u>that one</u> over there.*

1 ● *Look. Are _____ Tom's shoes here?*
 ○ *No. _____ over there are his. _____ here are Fred's.*

2 ● *After we turn on the computer, we need to put in a disk. Could you pass me _____ blue _____ on your desk, Bob?*
 ○ *Do you mean _____ here?*
 ● *Yes, _____, please.*

3 ● *I need some lights for my bike, please.*
 ○ *Yes, Sir. Have a look at _____ here.*
 ● *What about _____ over there?*
 ○ *They're good too, but _____ are better.*

4 Write *one/ones* or *the one/the ones*.

Example: ● *Excuse me. I'm trying to find a house. It's Number 73.*
 ○ *Do you see the three small <u>ones</u> there? Number 73 is <u>the one</u> on the left.*

1 ● *Go and say hello to Jim Baker.*
 ○ *Which _____ is he?*
 ● *He's _____ over there with dark hair.*

2 ● *I'd like some shoes from the shop window, please.*
 ○ *Of course. Which _____ would you like?*
 ● *They're _____ red _____ on the left.*

3 ● *Are David Frost and Roger West here?*
 ○ *Yes, they're by the window. David is _____ on the right, and Roger is _____ on the left.*

4 ● *Could I borrow some plates for my dinner party?*
 ○ *Of course. They're all in this cupboard. Which _____ would you like – _____ large _____ or _____ small _____ ?*

5 ● *Hello. You're from the band Magic Machine, aren't you? I'm Pete Price. I'm _____ who's interviewing you. Which of you is _____ who writes the songs?*
 ○ *I'm Paul, _____ who writes wites the music. Ron and Bob are _____ who write the words.*

55 *some or any*

We've got some olives.   We haven't got anything.

> Have we got any green olives?

> Yes, we've got some green olives, but we haven't got any black olives.

some or *any*

Use *some* in positive sentences with plural nouns and uncountable nouns.
> *There are **some green olives**.   There's **some tomato juice**.*

Use *any* in negative sentences with plural nouns and uncountable nouns.
> *There aren't **any black olives**.   There isn't **any orange juice**.*

Use *any* with plural nouns and uncountable nouns in *Yes / No* questions. The answer can be *Yes* or *No*.
- ● *Have we got **any** green olives?*   (○ *Yes.*)
- ● *Have we got **any** orange juice?*   (○ *No.*)

When we think the answer to our question is *Yes*, we use *some*.
> *Are you going to buy **some** things in town today?*

We also use *some* to make requests and offers sound positive.
> *Could I have **some** money, please?*
> *Would you like **some** money?*

We sometimes use *any* to talk about things that are possible, but uncertain.
> *If there are **any** calls, please tell me.*
> *Please send **any** letters to my new address.* (if there are any letters)

something or *anything*

We can use *some* and *any* to make these new words.

	thing	body/one	where
some	something	somebody	somewhere
any	anything	anyone	anywhere

We choose them as we choose *some* or *any*.
> *He told her **something**.* (like *some news* – positive)
> *We didn't see **anybody**.* (like *any people* – negative)
> *Are you singing **anything** tonight?* (like *any songs* – uncertain)

(See Unit 63 for more information about *something, anybody*, etc.)

We can use *any, anything* and *anybody* to mean 'it doesn't matter what'.
> *You can buy these at **any** supermarket.*
> *You can have **anything** you want. You choose.*
> *It's easy to make. **Anybody** can do it.*

Exercises

1 Write *some* or *any*.

Dear Aunt Lucy,

Well, here we are on holiday. We're having a good time, and there are <u>some</u> *great things about this place, but there are* [1]_____ *bad things too. The sea is great, but the hotel swimming pool isn't. There isn't* [2]_____ *water in the pool! There are* [3]_____ *interesting places to visit near here, but there aren't* [4]_____ *cars to hire. It's true, there are* [5]_____ *buses, but those are all in the middle of the day. There aren't* [6]_____ *in the morning or the evening.*

    Must stop. See you soon.

        Love, Sam

PS We'll bring you [7]_____ *local olives. They're really good!*

2 Write *some* or *any*.

Example: ● *Come and sit down. Now, have* <u>some</u> *coffee and biscuits.*

    ○ *I'm sorry, but I don't drink coffee. Have you got* <u>some/any</u> *tea?*

1 ● *I'm looking for _____ cups, but I can't find _____.*
  ○ *Perhaps there are _____ in the dishwasher.*

2 ● *Rod, could you lend me _____ money?*
  ○ *I'm sorry, Bob, but I haven't got _____. I wanted to ask you for _____ money!*

3 ● *I need _____ help with this work. Have you got _____ free time today?*
  ○ *OK. I can give you _____ time tonight.*

4 ● *Ben, would you like to spend _____ time with your grandparents this summer?*
  ○ *Well, they're very nice, but I haven't got _____ friends where they live.*

3 Write *some, any, somebody, anybody, something* or *anything*.

Example: ● *I'm getting* <u>some</u> *things at the market. Can I get you* <u>anything/something</u>?
    ○ *No, I don't need* <u>anything</u> *thanks.*

1 ● *Is there _____ good on TV tonight?*
  ○ *No, there isn't _____ really. There's just _____ about wildlife in India.*

2 ● *Listen! I think I heard a noise. Can you hear _____?*
  ○ *Do you mean that noise outside? I think _____ is coming to the front door.*

3 ● *Hello! Is _____ at home?*
  ○ *Oh, hello, Richard. Come in. You're just in time for _____ tea.*

4 ● *Could _____ please open the door for me? My hands are full.*
  ○ *Certainly. And would you like _____ help with carrying those things too?*

5 ● *You look hungry. I'll get you _____ to eat.*
  ○ *Thanks. I haven't had _____ to eat since yesterday.*

6 ● *Are there _____ people still living in the house?*
  ○ *No, we looked round, but there wasn't _____ there.*

4 Complete the answers. Use *any* (plus a noun from the question), *anything, anybody* or *anywhere*.

Examples: ● *Which car can we hire?*
    ○ *We can hire* <u>any car</u> *we like.*
    ● *I mustn't spend too much.*
    ○ *Don't worry. You can buy* <u>anything</u> *you want.*

1 ● *I like this car, but I don't like the colour.*
  ○ *You can have _____ you want, Sir.*

2 ● *I'm from Channel 5 TV, and I'd like to interview some members of the team.*
  ○ *You're welcome to interview _____ you want.*

3 ● *Are you sure you don't want to keep any of these things?*
  ○ *Yes, you can take _____ you want.*

4 ● *Are many people coming to the meeting?*
  ○ *I don't know, but we'll welcome _____ who comes.*

5 ● *Where shall we go on holiday this year, Tom?*
  ○ *You can go _____ you want to go, Penny.*

56 There, It and They

There's a hotel in the village.   *It's in the square.*

Excuse me ...

There is and There are

We can use *There is* and *There are* when we talk about something for
the first time.

● **Is there** a bakery in the town?   ○ Yes, **there's** one near the bank.

Use *There are* to talk about quantity with, eg *any, some, a lot (of),
several, a few, many.*

● **Are there any** other shops?   ○ Not **many**, but **there are a few**.

Use *There* with different forms of *be – will be, was/were, has/have been.*

Will there be time to buy some things?
There was no time to do any shopping in the last village.

It and They

We often use *It* and *They* after *There* to introduce something. *It* and
They refer back to that thing. We often use *It* like this for people (and
other living things).

There was a hotel in the last village, but **it wasn't** very nice.
There were some shops too, but **they were** closing.

It for time, weather and distance

Use *It* in expressions about time, weather and distance.

It's getting late. **It**'s time to go.
● What time is **it**?   ○ **It**'s 5.00.
It's cold. **It**'s going to rain.   **It** was a hot day. **It** was very sunny.
● Is **it** far to the village?   ○ **It**'s two miles.
● How far is **it** to London?   ○ **It**'s a long way.

It as a dummy subject

Use *It ... to* and *It ... that* in expressions like these.

It's a good/bad idea **to** stop.   **It** was good/lovely **to** see her.
It's sad/a pity **that** you can't stay.   **It**'s true **that** he's leaving.

Use *It ... verb + ing* in these expressions.

It's (not) worth **buying** that old car.
It's no use **talking**. He never listens.

The Church of St Peter, *Highfield*

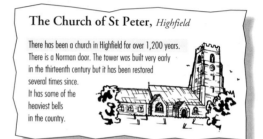

There has been a church in Highfield for over 1,200 years.
There is a Norman door. The tower was built very early
in the thirteenth century but it has been restored
several times since.
It has some of the
heaviest bells
in the country.

'It is better to be beautiful than to be good. But ... it is better
to be good than to be ugly.'

(Oscar Wilde, 1854–1900)

A Walk on the Wild Side?

Wessex Wildlife Trust invites you to take part in a
walk along the River Otter on Sunday 18th March.
There are two walks in different directions, both
starting in Marine Car Park at 11 am.

The Frozen Earth

Margaret Daley
£16.99 (Fiction)
ISBN 0 333 71166 1

MARGARET Daley's
first novel, *Goodnight My
Friend*, was one of last
year's most impressive
debuts. It is most unfair to
expect a second book of
the same excellence, and
The Frozen Earth doesn't
quite match up.

St Just:
Britain's most
westerly town

Oh ... and there are shops
and places to eat and
things to do when it's
wet. Then there are the
pubs – pubs you'll later
yearn for – The Star, The
Wink, The North Inn, The
Radjel, The Gurnard's
Head, The Tinners and
many more.

Exercises

1 Write questions and answers. Use *there* + the correct form of *be*.

Examples: *(sugar?) (Yes/over there)*
● *Is there any sugar?*
○ *Yes, there's some over there.*
(onions?) (No/buy some)
● *Are there any onions?*
○ *No, there aren't. I'll buy some.*

1 *(potatoes?) (Yes/in the bag)*
● _____
○ _____

2 *(coffee?) (No/buy some)*
● _____
○ _____

3 *(large pan?) (No/buy one)*
● _____
○ _____

4 *(carrots?) (No/buy some)*
● _____
○ _____

5 *(butter?) (Yes/in the fridge)*
● _____
○ _____

6 *(teapot?) (Yes/on the shelf)*
● _____
○ _____

2 Write *There was, There were, There wasn't* or *There weren't*.

Example: *There weren't many people at the party.*

1 _____ *much food in the house.*

2 _____ *no time to talk.*

3 _____ *many shops open after 9.00.*

4 _____ *a lot of strange noises outside in the forest.*

5 _____ *no bank in the village.*

6 _____ *only a few days left before the exams.*

7 _____ *very little time to do anything.*

3 Write *There* + the correct form of *be* and pronouns.

Examples: *There was a dog in our garden yesterday. It came from next door.*
There isn't any butter. We finished it yesterday.

1 _____ *some flowers for Ann.* _____ *'re from Tom.*

2 _____ *much sugar last night. Mum used most of* _____ *to make a cake.*

3 _____ *many people at the concert last night, but I think* _____ *enjoyed it.*

4 _____ *somebody on the phone for you. His name is Peter. Do you know* _____

5 _____ *any matches. Have you used* _____ *all?*

6 _____ *much water, so we'll have to use* _____ *very carefully.*

4 Complete the statements. Choose from these expressions.

It's	a good/bad idea to …
It was	good/lovely/sad to …
	sad that …
	a pity that …
	not worth …
	no use …

Example: *It was a bad idea to go camping in the middle of winter.*

1 _____ *see all the family together again today.*

2 _____ *walking ten kilometres yesterday just to see that boring view.*

3 _____ *shouting at the children. It doesn't do any good.*

4 _____ *we lost the match after we had done so much training.*

5 _____ *he died so young. He was only 32.*

57 Quantity
a lot of, many, much, a few, a little

With countable nouns use *a lot of, many* and *a few*. Use *a lot of* and *many* for a large number of things. The noun has an *s*, eg *a lot of cassettes* and *many videos*

With uncountable nouns use *a lot of, much* and *a little*. Use *a lot of* and *much* for a large amount of something. The noun has no *s*, eg *a lot of pop music* and *much time*. ·

Use *a lot of* with both countable and uncountable nouns. We use it in positive sentences more than in questions and negative sentences.

> She's got **a lot of cassettes**.   She's got **a lot of pop music**.

We can use the informal *lots of* instead of *a lot of*.

> He's got **lots of cassettes**.   He's got **lots of pop music**.

We can use short forms in answers to questions.

> ● *Are there many songs on the CD?*   ○ *Yes, there are **a lot/lots**.*

We usually use *many* and *much* in questions and negative sentences (but sometimes in formal positive sentences too). We can use *much* and *many* by themselves in answers to questions.

> ● *Are there **many** songs on the cassette?*
> ○ *No, **there aren't many**.* OR *Yes, **lots**.*
> ● *Is there **much** music on the cassette?*
> ○ *No, **not much**.* OR *Yes, **a lot**.*

We usually use *a few* and *a little* in positive statements, and also in requests and offers.

> There were **a few** people in the room.
> There was **a little** food on the table.
> Could I borrow **a few** stamps?   Would you like **a little** money?

a few is for a small number of something, but positive. *few* is also for a small number of something, but negative. The noun is plural.

> I'm going to see **a few friends** this evening. (positive)
> **Few people** live to 100. (negative)

a little and *little* are similar and are for a small amount of something. The noun has no *s*.

> We've got **a little time**, so let's have tea. (positive)
> Hurry! There's very **little time**. (negative)

Weather is cool, Chicagoans warm, location v. good. Lots of buildings to go up and down. You'd like it here. Hope all are well.

*Much love,
Mum and Dad xxx*

Ms J Turner,
23, Smith Street,
London EC1
UK

Everyday Etiquette

Q   When visiting friends for a weekend where it is likely that many bottles of wine will be drunk, how many bottles should one take? We always seem to take many, but receive few!
Peter Hargreaves, Plymouth

A   There are no strict rules here, but quality is more important than quantity. A host will generally prefer one really good bottle to a lot of something cheaper and not so enjoyable.

Wildlife Word Wizardry

How many words of three letters or more can you make out of the letters in the word **WILDLIFE**?

You can use each letter once only in each word. (No names allowed.) 6 - Good, 7–12 - Very Good, More than 12 - Excellent!

London Factfile

Check out the Houses of Parliament, Westminster Abbey, St Paul's Cathedral, Buckingham Palace, Trafalgar Square and the National Gallery, Madame Tussaud's, the Planetarium, the Tower of London ... These are just a few of the main attractions, but there is so much more to see. For more details, contact any tourist information centre. A lot of the pleasure in London is in just walking around and getting the atmosphere. Don't forget the shopping either. There are just so many good places, but places worth including on your list are Oxford Street, Knightsbridge, Covent Garden, Camden Lock Market.

Shadows on the Water By Steven Jones
£9.95 (Non-Fiction) ISBN 0 393 31676 9

With little experience of either ships or icebergs, Steven Jones cannot hope to compete with his fellow Titanic historians on mastery of detail in this cultural history of the disaster. His narrative is concerned not with the practicalities of the

Exercises

1 Complete the statements and questions. Use *a lot (of)*, *lots (of)*, *many* or *much*.

Example: ● *Have we got __much__ tea?*
○ *No, we haven't, but we've got __a lot of/ lots of__ coffee.*

1 *Let's hurry. There's _____ work to do, and there isn't _____ time.*

2 *Harry talks to _____ people in his work, but he hasn't got _____ close friends.*

3 *I haven't got _____ money. How _____ have you got?*

4 *Some people spend _____ time at the office, but they don't really do _____ work.*

5 ● *Are there _____ people in the shops today?*
○ *No, not _____ , even though _____ the shops are having sales.*

6 ● *How _____ time do you spend travelling every week?*
○ *_____ Probably about 20 hours.*

7 ● *How _____ times have you been to France?*
○ *Not _____ Three times altogether.*

8 ● *How _____ do you weigh?*
○ *Too _____ Nearly 85 kilos.*

2 Complete the statements and questions. Use *a few*, *few*, *a little* or *little*.

Examples: *You'd better go to the corner shop. We've only got __a few__ eggs and __a little__ milk.*
We'd better hurry. There's very __little__ time.

1 *We'd better go to the supermarket. There's only _____ orange juice, and there are only _____ tomatoes.*

2 *My motor-bike is very cheap to run. It uses very _____ petrol, and very _____ ever goes wrong with it.*

3 *Smoking is going out of fashion. _____ still smoke at work, but _____ of them think it's a good thing to do.*

4 *The soup isn't ready yet. I think it needs _____ cream and _____ more chopped vegetables.*

5 *We can only afford _____ small presents this year. We've got very _____ money.*

6 *Could you lend me _____ money? I only need _____ pounds.*

7 *The generals of the First World War were men with _____ ideas and _____ imagination.*

8 ● *I put on _____ weight while I was on holiday.*
○ *How much?*
● *Only _____ kilos.*

3 Complete the conversation. Choose from these forms.

a few, few, a little, little, a lot (of), lots (of), many, much

● *How's business, Fred?*
○ *It's quite good. We're getting __a lot of__ orders this year. Not like last year. Last year we had very ¹_____ work, and ²_____ of our staff lost their jobs. How's your company doing?*
● *It's still not very good, I'm sorry to say. We've only got ³_____ new orders at the moment, and not ⁴_____ of those are big ones.*
○ *I'm sorry to hear that.*
● *There's another big problem too. Some customers owe us ⁵_____ money from jobs that we did months ago.*
○ *That's terrible. How ⁶_____ money do they owe you?*
● *About £50,000. That's ⁷_____ for a small company like mine.*
○ *Can you do anything to make them pay?*
● *No, I can't really do very ⁸_____ If a company really decides not to pay me on time, there's very ⁹_____ that I can do about it.*
○ *Perhaps you should get them to pay you ¹⁰_____ each month.*
● *That's a good idea. I might try it.*

58 Partitives

All of, Most of, None of, Both of, Neither of, etc   every, each

Our weekend at Brill Adventure Centre

All of, Both of, etc

All of means 100% of a group. *None of* means 0% of a group.
> ***All/None of** us enjoyed rock climbing.*

Most of means nearly all. *A few of* means a small number. *Some of* is between *Most* and *A few*. (Other phrases: *A lot of, Half of, One or two of*.)
> ***Most/Some/A few of** us wanted to do more archery.*

Both of means 100% of a pair. *Neither of* means 0% of a pair.
> ***Both/Neither of** the instructors taught us sandsurfing.*

With *Both* and *All* + noun, you can leave out *of*. With *Both* + noun, you can also leave out *the*.
> ***Both (of) (the)** instructors helped **all (of)** the students.*

But you must use *of* before object pronouns and after *Most, Some, A few* and *Neither*.
> *Both of them, All of us, Most of you, One of them*
> *Most of the students, Neither of the instructors*

One of is different from *either of* and *any of*.
> *You can use **either of** the cars. (It doesn't matter which of the pair you use.)*
> *You can book **any of** the 200 rooms in the hotel. (It doesn't matter which of the rooms you book.)*

Compare *None of* and *Neither of* above with *not ... any of* and *not ... either of*.

	Subject	Object
Group:	*None of*	*not ... any of*
Pair:	*Neither of*	*not ... either of*

> ***None of** us enjoyed it. They did**n't** help **any of** the students.*
> ***Neither of** them taught us. We did**n't** like **either of** them.*

Compare talking about a group and talking in general.
> ***Most of** the students enjoyed it. (most of the groups of students)*
> ***Most** students work hard. (most of the group of students)*

Use *All, Some* and *No* to talk in general.
> ***All** cats like milk.   **Some** trees grow fruit.   **No** man can fly.*

every and each

We use *every* and *each* to talk about all members of a group. Use a singular noun and verb.
> ***Every** day was fun. (all group members together)*
> ***Each** day was different. (all group members one by one)*

Exercises

1 Complete the statements about the students. Use these words.

all, almost all, a few, most, one, some

A teacher checked her class register for the last 15 lessons.

NAME	PRESENT	ABSENT
John	14	1
Lisa	1	14
Lucy	4	11
David	15	0
Robin	8	7
Greg	12	3
Sally	6	9

Examples: John came to <u>almost all of the lessons.</u>
Lisa only came to <u>one of them.</u>

1 *Lucy only came to* _____

2 *David came to* _____

3 *Robin came to* _____

4 *Greg came to* _____

5 *Sally only came to* _____

2 Complete the second statement in each pair. Use these words.

all of, both of, most of, half of, a few of, us, you, them

Example: Rob and I don't always get to work on time.
<u>Both of us</u> were late again today.

1 *You and your brother look ill.* _____
need to see the doctor.

2 *The teacher put the class in two groups.*
_____ *prepared questions, and the other half prepared their answers.*

3 *Well, everybody, you did very badly in the test.*
_____ *got less than 50%. That's really not good enough!*

4 *The senior and the junior basketball teams are doing very well.* _____ *reached the national championships.*

5 *About 60 supporters went to the championships. The team coach took* _____ *in his car, but* _____ *went by bus. We had a great time.*

3 Complete the negative statements. Use these words.

any of, either of, neither of, none of

Examples: *The couple next door are strange. I don't like* <u>either of</u> *them much.*
<u>None of</u> *the children wanted to go home at the end of the party.*

1 *I asked Wayne and Brian, but* _____ *them could lend me any money.*

2 *I offered all the old people a trip to London, but* _____ *them wanted to go.*

3 *We looked at several restaurants, but we didn't like* _____ *them.*

4 *Peter tried two different hotel jobs, but he wasn't very good at* _____ *them.*

5 _____ *Joe's clothes fitted him any more because he was growing so fast.*

6 _____ *the teams scored, and the match ended at 0 – 0.*

7 *I test drove a number of new cars, but I didn't buy* _____ *them.*

8 *I took two exams, but because I hadn't done enough work, I didn't pass* _____ *them.*

9 *I've read both of these books and I didn't like* _____ *them. They were very boring.*

10 *I asked the class if* _____ *them would help me move the tables, but* _____ *them did. So I did it myself.*

4 Complete the paragraph. Use these words.

all, both, each, every

Jamie and his friends, Bob and Pete, go to judo classes <u>every</u> week. He and [1]_____ his friends love judo, and they never miss their class [2]_____ Friday evening. There are about 20 people in the class, and [3]_____ of them train very hard. To start with, they [4]_____ do exercises together. Then the teacher works with [5]_____ member of the class, one by one. [6]_____ student trains at his or her own standard. [7]_____ three months, they take a test. If they pass, they go up to the next grade.

59 Pronouns: subject and object
You can give it to me.

> We must get this package to the Manchester office fast.
>
> Give it to me. I'm going there tomorrow.

FORMS

		1st person	2nd person	3rd person		
Singular						
	Subject	*I*	*you*	*he*	*she*	*it*
	Object	*me*	*you*	*him*	*her*	*it*
Plural						
	Subject	*we*	*you*	*they*		
	Object	*us*	*you*	*them*		

Personal pronouns refer to people and things. We use pronouns instead of nouns, eg for people's names, when the meaning is clear.

First person pronouns refer to the speaker, or to the speaker and one or more other people.

> **We** *must get ...* (the two speakers)
> *Give it to* **me**. (the speaker)

Second person pronouns refer to the person or people listening.

> **You** *can give ...* (the listener)

Third person pronouns refer to either a person or people or a thing or things. These are outside the 1st and 2nd persons' conversation.

> *Give* **it** *to* **them**. (the package and some other people)

A personal pronoun can be the subject or the object of a sentence.

Subject	**Object**
I'm going home now.	*Peter doesn't know* **me**.
Is **she** *working tomorrow?*	*Sally called* **her** *three times.*
They *don't like loud music.*	*We answered* **them**.

An object pronoun can be either a direct object or an indirect object. (See Unit 62 for more information about direct and indirect objects.)

> *Joe sent* **it**. (direct object)
> *Joe sent it* **to her**. (indirect object)

You can use pronouns in short answers to questions. The other way of doing this – with object pronouns – is informal.

> ● *Who broke this dish?* ○ **I** *did./* **I** *didn't.* OR **Me**. */Not* **me**.
> ● *Who'll wash the car for me?* ○ **We** *will./* **We** *won't.*
> OR **Us**. */Not* **us**.

There are ways of talking about people in general. The pronoun *you* is informal.

> **You** *never know what's going to happen.*

The pronoun *one* is very formal.

> **One** *cannot judge people by the way they look.*

The pronoun *they* refers to other people in general, or to people who are in charge.

> **They** *say some people hardly ever sleep.*
> **They** *don't let foreigners visit without a visa.*

We all live in the same world
Make sure you are part of it.
Join
GREEN ISSUES
today
Don't leave it too late.

Jamie Jean *Run to me* ★★★

You should know the story, but if you don't, then check this: 'I'm your babe', 'He gives me fire' (remix), 'Let me be your lover', 'We can work together'.
They have three things in common – they all topped the charts, they were all taken from albums by different singers, Jamie Jean sang backing vocals on all four. She now has her own single, 'Run to me'. We'll see if she can have the same success on her own.

HAPPY BIRTHDAY!

With love from me to you

For your security, always ask me for my identity card and check it.

'You can lead a horse to water, but you can't make it drink.'

(Proverb)

Exercises

1 Read the conversation. Then write the meanings of the underlined pronouns.

Paul: *What are ¹you doing tomorrow?*

Bill: *²I'm going to a football practice in the morning.*

Paul: *³I'd like to go to that too. I love football. What time does ⁴it start?*

Bill: *At 10.00. Why don't ⁵you come with ⁶me? Then after that, we can meet Neil in town. ⁷He wants to see the new Batman film.*

Paul: *Oh, yes. People say ⁸it's good.*

Bill: *Yes, ⁹they say it's the best Batman film yet. So I think ¹⁰we should all go and see it together. What do you think?*

1 you = <u>Bill</u>   6 me = _____

2 I = _____   7 He = _____

3 I = _____   8 it = _____

4 it = _____   9 they = _____

5 you = _____   10 we = _____

2 Write the correct subject pronouns and short forms of *be*.

Example: ● *What are <u>you</u> doing, Sally?*
　　　　　○ *<u>I'm</u> making a cake.*

1 ● *Where are Tom and Bill going?*
　○ _____ *going to the cinema.*

2 ● *Susan looks great in that dress.*
　○ *Yes, _____ a beautiful girl.*

3 ● *What are _____ and the boys doing?*
　○ _____ *going to the swimming pool.*

4 ● *What's that dog doing in our kitchen?*
　○ _____ *taking our lunch!*

5 ● *Do you know Peter Wells?*
　○ *Yes, _____ the man with the big house at the end of our street.*

6 ● *How are _____ travelling round France, Fred?*
　○ _____ *travelling by bike.*

7 ● _____ *looking very happy today, Sally.*
　○ *Yes, _____ my birthday and _____ 18 today. _____ having a party tonight. Please come.*

3 Write the correct object pronouns.

Example: ● *Where did you put my hat?*
　　　　　○ *I put <u>it</u> on the table.*

1 ● *Do you know where Ann is?*
　○ *Yes. I can see _____ over there.*

2 ● *I'll be at home this evening.*
　○ *All right. I'll call _____ at 7.00.*

3 ● *I need to see Mr Brice, please.*
　○ *Certainly. You can see _____ at 3.00.*

4 ● *Do you like these shoes?*
　○ *Yes. I'm going to buy _____*

5 ● *Why does Peter always call _____ in the evening, Tony?*
　○ *Because he always wants _____ to help _____ with his homework.*

6 ● *Were there any calls for _____ while we were out?*
　○ *There weren't any calls for Bill, but there was a call for _____ . Mrs Tucker phoned and she wants _____ to call _____ back.*

4 Write the correct subject and object pronouns and short froms of *be*.

It's Tom's first day at the office.

Jim: *Tom, come and meet Ann Scott. <u>She's</u> our Finance Director. Ann, this is Tom Blake. ¹_____ our new sales assistant.*

Ann: *It's nice to meet ²_____ , Tom.*

Tom: *³_____ good to meet ⁴_____ too, Mrs Scott.*

Ann: *Oh, please call ⁵_____ Ann. ⁶_____ all use our first names here.*

Later the same day

Jim: *Tom, could ⁷_____ help ⁸_____ please?*

Tom: *Yes, of course. What can ⁹_____ do?*

Jim: *Take this report to Finance and give ¹⁰_____ to Ann. And give ¹¹_____ these papers too. ¹²_____ very important. ¹³_____ needs ¹⁴_____ for a meeting. ¹⁵_____ starting in a few minutes from now.*

Tom: *Right. ¹⁶_____ 'll go immediately.*

60 Pronouns: possessive

Is this your jacket?   *It's mine.*   *It's Tim's.*

> **Is this your jacket?**
> **No, this is mine.**
> **I think it's Tim's. Look!**

Possessive determiners and possessive pronouns

my, your, their, etc, come before a noun. They are determiners.
They are also posssessive – they show who or what owns something.

> *Is this **your** jacket?*
> *Where are **my** shoes? I can't see them.*

We can use *mine, yours, theirs*, etc, instead of a possessive determiner + noun. They are pronouns.

> *This jacket isn't **mine**. Is it **yours**?*
> *That car isn't **ours**. It's **theirs**.*

Note that *his* and *its* are determiners and also pronouns.
(But *its* as a pronoun is rare.)

> ● *Perhaps this is **his** bag.*
> ○ *No, it isn't **his**. It's **mine**.*

its is different from *it's*. *its* is a possessive determiner. *it's* is short for *it is* or *it has*.

> *Here's the camera, and this is **its** case.* (possessive)
> *Look. Now **it's** raining.* (***it's*** = it is)
> *There's the bus! At last **it's** arrived.* (***it's*** = it has)

Possessive with *'s*

Use noun + *'s* like a possessive determiner.
> *This is **her** coat.* → *This is Sally**'s** coat.*

Use noun + *'s* like a possessive pronoun.
> *This hat is **hers**.* → *This hat is Sally**'s**.*

After a plural noun with *s*, write noun + *s'*.
> *These are the **girls'** coats.*
> *These coats are the **girls'**, not the **boys'**.*

My other car is a Porsche

03 NTC

Exercises

1 Write possessive adjectives.

Example: *Hello.* __My__ *name is Bob.*

1 *Could you write _____ address here, please?*

2 *The boy fell down and hurt _____ arm.*

3 *Let's take _____ holidays at the same time and go away together.*

4 *Could you call at Mr and Mrs Hill's house and give back _____ books?*

5 *Is Sally Barrett here? This is _____ bag.*

6 *That's _____ pen! Give it back to me!*

7 *The cat wants _____ dinner. Look, it's waiting outside.*

2 Write the answers.

Example: ● *Are these shoes Sally's? (No/bigger)*
○ *No, they aren't hers. Hers are bigger.*

1 ● *Is that coat John's? (No/older)*
○ _____

2 ● *Are those magazines Julie's? (No/newer)*
○ _____
_____

3 ● *Is that car Tom's and Lucy's? (No/smaller)*
○ _____
_____

4 ● *Is that coat mine? (No/nicer)*
○ _____

5 ● *Are these reports ours? (No/longer)*
○ _____
_____

6 ● *Is this umbrella yours?*
○ *Yes, it is _____! Thank you very much!*

3 Write the answers.

Example: ● *Is this bag his or hers? (hers)*
○ *It's hers. Look, it's got her name inside.*

1 ● *Are these boots yours or mine? (yours)*
○ _____
_____

2 ● *Is this briefcase his or hers? (his)*
○ _____
_____

3 ● *Are these shoes ours or theirs? (theirs)*
○ _____
_____

4 ● *Is that jacket hers or yours? (mine)*
○ _____
_____

5 ● *Are those T-shirts hers or mine? (hers)*
○ _____
_____

6 ● *Is this book yours or his? (ours)*
○ _____
_____

4 Write *its* or *it's*.

Examples: *The dog ate* __its__ *food in less that a minute.*
__It's__ *1.00 and this is the News.*

1 *The sky has gone dark and _____ started to rain.*

2 *Here's the cassette, but I've lost _____ case.*

3 *Let's stay indoors. _____ too cold to go out.*

4 *I know _____ hard for you, but you must finish the work.*

5 *This is our cat. _____ name is Fluffy.*

6 *Don't try to move your leg. I think _____ broken.*

5 Complete the words with *'s* or *s'*.

Examples: *Look at Tony* __'s__ *pictures. They're lovely.*
The two boy __s'__ *bikes are in the garage.*

1 *My parent___ phone number is 345-321. You can call them any time.*

2 *My brother Peter___ phone number is 345-789.*

3 *Please, can you tell me Sally West___ room number?*

4 *A policeman___ job is often difficult.*

5 *The government has refused to raise hospital worker___ pay again this year.*

6 *Why did you laugh at Tony___ suggestions? I don't understand why you can't accept other people___ ideas.*

61 Pronouns: reflexive
You'll hurt yourself.

> Be careful, or you'll fall and hurt yourself.

Use a reflexive pronoun when the subject (S) of a verb (V) is also the direct object (DO) of the action. Compare the following.

S	V	DO		S	V	DO
You'll	*hurt*	*him.*		*You'll*	*hurt*	*yourself.*
He's	*cut*	*her.*		*He's*	*cut*	*himself.*

Use a reflexive pronoun when the subject of an action is also the indirect object (IO) of an action. Compare the following.

S	V	IO		S	V	IO
She	*talked*	*to me.*		*She*	*talked*	*to herself.*
He	*works*	*for us.*		*He*	*works*	*for himself.*

Use a reflexive pronoun as an indirect object with a direct object. (See Unit 62 for more information about direct and indirect objects.) Compare the following.

S	V	IO	DO	S	V	IO	DO
She	*bought*	*me*	*a book.*	*She*	*bought*	*herself*	*a book.*
We	*taught*	*them*	*Arabic.*	*We*	*taught*	*ourselves*	*Arabic.*

Note the singular → plural change in *self → selves*.
> *I enjoyed **myself** at the party.*
> *We enjoyed **ourselves** at the party.*

Also use a reflexive pronoun to emphasize the subject of an action. This type of reflexive comes after the object of the verb.
> ● *Let me buy the ticket for you.*
> ○ *No, thanks. I'll buy **it myself**.* (I want to do it – not you.)
> *Jamie's five now, so he can put on **his clothes himself/by himself**.* (He doesn't need his parents' help.)

Also use *by* + a reflexive pronoun to emphasize that the subject of an action does the action alone.
> *John climbed the mountain **by himself**.*
> *The teacher made Ann sit **by herself**, away from the other girls.*

This is one of those movies that takes itself a little too seriously. But there is some fine acting from the star cast

If you see someone in difficulties, don't put yourself at risk to rescue them.

Dial 999 and ask for the COASTGUARD.

People in the Third World don't want to live on hand-outs. All they want is the opportunity to work themselves out of poverty – and the chance to live dignified and independent lives.

Your £4 a month will help these people in their daily struggle to help themselves.

Please complete the coupon inside.

Exercises

1 Write the correct reflexive pronouns.

Example: *Stop shouting. Control* <u>*yourself.*</u>

1 *Tell the children to dry _____ or they'll catch cold.*

2 *The light turns _____ off automatically.*

3 *Her real name is Monica, but she calls _____ Mo.*

4 *I was tired, so I gave _____ a day off work.*

5 *Dan injured _____ badly at work.*

6 *We need to protect _____ from the sun. We'd better wear hats.*

7 *Don't play with knives or you'll cut _____*

8 *Children, while I'm out I want you to behave _____*

2 Write the correct verbs and reflexive pronouns. Use these verbs.

bought, burn, kill, look after, looked at, made, push, save, wash

Example: *Be careful with the pan. It's hot. Don't* <u>*burn yourself.*</u>

1 *The boat crashed into the rocks, but Fred managed to _____*

2 *Drive more slowly in future, or you'll _____ one day.*

3 *Tina tried on the hat, and then she _____ in the mirror.*

4 *I was tired when I got home, so I _____ a cup of tea.*

5 *Everybody in the team went to the sports shop and they _____ the same kind of baseball cap.*

6 *We're not doing enough training. We've got to _____ even harder if we want to win the championship.*

7 *Our cat is a very clean animal. It likes to sit in the sun and _____*

8 *I shall miss you both while you're away. Be careful and _____*

3 Write the correct types of pronoun.

Examples: *Then I saw Bob. He was quite near, so I called* <u>*him.*</u>
Sue bought some books, and she taught <u>*herself*</u> *to cook.*

1 *I looked at Sam. He looked back at _____*

2 *Look at _____ in the mirror! You're all in a terrible mess.*

3 *Sue doesn't think about other people. She only thinks about _____*

4 *Your house is very near ours. You must come and visit _____ soon.*

5 *Let's put on the cassette recorder, and then we can record _____*

6 *They never help us, so I don't want to help _____*

7 *My son is going to university soon. I shall miss _____ very much.*

4 Write the answers. Use reflexive pronouns for emphasis.

Example: ● *Did Alan's assistant send the letters?*
○ <u>*No, he sent them himself.*</u>

1 ● *Did your dad pay for your car?*
○ _____

2 ● *Does Sue's secretary prepare the reports?*
○ _____

3 ● *Is Steve's brother bringing the equipment?*
○ _____

4 ● *Will I have to tidy the children's room?*
○ _____
_____

5 ● *Are the boys going to clean our car?*
○ _____
_____

6 ● *I'm hungry! Are you going to make dinner now?*
○ _____
_____

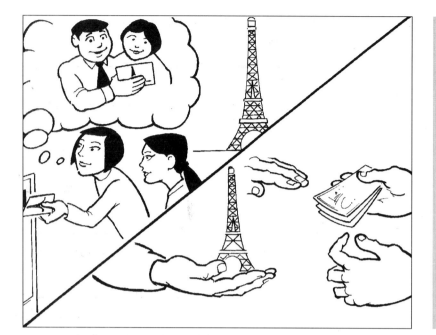

Some verbs (V) do not take a direct object (DO).

Susan **laughed**.   We **talked**.

Some verbs can be with or without a direct object.

Susan **studies**.   Susan **studies French**.

Most verbs must take a direct object.

Susan **sent a card**.   She **bought a souvenir**.

Some verbs take a direct object and an indirect object (IO) too.
After these verbs we introduce the indirect object with *to*: bring, give, lend, pass, pay, sell, show, take, teach, tell, throw.

S	V	DO	IO
He	*paid*	*the money*	*to her*.
Bob	*gave*	*his old car*	*to his brother*.

After these verbs we introduce the indirect object with *for*: bring, buy, cook, do, get, make, order, take.

S	V	DO	IO
I've	*brought*	*some books*	*for you*. Here you are.
I'm	*doing*	*a letter*	*for the boss*.

We can use *bring* and *take* with both *to* + indirect object and *for* + indirect object.

S	V	DO	IO
I	*took*	*the books*	*to the teacher*.
I	*brought*	*some flowers*	*for Mary*.

We often use Form 1 (see FORMS above) for emphasis.

Don't pass **the ball to him**! Pass **it to me**.

But we usually use Form 2.

He paid **her money**.   I've bought **you a book**.

In Form 3 there is no direct object, only an indirect object.

Sue laughed **at us**.   We smiled **at each other**.

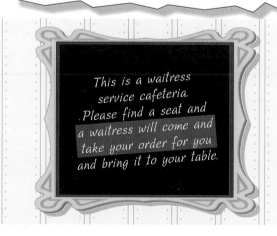

Exercises

1 Write statements with the indirect objects in the correct position.

Examples: *I'm writing a letter. (to my sister)*
<u>*I'm writing a letter to my sister.*</u>
I'm writing a card. (my brother)
<u>*I'm writing my brother a card.*</u>

1 *Ann gave a present. (her parents)*

_____

2 *Nick sent a book. (to his niece)*

_____

3 *Did you really buy it? (for me)*

_____

4 *Could you lend some money? (Harry)*

_____

5 *Susie's grandmother made a lovely dress. (her)*

_____

_____

6 *I'll take some magazines next time I visit her in hospital. (Celia)*

_____

_____

7 *Could you pass the report when he arrives? (to the boss)*

_____

_____

8 *I offered a place to stay as he had nowhere else to go. (Rob)*

_____

_____

2 Write replies. Use Form 1 indirect objects for emphasis.

Example: ● *Could you give Bob this magazine? (Kim)*
○ <u>*No, don't give it to Bob. Give it to Kim.*</u>

1 ● *I'm going to sell my pictures to Sally. (me)*
○ _____

2 ● *I'd better take the car to the garage in town. (one near my house)*
○ _____

_____

3 ● *I think I'll buy a computer game for Sally. (her brother)*
○ _____

_____

4 ● *I'm going to show this information about Mr Blake to him. (the police)*
○ _____

_____

5 ● *I think I'll cook the steak for the children. (the adults)*
○ _____

_____

6 ● *Do I have to pay the money to Tom's teacher? (the school secretary)*
○ _____

_____

7 ● *I'll buy a present for you while I'm in Paris. (the children)*
○ _____

_____

3 Complete the memo with *to* or *for*.

Memo
From: JJ
To: KL Date: 3rd March
Ken,
Could you do a few things <u>for</u> me while I'm away in Rome? Could you finish the report on my desk [1]_____ *me? I've been writing it specially* [2]_____ *the Head of Sales, so could you please give it* [3]_____ *him personally by midday on Thursday? Please explain the special items* [4]_____ *him. I've made some notes* [5]_____ *you, so you'll know what to write.*
We've ordered some new computer equipment [6]_____ *the Sales Department. Could you ask the men from Compu-Tech to take the equipment* [7]_____ *Room 508? Please give the cheque on my desk* [8]_____ *the men when they come.*
Thanks. I'll get some really good Italian olive oil [9]_____ *you while I'm in Rome.*
See you next week.
Jack

63 something, anybody, everyone, etc

There's something for everyone.

FORMS				
	thing	**body**	**one**	**where**
some	something (a thing)	somebody (a person)	someone (a person)	somewhere (in a place)
any	anything (a thing)	anybody (a person)	anyone (a person)	anywhere (in a place)
every	everything (all the things)	everybody (all the people)	everyone (all the people)	everywhere (in all the places)
no	nothing (no things)	nobody (no person)	no one (no person)	nowhere (in no place)

We can put *some, any, every* and *no* together with *thing, body, one* and *where* to form new words.

> My book is **somewhere** in this room.
> Has **anyone** seen my book?
> **Everybody**! Please help me find it!
> I looked, but I found **nothing**.

The words *something* and *anything*, etc, are like *some* and *any*.
Positive statements: *He told her **something**.*
Negative statements: *We didn't see **anybody**.*
Yes / No questions: *Did you go **anywhere**?*
Positive questions: *Did you find **something**?*
Offers: *Can I help **anyone**?*
Requests: *May I see **someone** in the office?*
Things that are possible, but not certain: *If **anybody** calls, tell me.*
(See Unit 43 for more information.)

All the words in this group are singular, including the words with *every*.

> Is **everyone** here now?   **Everything** takes a long time.

The words with *no* are negatives, so use the 3rd person singular positive forms of verbs.

> **Nobody** is happy with the plan.   **No one** wants to go out.

We can use an adjective, eg *strange, funny* and *boring*, after words with *some, any* and *no*, (but not usually after words with *every*).

> **Somebody** came to the door.   Is there **anything** funny on TV?

We can use *else* after all these words.

> We haven't got **anything else** to eat.
> There's **nowhere else** to go.

We can use the possessive *'s* form with the words that end with *body* or *one*.

> Is this **anybody's** jacket?   The accident was **no one's** fault.
> **Somebody's** car is in our parking space!

Life's but a walking shadow, a poor player, That struts and frets his hour upon the stage, And then is heard no more; It is a tale told by an idiot, Full of sound and fury, Signifying nothing.

(*Macbeth*, William Shakespeare, 1564 – 1616)

Exercises

1 Write *some, any, something, anybody, somewhere,* etc.

Examples: *I met* <u>some</u> *old friends yesterday.*
Yesterday I met <u>somebody</u> *who knows you.*

1 *I've got _____ free time tomorrow.*

2 *I can't think of _____ to do.*

3 *Have you got _____ money?*

4 *Tony must be _____ in the park.*

5 *Does _____ here know how to work this machine?*

6 *Could I take _____ paper, please?*

7 *If _____ asks for me, just say I'm busy.*

8 *Would you like _____ coffee?*

9 *She can't find her glasses _____*

10 *I've got _____ for you to do this afternoon.*

2 Complete the statements with the correct words beginning with *some-, any-, every-,* and *no-.*

Examples: *I don't know* <u>anybody</u> *as clever as Tom. (any-)*

1 *If _____ is here now, the meeting can begin. (every-)*

2 *_____ we went in Africa, we found the people very friendly. (every-)*

3 *Excuse me. I've got _____ important to say. (some-)*

4 *_____ in the world can run as fast as Steve. (no-)*

5 *If there's _____ still in the building, tell them to come out quickly. (any-)*

6 *Is there _____ quiet near here for us to talk? (any-)*

7 *Is there _____ I can do to help you? (any-)*

3 Write *something, anybody, everyone, nowhere,* etc.

● *Has* <u>anybody</u> *seen my new Bruce Springsteen cassette? I've been looking for it* [1]_____ *– all over the house.*

○ *I don't think it's* [2]_____ *in this room.*

● *Well, it must be* [3]_____ *round here. It can't have disappeared.* [4]_____ *must have seen it.*

○ *Did you lend it to* [5]_____ *Or did you take it* [6]_____ *with you – into town, for example?*

● *No, I've been absolutely* [7]_____ *since yesterday morning. I've just been at home. And* [8]_____*'s borrowed it either.*

○ *Wait. Look! There's* [9]_____ *under that chair. Is that it?*

● *Where? I can't see* [10]_____ *Oh, I see it now. You're right. That's it! Thanks very much!*

4 Complete the statements. Use the words in brackets.

Examples: *There's* <u>something good</u> *on TV tonight. (a good thing)*
We're all here now. There's <u>nobody else</u> *to come. (not another person)*

1 *There's _____ on TV tonight. (no interesting thing)*

2 *I haven't told you the whole story. I've got _____ to tell. (another thing)*

3 *This beach is too crowded. Isn't there _____ we can go? (another place)*

4 *I've looked for the money _____ _____ (all possible places)*

5 *Is _____ coming to dinner this evening? (a nice person)*

6 *There's _____ to look for the money. (no other place)*

145

64 Relative clauses 1

He's the person who caused the accident.

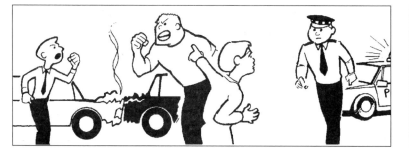

FORMS

He's the person	who that	caused the accident.
That's the car	which that	he was driving.

A clause is a group of words with a subject and a verb. It can be a complete, simple sentence, or it can be a part of a larger sentence. A relative clause is only a part of a sentence. It adds meaning to the main clause of a sentence.

who, *which* and *that* introduce relative clauses. They refer back to a noun and stand instead of the noun.

> He's **the person who** ...
> That's **the car which** ...

They introduce a new idea about the noun.
> ... **who caused the accident**.
> ... **which he was driving**.

Below, idea 2 shows which bus and which friends the speaker means. Idea 1 is the main clause. Idea 2 supports it and completes the meaning of the sentence. It is a defining relative clause.

1 *The bus is going to London.*
2 ~~The bus~~ (which) has just left.
→ The bus **which has just left** is going to London.

1 *I often see some old friends.*
2 ~~Some old friends~~ (who) live in Oxford. → I often see some old friends **who live in Oxford**.

Use *who* or *that* for people.
> **The man who/that** bought the coat is standing over there.

Use *which* or *that* for things and animals.
> Those are **the cars which/that** crashed.

Use defining relative clauses in general statements.
> People **who do dangerous jobs** are usually paid well.
> A nice car is something **which most people want**.

Use defining relative clauses to define and identify.
> Gold is a heavy metal **which is very valuable**.
> Bell was the man **who invented the telephone**.

We usually use *who* or *which* in more formal writing, eg in business letters and reports.
> Dear Sir,
> Thank you for the catalogue and price list **which** I recently requested. The person **who** spoke to me on the phone also promised to send some samples, but these ...

Barry Collins dies, aged 51

A popular Sidmouth saxophonist who helped raise money for disabled people has died, aged 51.

Barry Collins, who suffered from multiple sclerosis for many years, lived at Mayfield House, and last year joined a group of residents and helpers on a trip to Disneyworld, Florida, with money he had raised through a concert with his Sixties band, The Majestics.

Tomorrow's television

Sibling rivalry:
Why do brothers and sisters compete? Part three of *Baby Wars* looks at the tightrope that families walk between co-operation and conflict.

The Donkey Sanctuary is a haven for donkeys that have been mistreated, neglected, retired from working on the beaches or simply cannot be cared for any longer by their owners. Since Dr Elisabeth Svendsen founded the Sanctuary in 1969, over 7,000 of these gentle creatures have been taken into care, which makes it the largest sanctuary for donkeys in the world.

Exercises

1 Write *who, which* or *that*.

Arthur Penn is an old farm worker <u>who/that</u> lives in our village. He lives in a small house ¹_____ his family have had for 100 years. Recently, he was outside, moving a pile of stones and bricks ²_____ used to be an old garden shed. Suddenly his spade hit something ³_____ wasn't stone or brick. It sounded like metal. He dug a little more, and he found it was a very old box. He called to a friend ⁴_____ was passing the garden gate. They worked together until they were able to pull the heavy box out. 'Perhaps it's something valuable ⁵_____ somebody wanted to hide years ago,' Arthur said. 'Let's open it and see,' his friend said. 'Come on. You're the one ⁶_____ should do that.' Arthur broke open the box, but there was no gold or silver – just a set of old-fashioned garden tools! 'They're the tools ⁷_____ my grandfather used,' Arthur said. 'He was the one ⁸_____ built the shed 100 years ago.'

2 Join each pair of statements to make one statement with a relative clause.

Example: *A girl won the prize. She wrote the best essay.*
<u>The girl who/that wrote the best essay won the prize.</u>

1 A pilot escaped without injury. He crashed his plane in the lake.

_____

_____

_____

2 A student has got a place in the national team. He broke the 10,000-metre record.

_____

_____

_____

3 A bus broke down. It takes people to the airport.

_____

_____

4 A file is on the top shelf. It has all the information.

_____

_____

_____

5 A policeman has recevied an award. He rescued 15 people from a fire.

_____

_____

_____

6 A woman wanted to speak to you. She phoned last night.

_____

_____

_____

3 Write relative clauses with *who, which* or *that*. Use these endings.

It teaches Japanese.
She painted that picture.
They built the first aeroplane.
It will pay a better salary.
She was lost for five days.
They are warm and friendly.
He scored all the goals.
He discovered America.
He can repair my old car.

Example: *Were the Wright brothers the ones <u>who/that built the first aeroplane?</u>*

1 What was the name of the player _____

_____

2 I want to get a new job _____

_____

3 Where can we find a mechanic _____

_____

4 Ann wants to find a book _____

_____

5 I like people _____

_____

6 Do you know the artist _____

_____

7 Mountain rescuers have found the climber _____

_____

8 Columbus was the man _____

_____

The man we want is coming now.

Reduced relative clauses with objects

who, *which* and *that* can be the subject of a clause, or they can be the object. If they are the object, we can leave them out.

> **The man who wants us** *is coming now.* (subject – no change)
> **The man who we want** *is coming now.* (object – change possible) → **The man we want** *is coming now.*
> *Did you see* **the dress which she bought**? (object – change possible) → *Did you see* **the dress she bought**?

ing and ed participles with relative clauses

The verb in a relative clause can be in a continuous tense. If it is, we can leave out *who*, *which* or *that* and then just use the *ing* (present) participle.

> *His case is the one* **which is coming now**. → *His case is the one* **coming now**.
> *I was angry with the people* **who were shouting last night**. → *I was angry with the people* **shouting last night**.

The *ed* (past) participle can be part of a passive tense. If it is, we can leave out *who*, *which* or *that* and then use the *ed* participle.

> *His case is the one* **that is marked** *with a cross.* → *His case is the one* **marked** *with a cross.*
> *He's the man* **who was followed** *by the police.* → *He's the man* **followed** *by the police.*

With a continuous passive tense use *being + ed* participle.

> *He's the man* **who is being watched** *by the police.* → *He's the man* **being watched** *by the police.*
> *Those were the cases* **which were being checked** *by Customs.* → *Those were the cases* **being checked** *by Customs.*

Students contemplating a course that will help them develop or change their career will find the best range of options in the Department of Continuing Education.

The monument most visited by tourists in the United Kingdom last year was Stonehenge, the prehistoric stone circle on the Salisbury Plain. Next came the Tower of London in the centre of the capital, followed by Hampton Court, Henry VIII's palace, with its famous maze. The monument least visited was

And the man being chased off the pitch by officials has just disrupted the most important cricket fixture of the season.

Exercises

1 Join each pair of statements to make one statement. Use *who, which* or *that* as the subject of the relative clause.

Example: *The person wasn't there. She had sold the watch.*

   The person who/that had sold the watch wasn't there.

1 *The book has disappeared. It has all the answers.*
   _____
   _____

2 *We climbed over the fence. It separates the fields.*
   _____
   _____

3 *The old man can't see well. He crashed his car.*
   _____
   _____

4 *I'm going to give the boy some money. He found my camera.*
   _____
   _____

2 Join each pair of statements to make one statement. Use *who, which* or *that* as the object of the relative clause.

Example: *The house stood by the river. We bought it.*
   The house which/that we bought stood by the river.

1 *The girls seemed sad. We met them at the wedding.*
   _____
   _____

2 *I want to go to the museum. You told me about it.*
   _____
   _____

3 *The taxi finally arrived. I'd ordered it.*
   _____
   _____

4 *The flowers are dying. She gave us them.*
   _____
   _____

3 Write *who, which, that* or nothing (✗)

Example: *The house ✗ we bought stood by the river.*
   The person who/that had sold the watch wasn't there.

1 *The bus _____ we caught got to town early.*

2 *The man _____ will meet you is my brother.*

3 *Here's the money _____ I owe you.*

4 *Rob is the player _____ won the game.*

5 *This goes in the file _____ I put on the shelf.*

4 Write the active participle form of these verbs.

enter, finish, go, show, stand, wear

Example: *The police stopped a car _going_ at 220 kph.*

1 *We listened to the guide _____ us round the palace.*

2 *Did you see anybody _____ the house?*

3 *I took photos of people _____ the race.*

4 *Can you pass me the vase _____ on the cupboard?*

5 *I didn't like that man _____ a red jacket.*

5 Write the passive participle form of these verbs.

build, find, make, mend, paint, prepare, use, write

Examples: *This is the gun _found_ in the car.*
   The houses _being built_ in London Street will soon be ready.

1 *This was the plane _____ by the President on his trip to Australia.*

2 *I'm now going to show you a pot _____ by hand. Watch carefully.*

3 *As we watched, there were two ships _____ to go to sea.*

4 *This is a story _____ for young people.*

5 *That's the bridge _____ after the storm. It'll be closed for another week.*

6 *I prefer shoes _____ of real leather.*

66 Relative clauses 3

There was a time when you could live well.

FISHERMEN FACE HARD TIMES

The fishing industry is going from bad to worse. There are now fishermen whose debts are rising and pushing them out of business.

Tom Billings, aged 58, says, 'There was a time when you could live well from the sea. But not any more. All the best areas where we used to fish are dead now.'

The main reason why this has happened is the fishing industry itself. With too many boats and efficient modern methods, the fishermen have fished the sea to death.

Relative clauses with *whose*

whose is a relative pronoun like *who*, but it is also possessive like *his, her, its, their*, etc.

> 1 *There are many fishermen with debts.*
> 2 ~~Their~~ *(whose) debts are rising.* → *There are many **fishermen whose debts are rising**.*

We usually use *whose* with people. We sometimes also use it with things and animals too.

> *Mary Owen was **the girl whose** story won first prize.*
> *Japan is **a country whose** economy is very successful.*
> *The boys found **a bird whose** wing was broken.*

Relative clauses with *whose* are formal. We often use them in more formal writing. We do not use them much in conversation.

> *Dear Sir,*
> *I wish to complain about a member of your sales staff **whose behaviour towards my wife was very unpleasant**.*

Relative clauses with *when*, *where* and *why*

We can use several sorts of relative clauses about a 'time' noun.

> *There was **a time when** you could live well.*
> *There was **a time that** you could live well.*
> *There was **a time** you could live well.*

'Time' nouns include words like *summer, year, week, day*, and *moment*.

> *Do you remember that **summer when** we went to France?*
> *I shall never forget the **day when** my sister was born.*

We can also use *where* to refer to a 'place' noun such as *house, street, town* and *city*.

> *I remember the **house where** I grew up.*
> *That's the **street where** John lives.*

We can use *why* to refer to the noun *reason* in the same way.

> *He's lazy! That's the **reason why** he failed.*

WE'LL RESPECT YOUR PRIVACY

We occasionally make our customer lists available to carefully screened companies whose products or services we feel may interest you. If you do not wish to receive such mailings, please send an exact copy of your name and address to:

The Bodmin Clothes Company,
Data Protection Department, Admail 789.

CRITIC'S CHOICE

* WATCH OUT FOR THE JELLYFISH
Radio 4, 10 am, FM only

Series in which famous politicians remember their early years. This week, Michael Redfern returns to his boyhood in Paisley, where his grandfather ran a brewery.

BRAVE RAT SAVES FAMILY FROM FIRE

The Gamble family of Brixham will never forget the day when a rat called Fido saved their lives. The pet was in its cage at 2 am on Friday when an electric heater set fire to the carpet and furniture of the house in Brixham where Fido lives with his owners. Spotting the cage door was open, Fido jumped out, climbed 15 stairs and scratched at the bedroom door. The noise woke the family, who smelt smoke and managed to get out of the house. The fire brigade was called and quickly controlled the blaze. Later, Fire Chief Ron Walker said, 'We've all heard of people whose dogs or cats warn them of danger, but never a rat. We hope to give Fido a bravery award.'

Exercises

1 **Complete the questions with *whose, who, which* or *that*. Answer the questions.**

Examples: ● *What was the name of the man <u>who</u> first reached America from Europe in 1492?*
○ <u>*Christopher Columbus.*</u>
● *What is the name of the country <u>whose</u> capital is Kuala Lumpur?*
○ <u>*Malaysia.*</u>

1 ● *What is the English name for the three ancient man-made structures _____ stand near Cairo?*
○ _____

2 ● *What was the man _____ first flew in space called?*
○ _____

3 ● *Name the woman scientist _____ most important work was the discovery of radium.*
○ _____

4 ● *What was the name of the Italian _____ travelled to China and home again 700 years ago?*
○ _____

5 ● *What is the country _____ flag is a red circle on a white square?*
○ _____

6 ● *Name the US state _____ is famous for cowboys and _____ symbol is a yellow rose?*
○ _____

2 **Answer the questions. Use *whose* as the subject of the relative clause.**

Your friend is looking at a wedding party guest list and trying to remember people.

Example: ● *Who was Yvonne Laroche? (Her husband had a large beard.)*
○ <u>*She was the one whose husband had a large beard.*</u>

1 ● *Which one was George Barret? (His wife had a wonderful diamond necklace.)*
○ _____
_____
_____

2 ● *Do you remember the Schmidts? (Their children fell in the pool.)*
○ _____
_____

3 ● *Who was Lucy Rosser? (Her hat flew off in the wind.)*
○ _____
_____

4 ● *Do you remember the Lewis family? (Their car refused to start after the party.)*
○ _____
_____
_____

5 ● *And which ones were Mario and Maria di Stefano? (Their daughters wore lovely blue dresses.)*
○ _____
_____
_____

3 **Write statements about the underlined parts of the conversation. Use *when, where* or *why* as the subject of the relative clause.**

Example: ● *Do you remember that <u>time</u> on the river?*
○ *Oh, yes. Our boat nearly sank!*
They talked about the <u>time when their boat nearly sank.</u>

1 ● *Our boat nearly turned over because you turned it in front of that big river cruiser.*
○ *Yes, that was the <u>reason</u>.*
They talked about the _____
_____
_____

2 ● *And then we stayed at that <u>old hotel</u>.*
○ *Yes. <u>We dried out our clothes there.</u>*
They talked about the _____
_____

3 ● *And what about the <u>night</u> of the storm?*
○ *Yes. <u>The rain almost washed our tent away.</u>*
They talked about the _____
_____
_____

67 Relative clauses 4

He's the driver who won.   Alan Brant, who won in France, is …

NEW WORLD NUMBER ONE

Alan Brant, who yesterday won in France, is now Number One in the world. The race, which was watched by 100 million people world-wide, took place in temperatures of up to 40°C.

Compare defining relative clauses with another type – adding clauses.

FORMS

Defining relative clauses

Anna: *Who's that in the picture?*
Jean: *Alan Brant. He's the driver who won the big race yesterday.*
Anna: *What race was that?*
Jean: *The race which they showed on TV yesterday.*

Adding clauses

Alan Brant, who won in France yesterday, is now Number One in the world. The race, which was watched by 30 million people world-wide, took place …

CROSSCHECK

Defining relative clauses

These clauses explain which driver and which race. The sentences are not complete without these clauses.

> *He's the driver **who/that won the big race**.*
> *The race **which/that they showed on TV**.*

These clauses do not have commas. They are a main part of the sentence.

We can use *that* instead of *who* or *which*. We can often use reduced forms. (See Unit 65.)

> *We mended the window **which/that was broken.***
> *They'll only give jobs to pilots **who/that are very experienced**.*
> *Visitors should come on a day **when the castle is open**.*

which can refer to a noun phrase or a whole sentence.

> *I mended **the doll**, **which** was broken.*
> *They worked on the car all night, **which** helped Alan win.*

Most relative clauses are defining relative clauses. (See Units 64, 65 and 66.) We use them in speaking and in writing.

Adding clauses

These clauses add extra information to the basic sentences. The basic sentences are complete without these clauses.

> *Alan Brant, **who yesterday won in France**, is now …*
> *The race, **which was watched by 30 million**, took place …*

We separate this type of clause from the basic sentence with commas (,), dashes (–) or brackets ( ).

We cannot use *that* instead of *who* or *which*. But we can use *whose*, *when* and *where*.

> *We mended the kitchen window, **which was broken**.*
> *The pilots – **who are very experienced** – will be given jobs.*
> *Visitors should come on Sunday (**when the castle is open**).*

We use non-defining relative clauses mainly in writing. Newspaper reports use them a lot because they give a lot of information quickly.

Meanwhile, Kate Winslet has become a bit of a globetrotter. Her new film *Hideous Kinky* was filmed on location in Morocco. In this film adaptation of Esther Freud's novel, Winslet plays the English woman who takes her two young daughters to Marrakech and gets caught up in an exotic new life.

We invited our readers to tell us which member of the Royal Family from any period in history they would most like to have dinner with.

The royal that 78% of readers chose was, you guessed it, Diana, Princess of Wales. Other popular royals were Henry VIII and Queen Victoria, as well as our own queen, Queen Elizabeth II.

Warning: Not suitable for young children, who can choke on nuts.

Many tributes have been paid to the trombonist, George Chisolm, who died in December at the age of 82.

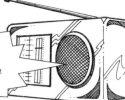

Legend says that the ancient city of Atlantis sank in a single day of earthquakes, rain and floods in about 9,000 BC! Some say it's the Greek island of Santorini. Others link it with the Bermuda Triangle, where ships and planes mysteriously disappear!

Exercises

1 Are the clauses in *italics* defining or adding? Write commas if necessary.

Example: *Beethoven*, *whose music is loved by millions*, *was born in 1770 and died in 1827.* <u>adding</u>

1 Dover Castle *which is a very impressive building* was built by the Normans. _____

2 The girl *who found the wallet* handed it in to the police. _____

3 The programme *that we watched last night* was awful. _____

4 The writer Pete Holmes *whose most famous book is 'Glory'* has died today. He was 75. _____

2 Join each pair of statements to make one statement with an adding clause with *who* or *which*.

Examples: *Harry Lane is a rich man now. He was at college with me.*

Harry Lane, who was at college with me, is a rich man now.

1 *Old Professor Jones is going to stop work soon. He's nearly 70.*

_____

_____

_____

2 *To the north of India are the Himalayas. They include the highest mountains in the world.*

_____

_____

_____

3 *I bought myself some good, new clothes. I needed them for my new job.*

_____

_____

_____

4 *Barry Stone has built his own house. He works as a computer programmer.*

_____

_____

3 Match the statements 1–7 and a–g. Join each pair changing a–g into adding clauses with *which*.

1 *The baby cried all night.*
2 *The old ship stayed in port.*
3 *I was out when Peter called.*
4 *The company has won the contract.*
5 *They've started doing road repairs.*
6 *They sun has come out at last.*
7 *The school is building a new gymnasium.*

a *That saved it from the storm.*
b *It's causing bad traffic delays.*
c *That was why I didn't hear the news.*
d *It meant I was tired all next day.*
e *That means we can go to the beach.*
f *It's going to help their basketball teams a lot.*
g *That's good news.*

1 – <u>d</u> 2 – ___ 3 – ___ 4 – ___ 5 – ___ 6 – ___ 7 – ___

1 <u>*The baby cried all night, which meant I was tired all next day.*</u>

2 _____

_____

_____

3 _____

_____

4 _____

5 _____

_____

6 _____

_____

7 _____

_____

_____

68 Adjectives 1

It's large.   It's a large suitcase.

Adjectives describe nouns and pronouns. They give us more information about things. Their form is the same with singular and plural nouns. They do not add *s*.

> *red, green, blue   dark, light, bright   large, small   beautiful, ugly*
> *Japanese, English   my, your, her   this, that, these, those* + noun

Word order 1

Most adjectives can go in two places. They can go before a noun and the pronouns *one* and *ones*.

> *I've got a **blue bag**.   **That one** is **my bag**.*

They can also go after a noun. Link verbs include *be, become, get* (become), *stay, feel, smell, sound, taste, look, seem* and *appear*.

> *The **bag** is **blue**.   **I**'m getting **tired**.   **He** seems **nice** – but is he?*

Word order 2

When you use two or more adjectives, put them in the right order. Put a 'feeling' adjective, eg *beautiful* and *terrible*, before an 'information' adjective, eg *red* and *dark*.

> *Ann bought a **beautiful red** dress.   It was a **terrible dark** night.*

Adjectives can give different types of information. We sometimes put different 'information' adjectives together. They go in the following order. We often put commas between several adjectives together.

1 Feeling	+	2 Size	3 Age	4 Shape	5 Colour	6 Origin	7 Material	+ Noun
ugly beautiful	+	big little	old new	square round	red blue	French German	metal wooden	+ Noun

> *I bought a **beautiful, old, round, French** clock.*
> *He saw an **ugly, little, blue, wooden** box.*

Adjective + *to* + infinitive

'Feeling' adjectives can take *to* + infinitive. The adjective usually follows *It*. Some common 'feeling' adjectives are *dangerous, delighted, difficult, easy, funny, important, pleased, safe, sorry* and *stupid*.

> *It's **dangerous to play** in the road.   I'm **pleased to meet** you.*

John and Margaret Hancock are delighted to announce the birth of their first daughter, Hannah, a sister for Toby.

Cornwall ...

Dozens of beaches – sandy, rocky, wild, windswept or sheltered, lie within 20 minutes' drive. For walkers, dreamers, lovers and dwellers in history, this is the place – wind-blown, sun-burnt, salt-sprayed, rain-drenched and lost in the mists of time.

Exercises

1 Complete the statements. Use these link verbs and adjectives.

Link verbs

feel, get, look, seem, smell, sound

Adjectives

angry, delicious, happy, right, terrible, tired

Example: *I'll have to check the sales figures again. They don't* <u>*look right.*</u>

1 ● *Dinner's ready.*
  ○ *Mmm! It* _____

2 *I didn't get enough sleep last night. I still*
  _____

3 *Don't try to take a dog's food away, or it'll*
  _____

4 ● *The children are all laughing.*
  ○ *Yes, they* _____ *really* _____

5 *Oh, no! Annie's doing her music practice again. It*
  _____

2 Write the words in the correct order.

Example: *(beautiful/a/flower/red)*
  <u>*a beautiful red flower*</u>

1 *(book/old/a/boring)*
  _____

2 *(blue/an/diamond/unusual)*
  _____

3 *(film/exciting/new/an)*
  _____

4 *(yellow/light/a/strange)*
  _____

5 *(an/clock/German/interesting)*
  _____

6 *(little/a/lovely/baby)*
  _____

7 *(green/a/valley/pleasant)*
  _____

8 *(a/man/tall/young)*
  _____

9 *(round/box/a/plastic)*

3 Report the answers. Use commas between the adjectives.

Example: ● *What was the snake like?*
  ○ *It was big! It was green! It was horrible!*
  <u>*It was a horrible, big, green snake.*</u>

1 ● *What was the man like?*
  ○ *He was little. He was old. He was funny.*
  _____

2 ● *What was the box like?*
  ○ *It was ugly. It was brown. It was metal.*
  _____

3 ● *What were the jackets like?*
  ○ *They were silk. They were new. They were Italian. They were beautiful.*
  _____
  _____

4 ● *What were the vases like?*
  ○ *They were tall. They were wonderful. They were Chinese. They were round.*
  _____
  _____

4 Complete the statements. Use these endings.

to go home.   to drive when you're tired.
to have you with us.
to meet you.   to play with matches.
to remember to post them.   to understand.

Example: *Goodbye for now. It was nice* <u>*to meet you.*</u>

1 *Put them down. It's dangerous* _____
  _____

2 *I've really enjoyed this holiday. I'll be sorry*
  _____

3 *Please don't forget these letters. It's very important*
  _____

4 *Of course you can come too. We'll be delighted*
  _____

5 *They were speaking very fast, so it was difficult*
  _____

6 *You should have a sleep before you go. It isn't safe*
  _____

69 Adjectives 2

The programme is interesting.   Alan is interested.

There are some pairs of important adjectives with the endings *ing* and *ed*.

CROSSCHECK

Adjectives with *ing* endings

These describe something, eg a TV programme, a film, a book or a person.

Compare these examples.

> *Ann thinks computer games are* ***boring***.
> *The football match was* ***exciting***.

> *Rod works at an* ***amazing*** *speed.*

> *A bad school report is very* ***depressing***.

Adjectives with *ed* endings

These describe your feelings about something, eg a TV programme, a film, a book or a person.

Compare these examples.

> *Ann gets* ***bored*** *when her brother plays computer games.*
> *Everybody at the match was* ***excited***.
> *We are* ***amazed*** *at the speed Rod works.*
> *Mum will be very* ***depressed*** *when she reads my school report.*

Be careful about the difference between these sentences. You will be embarrassed if you say the wrong one!

> *I'm* ***boring***!   *I'm* ***bored***!

(*I'm* ***boring***! means that other people are not interested in me.)

This is a list of common pairs of adjectives with *ing* and *ed* endings.

amazing/amazed
amusing/amused
annoying/annoyed
astonishing/astonished
boring/bored
confusing/confused
depressing/depressed
disappointing/disappointed
disgusting/disgusted
embarrassing/embarrassed
exciting/excited
exhausting/exhausted
fascinating/fascinated
frightening/frightened

horrifying/horrified
infuriating/infuriated
interesting/interested
irritating/irritated
puzzling/puzzled
relaxing/relaxed
satisfying/satisfied
shocking/shocked
surprising/surprised
terrifying/terrified
thrilling/thrilled
tiring/tired
worrying/worried

Exercises

1 Write the correct adjectives.

Example: *Thunderstar 2 is the most exciting film of the year. (exciting/excited)*

1 *Everybody was _____ when we reached the huge waterfall. (exciting/excited)*

2 *The map of the city was out of date, and I was soon _____ (confusing/confused)*

3 *One of the _____ things about Steve is his stupid laugh. (annoying/annoyed)*

4 *I was _____ by the engines in the Science Museum. (fascinating/fascinated)*

5 *We were all _____ after walking round town all day. (exhausting/exhausted)*

6 *The police have found the facts of this crime very _____ (puzzling/puzzled)*

7 *It's _____ that Tina is late. She's usually on time. (surprising/surprised)*

8 *The story of the Earth's development is _____ (amazing/amazed)*

2 Write the correct adjectives.

Example: *(bore)*
  ● *This programme is boring.*
  ○ *Yes, I'm bored with it too. Let's turn it off.*

1 *(astonish)*
  ● *I was _____ that Tim passed the exam.*
  ○ *Yes, he found it _____ too!*

2 *(shock)*
  ● *The way Sam talks to people is _____*
  ○ *I know. I was _____ when I heard him being so rude.*

3 *(embarrass)*
  ● *It was really _____ to ask for my money.*
  ○ *Why? You shouldn't be _____ to ask for the money they owed you.*

4 *(depress)*
  ● *I've failed my driving test again. I'm very _____ about it.*
  ○ *I remember the feeling. It certainly is _____*

5 *(interest)*
  ● *Here is an _____ job advert in the paper. Look.*
  ○ *Are you _____ in applying for it?*

6 *(disappoint)*
  ● *The team were very _____ that they only came fifth in the competition.*
  ○ *The trouble is, the way they played was so _____*

7 *(irritate)*
  ● *Don't you get _____ when you see the same TV commercial all the time?*
  ○ *Yes, there are some really _____ ones on TV at the moment.*

8 *(tire)*
  ● *I've been working all day, but I don't feel _____ at all.*
  ○ *Well, you're lucky. I find this job very _____*

3 Complete the statements. Use these words with the correct endings.

amuse, disgust, frighten, horrify, infuriate, relax, satisfy, terrify, worry

Example: *I don't like being high up. It's really frightening.*

1 *That boy always wants more to eat! He's never _____*

2 *The assistant manager lost his job because everybody was _____ by his lies.*

3 *Susan keeps refusing to eat and is losing weight. It's very _____*

4 *When we got back to town, we saw the _____ damage done by the storm.*

5 *The President is feeling _____ after a good holiday.*

6 *The film isn't very funny, but it's quite _____*

7 *Oh, no! The train is going to be late again. It's really _____*

8 *We thought the plane was going to crash. We were all _____*

70   Adjectives and adverbs

He's a slow worker.   *He always works slowly.*

That boy is a slow worker.

Yes, he always works slowly!

FORMS

Adjective or adverb

Noun + adjective   Verb + adverb

Adjective → regular adverb

slow   → *slowly*

Irregular forms

1   *good / well*
2   *hard, fast,* etc
3   *hard / hardly,* etc
4   *friendly, lively, likely,* etc

CROSSCHECK

Adjectives

Adjectives say more about nouns.

That boy is	**slow**.
	quick.
	bad.

This sentence uses a link verb, *is*. Other link verbs include *become, get* (become), *stay, feel, smell, sound, taste, look, seem* and *appear*.

That boy	**is**	**slow**.
	looks	
	seems	

Adverbs

Adverbs say more about verbs.

He works	**slowly**.
	quickly.
	badly.

This sentence uses an action verb, *works*. Other action verbs include *run, talk, drive* and *write*. Adverbs go with action verbs, not link verbs.

That boy	**works**	**slowly**.
	moves	
	runs	

Some verbs are both link and action verbs, but with different meanings.

*Ann **looked** happy.*

*I **felt** awful, so I went to bed.*

*The milk **tasted** bad.*

*Peter **looked** quickly in the cupboards.*

*The chef **felt** the vegetables carefully and bought the best ones.*

*I **tasted** the food nervously. It was OK.*

Adjective → regular adverb

We form most adverbs from adjective + *ly*, eg *slow* + *ly* → *slowly*.
     beautifully, carefully (note ... *l* + *ly*)*, coldly, freely, quickly, quietly, sadly, safely, warmly*

We form other adverbs according to special spelling rules. (See Appendix 2.)
     angry → angrily, easy → easily, lucky → luckily
     comfortable → comfortably, gentle → gently, possible → possibly
     true → truly, whole → wholly

Who's at risk?

If you drink at all, you're affected by alcohol. Generally, if you only drink a little and if you don't drink very frequently, the risks are very small. But the more you drink and the more frequently you drink, the higher the risks.

That's why it's important to look carefully at your drinking habits. This booklet will help you to find out if you are a sensible drinker, or what you can do to become one.

Readers' hobbies:
your questions answered ...

Q   I've heard that you can blend aromatherapy essential oils together, but how do you know which ones work well together?

A   *Well, luckily, there are just a few sensible guidelines you can ...*

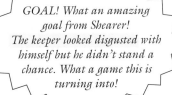

GOAL! What an amazing goal from Shearer! The keeper looked disgusted with himself but he didn't stand a chance. What a game this is turning into!

Irregular forms

good → *well*

Note this irregular form – *good* → *well*. *well* is also an adjective.

> *The car goes **well**.*
> ● *Is she **well**?*   ○ *No, she's ill.*

hard, fast, etc

These are both adjectives and adverbs: *deep, direct, early, far, fast, free, hard, high, late, long, low, near, right, short, straight, wrong.*

> *It's a **deep** swimming pool.   He dived **deep** into the water.*
> *It's a **fast** car.   He climbed the tree **fast**.*
> *We must catch the **late** bus.   He didn't want to arrive **late**.*

hard/hardly, etc

A few words have two adverb forms – one form is like the adjective and one form ends in *ly*. They have different meanings. Compare the sentences in CROSSCHECK below.

> *direct/directly, free/freely, hard/hardly, high/highly, late/lately, near/nearly, short/shortly*

CROSSCHECK

Adjective/adverb form	*ly* form
*I went **direct** from the station to the wedding.* (straight)	*I'll phone you **directly** I hear anything.* (immediately after)
*Airline staff can fly **free**.* (without paying)	*The animals can move round **freely**.* (without control)
*We worked **hard** all night.* (with a lot of energy)	*We had **hardly** any sleep that night.* (almost no)
*John works **high** above the city, on the 183rd floor.* (above)	*This snake is **highly** poisonous. Don't touch it!* (very)
*I have to work **late** this evening.* (a long time after normal)	*What's Sue doing these days? I haven't seen her **lately**.* (recently)
● *Is the hotel far?* ○ *No, it's quite **near** now.* (close)	*We've **nearly** run out of bread. I'll buy some more.* (almost)
*My brother was very ill, so we cut **short** our holiday and went home.* (reduced)	*The bus will be here **shortly**.* (soon)

ly adjectives

These adjectives end in *ly*: *deadly, friendly, likely, lively, lonely, lovely, silly, ugly.*

> *They're a very **friendly** family.   That poor girl is **lonely**.*

We cannot use them as adverbs. We have to say something like *in a* + adjective + *way*.

> *He spoke **in a lively, friendly sort of way**.*
> *He always speaks **in that silly way of his**.*

159

Exercises

1 Write an adjective after a link verb or an adverb after an action verb.

Examples: *The old man looked <u>sad.</u> (sad)*
The old man spoke <u>sadly</u> to us. (sad)

1 *We finished the work _____ so we could go home early. (quick)*

2 *Ann looks very _____ in that dress. (nice)*

3 *This soup tastes _____ What's in it? (wonderful)*

4 *Have a good trip home. It's a little foggy so drive _____ (safe)*

5 *Spring is coming and the weather is getting _____ (warm)*

6 *Mrs Pearce greeted the new neighbours _____ and she invited them for coffee _____ (warm) (immediate)*

7 *Old Tom seems very _____ , but he's really very _____ (hard) (kind)*

8 *The back of the ship rose _____ high into the air, and then the whole ship slid _____ into the cold, black sea. (slow) (quiet)*

2 Write the correct adjectives or adverbs.

Example: *(slow/slowly)*
● *Arthur is a <u>slow</u> worker.*
○ *Yes, he's very <u>slow.</u> He does everything very <u>slowly.</u>*

1 *(proper/properly)*
● *Is this the _____ tool for the job?*
○ *No, I'm afraid this one won't do the job _____*

2 *(quiet/quietly)*
● *Lucy is a very _____ person, isn't she?*
○ *Yes, she talks so _____ that it's sometimes difficult to hear her.*

3 *(smooth/smoothly)*
● *I drove the new Mitsui Tiara the other day. It was a very _____ drive.*
○ *I agree. And it handles extremely _____ in wet road conditions too.*

4 *(pleasant/pleasantly)*
● *The weather is very _____ at this time of year.*
○ *And the garden looks really _____ now, with all the flowers coming out.*

5 *(intelligent/intelligently)*
● *Sally dealt with the problem very _____ , I thought.*
○ *Yes, she's a very _____ woman.*

6 *(bad/badly)*
● *Look, the builders have built this wall really _____*
○ *You're right. They've done a very _____ job. They'll have to do it again.*

7 *(effective/effectively)*
● *Which of these cleaning chemicals is more _____ , do you think?*
○ *Well, Clean-ezy works more _____ with really heavy dirt, but Clean-up seems just as _____ as Clean-ezy for most jobs.*

3 Write the correct adverbs.

Examples: *Ann sang that song <u>beautifully.</u> (beautiful)*

1 *Ellen didn't panic after the accident. She acted very _____ (sensible)*

2 *We were able to cut through the dead wood _____ (easy)*

3 *The pilot is looking for somewhere to land _____ (safe)*

4 *The astronauts completed all their tasks _____ (successful)*

5 *I had forgotten to take any cash. _____ , I had my cheque book with me. (lucky)*

6 *We don't usually think _____ , but this time I agree _____ with you. (similar) (whole)*

7 *_____ , everything went wrong with my plan and now I'm _____ and _____ sorry for the problems I've caused you all. (unfortunate) (real) (true)*

4 Complete the statements. Use these irregular adverbs.

direct, early, far, hard, high, late, low, short, straight, well, wrong

Example: *The horse jumped __high.__ It got over every fence.*

1 *We got home very _____ that night.*

2 *They'll have to leave _____ in the morning, or they'll miss the train.*

3 *The bus goes _____ from Oxford to London without stopping.*

4 *They worked _____ all night to get the car working again.*

5 *The plan seemed to be working, but then everything went _____ at the last minute.*

6 *I tried to throw a rope up to the girl, but it fell _____*

7 *The Clark family don't live _____ from here – just five minutes on foot.*

8 *The children sang _____ in the concert.*

9 *You don't need to ask the hotel telephone operator. You can call any outside number _____*

10 *The helicopter flew _____ over the trees and then landed near them.*

5 Write the correct forms of the adverbs.

Example: *(late/lately)*
   a) *Have you seen Peter __lately?__*
   b) *He'll be in trouble if he goes back to college __late.__*

1 *(hard/hardly)*
   a) *The people in this part of Africa have got _____ any food left to eat.*
   b) *The UN are fighting _____ to get help to the people soon.*

2 *(high/highly)*
   a) *Our pilots are all _____ aware of the need for safety in the air.*
   b) *They watch the plane's control systems at all times as they fly _____ above the ground.*

3 *(near/nearly)*
   a) *The ball landed on the ground _____ the house.*
   b) *It very _____ hit the kitchen window.*

4 *(free/freely)*
   a) *After the borders were opened, people like us were able to move much more _____ round Europe.*
   b) *As we were students, we couldn't afford to pay much for our travel, but we often travelled _____ by hitchhiking.*

5 *(short/shortly)*
   a) *Unfortunately, we have fallen _____ of our sales target for this year.*
   b) *However, the economy is getting better, and we expect better sales _____*

6 *(direct/directly)*
   a) *Please call me _____ you get any more news.*
   b) *You can call me _____ on this number.*

6 Write the correct adverbs or adjectives. Choose from these changing the form where necessary.

early, easy, hard, late, quick, serious, tired

Ann: *Hi, Tom. I haven't seen you for ages. What have you been doing __lately?__*

Tom: *Good to see you, Ann. I've been working really [1]_____ to pass my exams.*

Ann: *Oh, I'm sure you'll pass them [2]_____ No problem. You should relax more. Why not finish work [3]_____ this evening and come out with us for an hour or two? You don't need to stay out very [4]_____*

Tom: *No, sorry, I don't think I should. I'm feeling really [5]_____ and I'd like to finish as [6]_____ as possible and then just go to bed.*

Ann: *Well, all right, but I think you should take life a bit less [7]_____*

71 Adverb positions

He drove slowly.   *He slowly drove.*

Front position

We often use an adverb in front position to show a feeling or for special emphasis. The adverb adds its meaning to the whole sentence.

> *Luckily* he was only driving slowly. (speaker's feeling)
> *Slowly* the car began to move. (special emphasis)
> *Finally* we all decided to go. (special emphasis)

Middle position

Main verb only – put the adverb before the main verb.

> He *usually* drives a long way.
> We *quickly* finished dinner.

Auxiliary verb only – put the adverb after a positive auxiliary verb.

> He *is certainly* the best player.

We often put the adverb before a negative auxiliary verb.

> You *certainly weren't* very good today.

Auxiliary + main verb – put the adverb between the auxiliary and the main verb.

> He was *only* driving a short distance.
> Ron has *always* lived in London.

End position

We often put the adverb after the verb, at the end of a sentence. An adverb of time goes after any other adverb or an adverbial phrase.

> He was driving **slowly today**.
> I'll be working **over there tomorrow**.
> We're living **in London now**.

Questions

We do not usually put the adverb in front position in questions. The adverb usually goes in middle or end position.

> Has Ron **always** lived in London?
> Where has Ron **always** lived?
> Was he driving **slowly**?
> Who was driving **slowly**?

East Salterton *Welcomes You*

Please drive slowly through the village

'Are you in earnest? Do you truly love me? Do you sincerely wish me to be your wife?'
'I do: and if an oath is necessary to satisfy, I swear it.'
'Then, sir, I will marry you.'

(*Jane Eyre*, Charlotte Brontë, 1816 – 1855)

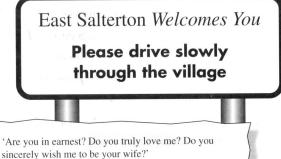

Another important factor in preventing osteoporosis is getting out into the sunshine. Ultraviolet light helps the body make its own Vitamin D, which is essential for the absorption of calcium. You only need 15 minutes a day outside during the summer months, so you won't put yourself at risk of premature ageing and skin cancer. Always remember to use the right factor sunscreen.

IN A DOME

Bubble pop

If the surface becomes dirty, wipe it gently with a soft cloth.

Exercises

1 Write these adverbs in front position.

Speaker's feeling
amazingly, frighteningly, hopefully, luckily, sadly

Special emphasis
angrily, finally, quietly, stupidly

Example: <u>*Amazingly,*</u> *John learned French in a month.* (Speaker's feeling)

1 _____ *we'll be able to finish work in time to go to the cinema.* (Speaker's feeling)

2 _____ *I forgot to take my passport with me to the airport.* (Special emphasis)

3 _____ *the boss banged his desk and shouted, 'Get out!'* (Special emphasis)

4 _____ *pieces from the ceiling started to fall around us.* (Speaker's feeling)

5 _____ *the bus arrived – 45 minutes late!* (Special emphasis)

6 _____ *Bob moved past the sleeping dogs and escaped.* (Special emphasis)

7 _____ *the great painter died before finishing the picture.* (Speaker's feeling)

8 _____ *the burning plane managed to land without crashing.* (Speaker's feeling)

2 Write the adverbs in middle position.

Example: *(is flying) (probably)*
John <u>*is probably flying*</u> *home now.*

1 *(get) (always)*
I _____ *to work at 8.30.*

2 *(only) (was trying)*
Everybody was angry with Sam, but he _____ *to help them.*

3 *(sometimes) (can see)*
You _____ *France from England.*

4 *(will be) (only)*
Peter _____ *here for two days.*

5 *(don't work) (usually)*
We _____ *on Saturdays.*

6 *(clearly) (has been failing)*
Alan _____ *to do this job properly.*

7 *(have you been) (ever)*
_____ *to Japan before?*

8 *(must talk) (never)*
You _____ *like that again.*

3 Write the adverbs in end position.

Example: *(all day) (very hard)*
I've been working <u>*very hard all day.*</u>

1 *(very soon) (there)*
Don't worry. We'll be _____

2 *(in America) (for five years)*
Brian lived _____

3 *(yesterday) (very heavily)*
It snowed _____

4 *(since last September) (much harder)*
Lisa has been studying _____
_____

5 *(as soon as possible) (over here)*
Please get _____
_____

6 *(wrong) (all the time)*
Poor old Paul. He gets things _____
_____

4 Write these adverbs in the letter.

over here, usually, last week, sadly, last year, definitely, this time, soon

Dear Chris,
It was good to hear from you [1]_____ *. We were pleased to hear you'll be travelling* [2]_____ *.*
[3]_____ *, we were away when you visited Miami* [4]_____ *. So you* [5]_____ *must stay with us* [6]_____ *We're* [7]_____ *at home in the evening, so call us* [8]_____ *.*

163

Adverbs of manner (*fast, quickly*, etc)

These usually go in end position and sometimes middle position. Irregular adverbs, eg *fast, well*, etc, go in end position. Use front position for emphasis.

> Peter **quickly** stopped.
> Peter stopped **quickly**.
> **Quickly** Peter stopped.

Adverbs of place (*there, outside*, etc)

These usually go in end position. They do not go in middle position. Use front position for emphasis. An adverb of place usually goes after an adverb of manner.

> The children are playing **outside**.
> I know I'll find her **somewhere**.
> **Somewhere** I know I'll find her.

Adverbs of time (*today, tomorrow*, etc)

These usually go in front position or end position. In end position, a time adverb goes after any other adverb.

> **Tomorrow** we're all going to the beach.
> We're all going to the beach **tomorrow**.

Adverbs of frequency (*usually, always*, etc)

These usually go in middle position. Adverbs of frequency include *always, almost always, usually, generally, normally, often, frequently, sometimes, occasionally, hardly ever, rarely* and *never*. (See the diagrams on the facing page for more information.)

> I **always** go to bed at 10.30.
> Pete **usually** plays football on Sundays.
> It's sad, but I **hardly ever** see my brother because he lives in Australia.
> They **never** ate sweets when they were children.

'Tomorrow never comes.'   (*Proverb*)

'Have you given him up?'
'No, father,' she answered.
He looked at her again for some moments without speaking.
'Does he write to you?' he asked.
'Yes, about twice a month.'
The Doctor looked up and down the valley, swinging his stick; then he said to her, in the same low tone,
'I am very angry.'

(*Washington Square*, Henry James, 1843 – 1916)

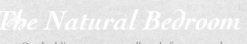

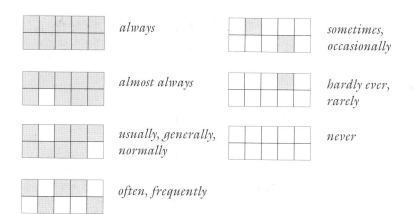

always		sometimes, occasionally
almost always		hardly ever, rarely
usually, generally, normally		never
often, frequently		

We often use *ever* in questions about frequency.

● *Have you **ever** visited London?*   ○ *Yes, I've often been there.*

You can show frequency with adverbial phrases like these. They usually go in end position.

once		day
twice	a	week
three times		month
several times		year

*Most people eat **three times a day**.*
*I take the medicine **once a day**.*

Adverbs of degree (*very, quite*, etc)

Use these adverbs to make an adjective or another adverb weaker or stronger.

Weak: *slightly, a little, a bit* (informal)
    *I felt **slightly** ill, but I didn't stop.*

Stronger: *quite, fairly, rather, pretty* (informal)
    *It isn't snowing, but it's **quite** cold. Bring some warm clothes!*

Strongest: *very, extremely*
    *Eddy is **extremely** good at tennis. In fact, he's Number 10 in the world.*

Be careful. *very* and *too* are different. *too* means more than a certain amount. (See Unit 75.)
    *I was **very** tired, but I went on walking.*
    *I was **too** tired to walk. I had to stop.*

Sentence adverbs (*luckily, probably*, etc)

Sentence adverbs often go in front position. They give their meaning to the whole sentence. They show the speaker's feeling about the information in the sentence. Sentence adverbs include *luckily, sadly, surprisingly, disappointingly, obviously, certainly, probably* and *perhaps*.
    *Then we ran out of petrol. **Luckily** there was a petrol station 300 metres along the road.*
    ***Sadly** Alan is ill and can't be with us.*
    *The train will **probably** be late, and then we **obviously** won't get to the meeting.*

Exercises

1 Find and write the adverbs.

Example: *My brother arrived yesterday.* <u>yesterday</u>

1 *The boys are working upstairs.* _____

2 *The train is definitely late.* _____

3 *Time passed slowly as we waited.* _____

4 *I'm tired, so I'm going to bed now.* _____

5 *This book is very hard to understand.* _____

6 *John always does what he promises.* _____

7 *Luckily the tree fell just behind our car.* _____

2 Name the types of adverb and adverbial phrase in *italics*. Choose from these.

degree, frequency, manner, place, sentence, time

I remember one Japanese national holiday ¹*well*. Some friends and I decided to go to the mountains 100 kilometres from Tokyo in two cars. The problem was that everybody else in Tokyo seemed to be going ²*there* too. The road was ³*very* busy and we moved ⁴*extremely* ⁵*slowly*. We travelled ⁶*all night* and we ⁷*finally* got to the house ⁸*at 6.00*. We were ⁹*terribly* tired, and we went to sleep ¹⁰*immediately*.

We enjoyed the next three days ¹¹*a lot*. We walked through the woods to the village ¹²*once a day* to buy food. And ¹³*every day* we cooked our meals ¹⁴*outside* on a barbecue. Time went ¹⁵*quickly*, and the last day came. We ¹⁶*certainly* didn't want to return to Tokyo but, ¹⁷*sadly*, we had to go.

'Let's leave ¹⁸*late*,' somebody said. 'That way the roads will be quieter.' ¹⁹*Unfortunately* everybody else had the same idea. The journey home was just as slow as the trip from Tokyo. We seemed to get ²⁰*nowhere* in the long, long line of cars. At 2.00 the people in the first car ²¹*suddenly* left the main road to try a smaller road. We followed in the second car. Five more cars followed us, so we thought, 'This must be a good road. The Japanese are using it too.'

²²*Strangely*, the road became narrower. At 2.45 it came to an end. We were back in the mountains again. The cars stopped, and everybody ²³*slowly* got out. The Japanese were embarrassed. 'We didn't know you were foreigners,' one of them said. 'You ²⁴*definitely* seemed to know the way, so we followed you.' Everybody laughed ²⁵*politely*, but we all felt ²⁶*really* tired.

We reached Tokyo ²⁷*early in the morning*, and ²⁸*then* we all had to go to work.

²⁹*After that* I ³⁰*always* stayed at home during national holidays!

1 *well* – <u>manner</u>

2 *there* – _____

3 *very* – _____

4 *extremely* – _____

5 *slowly* – _____

6 *all night* – _____

7 *finally* – _____

8 *at 6.00* – _____

9 *terribly* – _____

10 *immediately* – _____

11 *a lot* – _____

12 *once a day* – _____

13 *every day* – _____

14 *outside* – _____

15 *quickly* – _____

16 *certainly* – _____

17 *sadly* – _____

18 *late* – _____

19 *Unfortunately* – _____

20 *nowhere* – _____

21 *suddenly* – _____

22 *Strangely* – _____

23 *slowly* – _____

24 *definitely* – _____

25 *politely* – _____

26 *really* – _____

27 *early in the morning* – _____

28 *then* – _____

29 *After that* – _____

30 *always* – _____

3 Write the adverbs and phrases of manner, place and time in end position.

Example: *(soon) (somewhere)*
I'm tired of driving. Let's stop <u>*somewhere*</u> *<u>soon.</u>*

1 *(before midday) (there)*
Hurry up! We have to get _____
_____

2 *(beautifully) (yesterday)*
The team played _____

3 *(for a year) (everywhere)*
The police looked for the two men _____
_____

4 *(angrily) (last night) (at the meeting)*
A lot of people spoke _____
_____

5 *(at college) (these days) (well)*
Harry is doing _____
_____

4 Write the adverbs and phrases of frequency in the most usual position – middle or end.

Examples: *Jack goes into town. (sometimes)*
<u>*Jack sometimes goes into town.*</u>
A ship visits the island. (twice a month)
<u>*A ship visits the island twice a month.*</u>

1 *I do the washing on Monday. (usually)*
_____
_____

2 *Do you visit your old school? (ever)*
_____
_____

3 *Flights to New York leave. (once an hour)*
_____
_____

4 *You have to take the medicine. (twice a day)*
_____
_____

5 Emphasize the speaker's feeling. Change the adjective in the second sentence into an adverb in front position. Leave out unnecessary words.

Example: *I fell. It was lucky that I managed to catch a tree branch.*
I fell. <u>*Luckily, I managed to catch a tree branch.*</u>

1 *I called Ann at 7.00. It was sad that she'd already gone.*
I called Ann at 7.00. _____
_____

2 *Bill is getting better. We're hopeful that he'll be well soon.*
Bill is getting better. _____

3 *My wife and I are scientists. We were surprised that our children were good at Art.*
My wife and I are scientists. _____
_____

4 *The prize goes to Clint Starr. It's unfortunate that he isn't here to receive it.*
The prize goes to Clint Starr. _____
_____

6 Write the words in the best order.

Example: *(will be) (probably)*
Ann <u>*will probably be*</u> *late home.*

1 *(has finished) (definitely)*
The football game _____
_____ *now.*

2 *('ll visit) (never)*
I _____ *that place again!*

3 *(are delivered) (always)*
New books _____ *on Monday morning.*

4 *(hasn't understood) (clearly)*
She _____
anything I've said.

5 *('ll see) (hardly ever)*
If you move, I _____ *you again.*

FORMS

Comparison with adjective + *er/est*

The Highlight is cheaper than the Gazelle. It's the cheapest of the three.

Comparison with *more/most, less/least* + adjective

The Rebel is more expensive than the Gazelle. It's the most expensive car.

Comparison with two-syllable adjectives

He wants the Rebel, but she is happier with the Gazelle.

Comparison with adverbs

The Rebel accelerates more quickly than the others. It accelerates the most quickly.

We use a comparative form of an adjective (adjective + *er* or *more* + adjective) to compare two things. We use a superlative form of an adjective (adjective + *est* or *most* + adjective) when one of a group is beyond the others, eg *the cheapest* and *the most expensive*. Compare the following comparative and superlative forms.

Comparative adjectives: *cheaper (than)*   *more | expensive (than)*
                                                            less

Superlative adjectives: *(the) cheapest*   *(the) most | expensive*
                                                            (the) least

We usually use *than* after a comparative form. It connects the two things that we are comparing. We usually use *the* before a superlative form. It refers to the thing which we are describing.

Comparison with adjectives + *er/est*

We use *er/est* with nearly all one-syllable adjectives. Note the spelling changes. (See Appendix 2 for more information on spelling rules.)

Adjective	+ *er*	+ *est*	Adjective	+ *r*	+ *st*
small	smaller	smallest	nice	nicer	nicest
slow	slower	slowest	large	larger	largest

Adjective + doubled consonant	+ *er*	+ *est*
big	+*g*	bigger	biggest
hot	+*t*	hotter	hottest

> *His house is **smaller** than hers.*
> *Mexico City is the **largest** city in the world.*
> *Today is the **hottest** day of the year.*

Comparison with *more/most* or *less/least* + adjective

We use *more/most* or *less/least* for all adjectives with three syllables or more. We also use these forms for all adjectives ending in *ing* or *ed*, eg *pleasing/pleased, tiring/tired, worrying/worried* and *embarrassing/embarrassed*.

> *Cars are **more reliable** now than they were 20 years ago.*
> *She's the **most beautiful** girl in the world!*
> *I'm **less tired** than I was yesterday.*   *It's the **least tiring** job.*

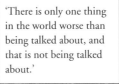
'There is only one thing in the world worse than being talked about, and that is not being talked about.'

(Oscar Wilde, 1854 – 1900)

We can also use these forms for all adjectives with two syllables.

> *Jack is the **most lazy** boy I know.*
> *John's work is **less careful** than it should be.*

We can also use *more/most* and *less/least* like *fewer/fewest* to talk about quantity.

Comparison with two-syllable adjectives

You can use *more/most* and *less/least* for all adjectives with two syllables. But we often use *er/est* with two-syllable adjectives.

> *The road is **more narrow/narrower** here.*
> *He's the **most lazy/laziest** boy in the class.*

We often use *er/est* with these very common two-syllable adjectives: *clever, cruel, gentle, narrow, pleasant, polite, quiet, simple, stupid, tired.*

> *Ann is **politer** than her sister.*
> *Tom is the **cleverest** boy in the class.*

We also often use *er/est* with two-syllable adjectives ending in a consonant + *y*, eg *dirty, easy, funny, happy, lazy, lovely, pretty, silly, sunny* and *tidy*. They change like this: *dirty + ier/iest → dirtier/dirtiest.*

> *Jack is the **laziest** boy I know.*
> *Question 2 is **easier** than question 1.*

Comparison of adverbs

We use a comparative form of an adverb (adverb + *er* or *more* + adverb) to compare two actions. We use a superlative form of an adverb (adverb + *est* or *most* + adverb) when one of a group does something beyond the others, eg *... accelerates the most quickly.*

Many adverbs have the form adjective + *ly*, eg *quickly, slowly* and *nicely*. (See Unit 70 for more information on adjectives, adverbs and adverb formation.) Just like longer adjectives, these *ly* adverbs take the forms *more/most* and *less/least*.

> *Rob works **more quickly** than Steve.*
> *Jane sings the **most beautifully** in the class.*

Some adverbs look like short adjectives which take *er/est*, eg *deep, early, fast, hard, high, late, long* and *near*. Just like these short adjectives, these adverbs usually take the forms *er/est*.

> *The Rebel goes **faster** than the Gazelle.*
> *I arrived the **earliest** at the meeting.*

Note the irregular forms.

Adjective	Adverb	Comparative	Superlative
good	well	better	best
bad	badly	worse	worst
far	far	farther/further	farthest/furthest

> *This year's results are **better** than last year's.*
> *My headache is getting **worse**.*
> *We can't go any **farther** tonight.*

Exercises

1 Write the *er* and *est* forms.

Adjective	*er* form	*est* form
1 short	shorter	shortest
2 pretty	prettier	prettiest
3 long	_____	_____
4 ugly	_____	_____
5 large	_____	_____
6 big	_____	_____
7 small	_____	_____
8 nice	_____	_____
9 cool	_____	_____
10 easy	_____	_____
11 simple	_____	_____
12 fine	_____	_____
13 thin	_____	_____
14 hot	_____	_____

2 Write the correct *er* forms of the underlined adjectives.

Example: *Bill has a <u>large</u> car. It's even <u>larger</u> than my brother's.*

1 *Yesterday's test was <u>easy</u> – much _____ than last month's.*

2 *Question 2 was <u>simple</u>. It was certainly _____ than question 1.*

3 *My cousin is <u>nice</u> – a lot _____ than my brother.*

4 *It's been <u>hot</u> today, and it'll be even _____ tomorrow.*

5 *The job took a <u>long</u> time. It took _____ than I thought.*

3 Write the *est* forms. Use these adjectives.

early, fit, funny, late, narrow, quick

Example: *There's a train at 5.30 am. That's the <u>earliest</u> one.*

1 *This is the _____ model. It's just come out.*

2 *Which is the _____ way to Paris, please?*

3 *We're coming to the _____ part of the river now. Here it's only five metres wide.*

4 *Rod is the _____ member of the team. He's been training very hard.*

5 *He was the _____ man I've ever heard. I couldn't stop laughing.*

4 Complete the radio adverts with regular *er* and *est* forms. Use these adjectives.

easy, fast, fine, fit, low, white

Example: *SPEED CLEAN was always the <u>fastest</u> home cleaner. Now it's <u>faster</u> than ever before. It does the job in seconds.*

1 *You'll be _____ in just three days with the HOME EXERCISER. And after a month you'll be the _____ you've ever been in your life.*

2 *There's no _____ watch in the world than the perfect TIME PERFECTA. Remember, we've been makers of the _____ watches in the world for 30 years.*

3 *You'll find the _____ prices in town at GOOD WAY SUPERMARKETS. And that's a promise. If you can find _____ prices anywhere else, we'll give you your money back.*

4 *GLEAM CREAM cleans your teeth _____ than white. For the _____ , cleanest teeth of all, choose GLEAM CREAM.*

5 *Do you hate all those video controls? Well, now TELE-SELECT is here. It's the _____ thing in the world to use. Just talk to it. Tell it the time, the channel and the film to record, and TELE-SELECT does the rest. What could be _____ than that?*

5 Complete the conversations. Use *more/most, less/least* or *fewer/fewest*.

Example: ● *I've just moved to a bigger apartment in the same building.*
   ○ *Do you have to pay <u>more</u> rent?*
   ● *Yes, it's the biggest in the building, so it costs the <u>most.</u>*

1 ● *Bob seems to get richer, but meaner every day. I can't stand him these days.*
   ○ *Yes, he's got _____ money than ever before, but he's got _____ friends!*

2 ● *I'm still hungry. Is there any _____*
  ○ *But you've already had the _____ out of everybody. Don't be so greedy!*

3 ● *This motor-bike is certainly quite cheap. It costs _____ than all the other models we've looked at.*
  ○ *I've read that it also costs the _____ to run out of all the bikes this size. And I've also heard that it has the _____ mechanical problems.*
  ● *But if there's a mechanical problem, spare parts are very expensive. In fact, they cost the _____ out of all the models in the 750cc class.*

6 Write the comparative and superlative forms of the adjectives.

Example: *No language is easy to learn, but Italian is <u>less difficult</u> than I thought. In fact it's the <u>least difficult</u> language I've ever studied. (difficult)*

1 *Joe is doing well at art college. He isn't the _____ student in his year, but he's _____ than 90% of the other students. (talented)*

2 *Why do you always have to buy the _____ thing in the shop? Couldn't you choose something _____ (expensive)*

3 *I think rock climbing is even _____ than deep sea diving. In fact, I think it's one of the _____ outdoor activities you can do. (dangerous)*

4 *Uncut diamonds are _____ than diamonds that are cut. A diamond that was recently sold for $975,000 is the _____ one in the world at the moment. (valuable)*

5 *I don't like Robin Black's new book as much as his last one. It's _____ In fact, I think it's the _____ book he's ever written. (interesting)*

7 Complete the statements with a verb and comparative adverb.

Examples: *Ann is a quicker worker than Sue.*
Ann <u>works more quickly</u> than Sue.

1 *Grandad is a slower driver than his me.*
Grandad _____ than me.

2 *Stephen Prince is a more exciting writer than Sid Shelley.*
Stephen Prince _____ than Sid Shelley.

3 *Don is a lighter sleeper than his brother.*
Don _____ than his brother.

4 *Ron is always an earlier arrival at work than Bob.*
Ron always _____ at work than Bob.

5 *Joe is a less intelligent football player than Steve.*
Joe _____ than Steve.

8 Write statements with superlative adverbs.

We tested three washing machines – the Crystal, the Wash-Tech and the Snowline. Here are the results.

Examples: *(Snowline/wash/+ good/Crystal/wash/ - effective)*
<u>The Snowline washed the best, and the Crystal washed the least effectively.</u>

1 *(Crystal/perform/+ reliable/Wash-Tech/perform/ - reliable)*

_____
_____
_____
_____

2 *(Wash-Tech/run/- economical/Crystal/run/+ cheap)*

_____
_____
_____

3 *(Crystal/finish/+ fast/Snowline/finish/- quick)*

_____
_____
_____

74 Comparison 2: sentence patterns

Hill finished faster than Rossi.   He's the fastest man in the world.

Sentence patterns with comparatives

A comparative sentence compares two things. When we mention both things, we link them with *than*.

> Hill is **faster than** Rossi.   A CD lasts **longer than** a cassette.

When we compare with an adjective, we do not always mention both things.

> ● *Which is your jacket?*   ○ *The **bigger one**.*

Sentence patterns with superlatives

We usually use *the* before superlative adjectives.

> *Paul is **the tallest** person here.*

We do not often use *the* before superlative adverbs. Compare the following.

> ● *Which is **the best** song?*   ○ *I like Sad Heart **best**.*

We can use *in* or *of* after a superlative. Use *in* to talk about places and groups. Use *of* to talk about other things, including numbers.

> *I'm the **tallest boy in the class**.*
> *July is the **warmest month of the year**.*

Sentence patterns with (not) as ... as

Use *as ... as* to say that two things or actions are equal.

> *Paul is **as tall as** his father now.*   *I drive **as well as** Tom.*

Use *not as ... as* (or *not so ... as*) to say that two things or actions are not equal.

> *English **isn't as difficult as** Maths.* (Maths is harder than English.)
> *He **can't work as quickly as** I can.* (I can work faster than he can.)

Comparison and object pronouns

After a comparative with *than* or *as ... as*, we often talk about another person. If we use a name we can do it in these two ways.

> *I drove faster **than Carlo did**.*   *I drove faster **than Carlo**.*

If we use a pronoun, the subject pronoun + auxiliary verb change to an object pronoun.

> *I drove faster **than he did**. → I drove faster **than him**.*
> *He can't run as quickly **as I can**. → He can't run as quickly **as me**.*

For art lovers, *St Just* is an excellent base to tour the many galleries of the area – quieter and less expensive than St Ives. And for those who like hitting small balls all over the place, there is a magnificent 18-hole golf course nearby.

'You know,' he said very gravely, 'it's one of the most serious things that can possibly happen to one in a battle – to get one's head cut off.'

(Through the Looking-Glass, Lewis Carroll, 1832 – 1898)

Exercises

1 Write statements with comparative adjectives.

Example: Tom is 17. Sam is 19. (old)
Sam is older than Tom.

1 Sue is 10. Ann is 12. (young)
_____

2 The Honda costs £10,000. The Toyota costs £12,000. (expensive)
_____
_____

3 Robin can do 100 metres in 10 seconds. Jack runs 100 metres in 10.5 seconds. (fast)
_____
_____

4 Five climbers have died on Mount George. Eleven climbers have been killed on Mount Egmont. (dangerous)
_____
_____

5 The journey by sea is an hour. The journey by tunnel is only half an hour. (short)
_____
_____

2 Write statements with superlative adjectives and *be* in the correct form.

Example: (the new Boeing/be/big/plane in the world)
The new Boeing is the biggest plane in the world.

1 (yesterday/be/hot/day of the year)
_____
_____

2 (the XL400/be/popular/car in Europe this year)
_____
_____

3 (Tom and Sam/be/good/players in last year's team)
_____
_____

4 (some people say Casa Blanca/be/fine/film ever)
_____
_____

3 Correct the statements. Use *isn't nearly as ... as ...*

Example: ● *Kuwait is larger than Saudi Arabia.*
○ *That's not right.* *Kuwait isn't nearly as large as Saudi Arabia.*

1 ● *A Jumbo 747 is faster than a Concord.*
○ *That's wrong.* _____
_____

2 ● *Britain is warmer than Egypt.*
○ *I'm afraid that's not quite right.* _____

3 ● *Silver is more expensive than gold.*
○ *I'm sorry, but that's wrong.* _____
_____

4 ● *Rome is older than Athens.*
○ *No, it's the opposite.* _____

5 ● *English food is better than French food.*
○ *I'm afraid I don't agree.* _____

4 Write the correct pronouns.

Examples: *He's cleverer than* they *are.* (they/them)
He's cleverer than them. (they/them)

Tom: *Sue, why did you give the mailroom manager's job to Tim. Ann is twice as clever as* [1]_____ *is.* (he/him)

Sue: *Yes, but he knows the work better than* [2]_____ (she/her) *Remember, he's been with the company much longer than* [3]_____ *has.* (she/her)

Tom: *Well, what about Alan and Emma? Tim hasn't been here any longer than* [4]_____ *have.* (they/them) *And he certainly doesn't know the work any better than* [5]_____ (they/them)

Sue: *Yes, but they're both cleverer than* [6]_____, *and I'm going to give them better jobs.* (he/him)

Tom: *Well, I still don't agree about Tim.*

Sue: *Believe me, you don't know him as well as* [7]_____ *do.* (I/me) *If you did, I'm sure you'd make the same decision as* [8]_____ (I/me)

75 *too* and *enough*
He's too young.   He isn't old enough.

too and *enough*

We use *too* and *enough* when we talk about the right amount of something, eg *money, clothes size, exam marks* and *age*.

too and *enough* go with adjectives and adverbs. *too* goes before an adjective/adverb. *enough* goes after an adjective/adverb.

Adjectives
*Len is **too young** to get the job.*
*Len isn't **old enough** to get the job.*

Adverbs
*Slow down! We're going **too fast**.*
*Hurry! We aren't going **fast enough**.*

too + adjective/adverb

too means more than the right amount. *not too* means the right amount. Note that we often leave out the last part in brackets.

> *Ron is 50, so he's **too old** (to get the job).*
> *Bob is 25, so he is**n't too old** (to get the job).*
> *The plane won't take off. It's going **too slowly** (to take off).*

too is not the same as *very*. Compare the following. (See also Unit 76.)

> *Harry was **very old**, but he kept on working.*
> *Harry was **too old** to work. He had to stop.*

Adjective/adverb + *enough*

enough means the right amount – not more, not less. *not enough* means less than the right amount. Note that we often leave out the last part in brackets.

> *Bob is 25, so he's **old enough** (to get the job).*
> *Len is only 20, so he is**n't old enough** (to get the job).*

Further patterns

enough can go with a noun – before, not after. *too* needs *much* or *many* to go with a noun. (We sometimes also say *too little/too few*.)

> *Is there **enough orange juice**?   We haven't got **enough sandwiches**.*
> *There's **too much orange juice**.   Have we got **too few sandwiches**?*

After *too* and *enough* we can use *to* + infinitive + noun or *for* + noun.

> *He's **too young to get the job**.   He isn't **old enough for the job**.*

We can also use them together.

> *This shirt is **good enough to wear** at home, but it's **too old-fashioned for the party** tonight.*

Tom appeared on the sidewalk with a bucket of whitewash and a long-handled brush. He surveyed the fence, and the gladness went out of nature, and a deep melancholy settled down upon his spirit. Thirty yards of broad fence nine feet high! ...

He began to think of the fun he had planned for this day, and his sorrows multiplied. Soon the free boys would come tripping along on all sorts of delicious expeditions, and they would make a world of fun of him having to work. He got out his worldly wealth and examined it – bits of toys, marbles and trash; enough to buy an exchange of work maybe, but not enough to buy so much as half an hour of pure freedom.

(*The Adventures of Tom Sawyer*, Mark Twain, 1835 – 1910)

Exercises

1 Write *too* + these adjectives or adverbs.

Adjectives	Adverbs
late, strong, young	quickly, quietly, slowly

Example: *Can't you work faster? You're working*
too slowly.

1 *I'm only 15, so I can't drive yet. I'm* _____
2 *Time goes* _____ *when you're having fun.*
3 *I couldn't hold the thief. He was* _____
4 *I ran, but I missed the train. I was* _____
5 *Tell Ann to speak up. She's talking* _____

2 Write these adjectives or adverbs + *enough*.

Adjectives	Adverbs
big, good, soon	carefully, hard, quickly

Example: *Can't you work faster? You aren't working*
quickly enough.

1 *I can't climb through the window. It isn't*
_____
2 *I can tell you the answer tomorrow. Is that*
_____
3 *The engine broke down. The engineers hadn't checked it*
_____
4 *Nick is going to lose the race. He hasn't trained*
_____
5 *I'm going to buy the smaller sound system. It isn't the best, but it's* _____

3 Complete the dialogues. Use *too + little/few*, *enough* or *not/n't ... enough*.

Mr Simpson and his assistant are checking stock in his small stationery shop.

1 (✓ A5 paper/✗ A4 paper/✗ brown envelopes)
Mr S: *We've got* enough A5 paper, *but we have* n't
got enough A4 paper.
Asst: *And we've got* too few brown envelopes.

2 (✗ large paper clips/✗ medium clips/✓ small clips)
Mr S: *We have* ___ *got* _____
_____ *and we have got*
_____
Asst: *But we've got* _____

3 (✗ brown sticky tape/✗ clear tape/✓ elastic bands)
Mr S: *We've got* _____
_____ *and we have* ___ *got*
_____
Asst: *But we've got* _____
_____

4 (✗ glue/✗ stapling machines/✗ staples)
Mr S: *We've got* _____ *and we've*
got _____
_____
Asst: *And we have* ___ *got* _____

4 Write statements.

Example: *The boys don't like the weather. It's too hot.*
The weather is too hot for the boys.

1 *I really want a holiday. I haven't got enough money.*
_____
_____
2 *Your mother won't like this coffee. It's too strong.*
_____
_____
3 *The family are all very happy with the new house. It's big enough.*
_____
_____

5 Write statements.

Example: *I don't want to go out. It's too hot.*
It's too hot to go out.

1 *We don't want to go out. It isn't warm enough.*
_____
2 *They tried to catch the bird. It was too fast.*
_____
3 *We wanted to catch the bus. We were too late.*
_____
_____
4 *The plane missed the mountain. It was flying just high enough.*
_____
_____

a bit, very, etc + adjective/adverb

Use these words to give an adjective or an adverb a weaker or stronger feeling. *a bit*, *pretty* and *really* are informal. Use them in friendly conversation.

Weakest	Weak	Stronger	Strongest
not (+ verb) + *very*	*slightly, a little, a bit*	*quite, rather, fairly, pretty*	*very, extremely, really*

*He did**n't feel very well**. In fact, he felt **quite ill**.*
*Eddy is **extremely good** at tennis. He's Number 10 in the world.*

very and *too* are different. Compare the following. (See also Unit 75.)
*He was **very** tired, but he went on climbing.*
*He was **too** tired to walk. He had to stop.*

much, a lot, etc + comparative adjective/adverb

Use these words to give a comparative adjective or adverb a weaker or stronger feeling.

Weak	Strong	Strongest
slightly, a little, a bit	*much, a lot*	*far*

*Could you please talk **a little more quietly**?*
*I felt **a lot better** after a good night's sleep.*
*Susan can speak Japanese **far better** than she can write it.*

CROSSCHECK

so + adjective/adverb

Use *so* to make an adjective or adverb very strong.

*The film was **so boring**!*
*What took you **so long** to get here?*
*I didn't see. It happened **so quickly**!*

We can add a *that* phrase to show the result of the *so* part of the sentence.

*The story was **so exciting that** I couldn't stop reading.*
*I was **so cold that** I wore two sweaters.*

such (+ adjective) + noun

Use *such* (+ adjective) + noun in the same way.

*He always talks **such rubbish**!*
*What took you **such a long time**?*
*This is such **a beautiful house**.*

We can do exactly the same with a sentence containing *such*.

*It was **such an exciting story that** I couldn't stop reading.*
*It was **such a cold day that** I wore two sweaters.*

Our verdict on what's on offer in the High Street

Outdoors	Mayfield XCS	CAT
***	**	****
Classic brown leather boots	Black leather and rubber training boots	Oxford Boots
£85	£75	£79.99
Not really my style, but very comfortable and *SO* light.	A bit heavy, but with the right trousers very cool and stylish.	These are my favourites. Very stylish and comfortable. I would feel so good in them, I could wear them anywhere.

'It is a far, far better thing that I do, than I have ever done;
it is a far, far better rest that I go to, than I have ever known.'

(Sydney Carlton's last thoughts before being guillotined.)
(*A Tale of Two Cities*, Charles Dickens, 1812 – 1870)

So good, it's a pity to share them ...

Ego chocolates

...They make you selfish

... and that was our last review tonight in Movie Spot. It's been such a good week for movies but that last one is great for a date. So scary you'll spend all evening in each other's arms ...

Exercises

1 Complete the statements. Use these words.

a bit, not very, quite, very

Example: *The traffic was travelling at 5 kph. The journey was __very__ slow.*

1 *Sally is doing much better at Maths now, but she's still _____ slow.*

2 *I like football, but I'm _____ good at it.*

3 *I'm _____ hungry. I need food now!*

4 *The new XR200 is _____ a good car, but it isn't my favourite.*

5 *Don't climb on that old fence. It's _____ strong.*

2 Complete the statements. Use these words.

a little, far, much

Example: *Tony is still very ill, but he's getting __a little__ better every day.*

1 *These shoes look the same, but these are £50 more than those. They're _____ more expensive.*

2 *I failed my driving test badly the first time, but I did _____ better the second time, and I passed.*

3 *Sue is _____ older than Tim. She's 10 and he's 9.*

4 *Our new house is _____ bigger than our old one. It's got four bedrooms instead of two.*

5 *Tony drives _____ more carefully than he did a few years ago, but he still frightens me!*

3 Complete the conversation with *so* or *such*.

- *You're __so__ quiet! Is anything wrong?*
- *It's my exams. They're* [1] *_____ soon, and I've got* [2] *_____ a lot of work. I've got to stay up all night.*
- *Don't be* [3] *_____ an idiot! You're obviously* [4] *_____ tired that you can't work properly. It would be* [5] *_____ a waste of time if you stayed up all night! What's more, you'd be* [6] *_____ exhausted tomorrow that you'd waste the whole day!*
- *But I'm* [7] *_____ worried! If I don't pass, it'll be* [8] *_____ a disaster!*
- *You'll pass. The trouble with you is that you're* [9] *_____ a worrier, and you've really* [10] *_____ little to worry about!*

4 Match statements 1–8 and a–h. Then join them using *so* or *such … (that)*.

1 *The weather was bad.*
2 *The students are making a noise.*
3 *The birds are friendly.*
4 *The children made a mess.*
5 *Everybody is busy.*
6 *I haven't driven for a long time.*
7 *After the trip we were all tired.*
8 *They took a long time to get ready.*

a *All the neighbours are complaining.*
b *They nearly missed their plane.*
c *We went straight to sleep.*
d *They even take food from your hand.*
e *We gave up our holiday and went home.*
f *Nobody is answering the phone.*
g *I feel quite nervous about going on the road.*
h *It took an hour to clean the room.*

1 – *e*　2 – ___　3 – ___　4 – ___　5 – ___　6 – ___
7 – ___　8 – ___

1 *__The weather was so bad (that) we gave up our holiday and went home.__*

2 _____

3 _____

4 _____

5 _____

6 _____

7 _____

8 _____

The prepositions in this unit express their place or movement. The preposition refers to the noun which always follows it. (See Unit 78 for differences between the prepositions of place *in*, *on* and *at*.)

> The hotel is **down** the hill. (place)
> The Wood family are walking **down** the hill. (movement)

on, on top of

> There's a suitcase **on** the chair.
> There's another suitcase **on top of** the cupboard.

on, onto, off

> Nick Wood is putting a pile of clothes **onto/on** the bed.
> His cap is falling **off** the pile.

in, into, out of

> There are some clothes **in** the suitcase.
> He's putting them **into/in** the case.
> Nick is taking some more clothes **out of** the cupboard.

down, up

> Nick is taking his case **down** the stairs.
> His sister is going **up** the stairs.

inside, outside

> There are two sports bags **inside** the front door.
> There are some beach things **outside** the front door.

behind, in front of, around, round

> The car was in the garage **behind** the house.
> Now it's **in front of** the house.
> Mr Wood has brought it **around/round** the house.

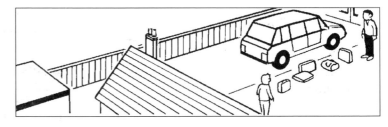

next to, by, beside

The car is **next to/by/beside** the garden fence.
There are some pieces of luggage **next to/by/beside** the car.
Mr Wood is standing **next to/by/beside** the car.

across, along

Mrs Wood is going **across** the road.
A friend is coming **along** the road.

near, from, to

The Wood family live in Sandford **near** Oxford.
Today they're driving **from** Sandford **to** Heathrow Airport.

away from, towards, past

They're driving **away from** Sandford.
They're going **towards** the motorway.
They're driving **past** the motorway sign.

over, under, through

They've just driven **over** a bridge. (**across** a bridge is also possible.)
There's a river **under** the bridge.
They're going to drive **through** a tunnel.

above, below

The Wood family catch their plane. Soon it's **above** the clouds.
Nick watches the clouds **below** the plane.

between, among, opposite

The Woods finally reach their hotel. It's **between** the hills and the sea.
It stands **among** a lot of trees.
It's **opposite** a small island.

Exercises

1 Look at the picture. Then complete the statements with these prepositions.

above, behind, between, in, in front of, near, next to, on, opposite, under

Example: *There is a light ___near___ the window.*

1   *There is a desk _____ the window too.*

2   *There is a light _____ the desk.*

3   *There is a chair _____ the desk.*

4   *There is a lamp _____ the desk.*

5   *There is a paper bin _____ the desk.*

6   *There is an empty box _____ the paper bin.*

7   *There is a phone _____ the desk.*

8   *There is a filing cabinet _____ the desk.*

9   *There is a large wall map _____ the window.*

10 *The desk is _____ the window and the wall map.*

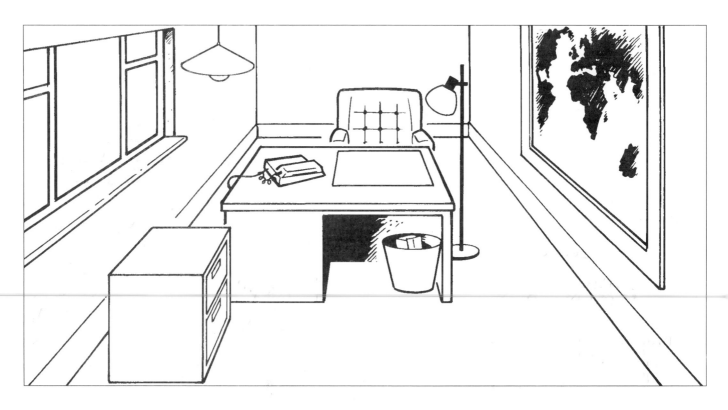

2 Write the correct prepositions.

Example: *There were a lot of people ___outside___ the cinema before the doors opened. (inside/outside)*

1   *There's someone ___ the door. Could you answer it, please? (in/at)*

2   *Is Lucy ___ home today? (in/at)*

3   *Listen! I think I can hear somebody ___ the garden. (in/at)*

4   *I'm sorry. Mr Davis isn't ___ his office just now. He's seeing the Director. (in/at)*

5   *There's a newspaper shop on the other side of the road, _____ our house. (opposite/in front of)*

6   *Please don't stand _____ the children. They can't see what's happening. (opposite/in front of)*

7   *Look! Can't you see your glasses now? They're right _____ you. (opposite/in front of)*

8   *Swindon is a large town that stands on the road _____ London and Bristol. (between/among)*

9   *_____ all the white sheep in the field there were a few black ones. (between/among)*

10 *The woods are lovely there, and we camped _____ the trees by the stream. (between/among)*

3 Look at the picture. Then complete the statements with prepositions.

Example: *(across, along, into, past, through)*
         The cat walked <u>along</u> the road for a while.

1 *It went _____ the bus stop.*

2 *Then it suddenly ran _____ the road.*

3 *It came _____ our garden.*

4 *It came in _____ the gate.*

   (along, over, round, towards, up)

5 *It walked a little way _____ the garden path.*

6 *Then it ran _____ the tree.*

7 *Next it went _____ our summer house.*

8 *It jumped _____ the flower bed on the way.*

9 *It climbed _____ one side of the summer house.*

   (away from, down, inside, out of, under)

10 *And it climbed _____ the other side.*

11 *It crawled _____ the summer house.*

12 *Then it went _____ the summer house for a moment.*

13 *But then it jumped _____ the window.*

14 *Finally, it ran _____ the summer house and left the garden.*

at

Use *at* to talk about an exact place.

> *He lives **at Number 25, Park Road**.*
> *Where's Mary? She isn't **at her desk**.*
> *I'll meet you **at the cinema entrance**.*

Use *at* to talk about an event.

> *Were you **at the football match**?*
> *Over 100 people were **at the meeting**.*

in

Use *in* when there is something around, eg a person in a country or a pen in a pocket.

> *He lives **in Sandford, in England**.*
> ● *Is she **in the TV room**?*   ○ *No, she's **in the garden**.*
> *Did you put the pen **in your pocket**?*

Compare the use of *in* and *at*.

> *The meeting was **in Room 93**. (the place)*
> *Over 100 people were **at the meeting**. (the event in the place)*

on

Use *on* for any surface.

> *Nick was standing **on the chair**.*   *Her name is **on the door**.*
> *There's a mark **on the ceiling**.*   *The answer is **on page 75**.*

Use *on* for a line that runs between two places.

> *Sandford is **on the River Thames, between Oxford and Abingdon**.*
> *The Wood family were **on the road to the airport**.*
> *There were guards **on the frontier between India and Pakistan**.*

Note these common expressions of place.

at	in	on
at school/work/home/college	in hospital/town	on holiday/business
at the library/bus station/ cross roads	in the country/ shopping centre	on the beach/lake/ island
at the (third) turning	in the middle of the road	on the right/left
at the top/bottom of the hill	in the middle/centre of the city/town/village	on the edge/outskirts of town/the city
at a party/meeting/lesson	in a group/queue/line	on the front/back of an envelope/a book
at the front/back of a queue/hall/bus	in the front/back of a car	on TV/cassette/disk
at the end of a corridor/ queue		

Saint Catherines
Woodbridge

The present church was begun in the 13th century. The tower was added in 1409 with fascinating gargoyles at each angle.

Pack your bags

A selection of last-minute holidays and travel opportunities at home, on the continent, further afield; in the country, on the coast, near national parks; many at bargain prices. Phone GETAWAY BREAKS, the last-minute specialists **on 0171 599 3111**.

> After my work in the City, I like to be at home. What's the good of a home, if you are never in it? 'Home, Sweet Home', that's my motto.

(The Diary of a Nobody, 1892, George & Weedon Grossmith)

The Thelma Hulbert GALLERY

The Thelma Hulbert Gallery is situated in Elmfield House, Honiton. The Gallery incorporates a changing display of paintings by artist Thelma Hulbert together with temporary exhibitions of contemporary art and craft.

Thelma Hulbert was born in Bath, Somerset, in 1913. She studied painting and design at Bath School of Art before moving to London in the early 30s.

> Breathless, we flung us on the windy hill, Laughed in the sun, and kissed the lovely grass.

(The Hill, Rupert Brooke, 1887 – 1915)

Exercises

1 Match statement halves 1–10 and a–j. Then write the complete statements.

1 Tom lives at
2 There's a notice on
3 Ann is buying some things in
4 Dad is having a sleep in
5 My aunt lives in
6 Come and meet all the trainees in
7 I want you to introduce me to everyone at
8 There are two men working up on
9 Sally put the vase of flowers on
10 Both London and Oxford are on

a the shopping centre.
b Room 564.
c a small town outside London.
d the small bedroom.
e the roof.
f the party.
g Number 25, North Street.
h the River Thames.
i the wall outside my office.
j the table.

1 – _g_   2 – ___   3 – ___   4 – ___   5 – ___   6 – ___
7 – ___   8 – ___   9 – ___   10 – ___

1 _Tom lives at Number 25, North Street._
2 _____
3 _____
4 _____
5 _____
6 _____
7 _____
8 _____

9 _____
10 _____

2 Complete the statements. Use these phrases.

at that desk, at the entrance, at the meeting, in a village, in the garden, in the middle of, on that wall, on the way, on the bottle, on the edge of

Example: Sally lives _on the edge of_ London. She can see the country from her house.

1 I live _____ London. It takes an hour to get out of the city.
2 We can stop for some petrol _____ to the shops.
3 A lot of people spoke _____ meeting.
4 Let's put this picture _____.
5 What does the label _____ say?
6 My brother usually works _____.
7 You can buy your ticket _____.
8 Mary is picking some flowers _____.
9 My sister lives _____ near Oxford.

3 Complete the dialogues. Use in, on or at.

● Excuse me. Where can I find a photocopier?
○ There's one _in_ Room 303. Go upstairs and turn right ¹___ the top of the stairs. It's ²___ the right ³___ the end of the corridor.

● Look. There's a note ⁴___ the front door.
○ Oh, yes. It's written ⁵___ the back of an envelope. It's from Jenny. She says she's ⁶___ a meeting ⁷___ college. She'll be back for dinner.

● Is Sue ⁸___ home this afternoon?
○ No, sorry. She's ⁹___ the library.
● Is that the one ¹⁰___ Bath Street ¹¹___ town?
○ No, she always uses the one ¹²___ the shopping centre ¹³___ the edge of town.

at, in, on   past, to

at, in and on

The Wood family had their holiday in July.
They left on Saturday.
They left on 7th July.
They left at 7.20.

past and to

They left at twenty past seven.
They arrived at twenty to one.

at

Use *at* for time.

> *Lunch will be at 1.00.*
> *Mum called us at dinner time.*

Use *at* for a known point in the past or the future.

> *They married young. At that time, they were poor.*
> *We will arrive at 10.00. At that point, you will open the main door.*

Use *at* for special days, short holidays and festivals.

> *We always have a party at New Year.*

in

Use *in* for centuries, years, months and seasons.

> *The car was invented in the 19th century.*
> *We bought our house in 1989.*
> *School started again in September.*
> *We always go skiing in (the) winter.*

Also use *in* for periods of time.

> *We don't do much work in the holidays.*
> *Are you going away in the summer break?*

Compare these examples with *at* + short period of time.

> *We always have a party at New Year.*
> *What are you doing at the weekend?*

Use *in* for parts of the day (but not usually with the word *night*).

> *I ate in the morning/afternoon/evening.*
> *We arrived late at night.*

Use *in* for a measured time.

> *Tony finished the job in three weeks.*
> *Your pizzas will be ready in ten minutes.*

August 6, Bank Holiday.

As there was no sign of Lupin moving at nine o'clock, I knocked at his door, and said we usually breakfasted at half-past eight, and asked how long would he be? ... he said he could do with a cup of tea, and didn't want anything to eat.

Lupin not having come down, I went up again at half-past one, and said we dined at two; he said he 'would be there'. He never came down till a quarter to three.

(*The Diary of a Nobody,* 1892, George & Weedon Grossmith)

At half past twelve I left home. I walked to the centre of town. I wanted to arrive on time for my appointment with the bank manager at a quarter to one. When I arrived at the bank ten minutes later, I didn't notice anything unusual at first. It was only when I knocked on the manager's door, that I realised the building was completely empty.

Toni Morrison was born in 1931 in a small steel town in Ohio in the United States. In those days blacks lived separately from whites, but Morrison says she never felt inferior because of her colour. She was more aware of being poor than black.

Rehearsals start for Mozart Mass

REHEARSALS for the Exmouth Choral and Orchestral Society's 'Mass in C Minor' by Mozart started on Monday at Glenorchy Church, Exeter Road.

The mass will be performed at Holy Trinity Church on April 25.

★ *Five Cornish Artists* ★

invite you to a private view of their work
on Sunday 10th May from 4.30 to 6.30 pm

(thereafter 11.00 – 5.00 from Tuesday 12th May to Saturday 30th May)
at the Brick Street Gallery, Penzeen (just behind the Corn Market)

on

Use *on* for days and dates.

> *They arrived **on Saturday**.*
> *We left **on 7th July**.*

Use *on* for special days.

> *I visited my parents **on New Year's Day**.*
> *I didn't have a party **on my birthday**!*
> *Did things go well **on your wedding day**?*

Use *on* for parts of a particular day. Compare the following.

> *Did they go **on Saturday morning**?*
> *Did they go **in the morning**?*

Do not use *in* or *on* with *this, last, next, yesterday, tomorrow, each* and *every*.

> *I came to work late **this morning**.*
> *Did you go away **last weekend**?*
> *Tom cleans his car **every weekend**.*

Note these common expressions of time with *at, in* and *on*.

> *He's usually happy, but **at times** he feels sad.* (sometimes)
> *He's rich now, but **at one time** he was very poor.* (for a time in the past)
> *The soldiers climbed the ropes three **at a time**.* (three together)
> *We met **in time** to talk before the film.* (with enough time)
> *The plane took off **on time**.* (at the right time – not too early, not too late)
> *You must always get to work **on time**.* (You must not be late for work.)

past and to

We can tell these times in different ways.

> *12.15 → twelve fifteen* OR *quarter past twelve*
> *12.30 → twelve thirty* OR *half past twelve*
> *12.45 → twelve forty-five* OR *quarter to one*
> *12.50 → twelve fifty* OR *ten to one*

We can also tell these times in different ways. If you use the second way, you must say *minutes*.

> *1.03 → one oh three* OR *three minutes past one*
> *1.39 → one thirty-nine* OR *twenty-one minutes to two*

Exercises

1 Complete the conversation. Use *at*, *in* and *on*.

Tony and his mother are talking on the phone.

Mum: *So can you come home <u>on</u> Saturday, Tony?*

Tony: *I'm sorry, Mum, but I can't come [1]___ the weekend this week or next week.*

Mum: *Well, are we going to see you [2]___ the holidays? Can you get away from London [3]___ the last week of December?*

Tony: *Well, I can get away [4]___ the 30th.*

Mum: *The 30th. That'll be a Thursday, won't it?*

Tony: *That's right. And I can stay for three days.*

Mum: *Good! So you'll be with us [5]___ New Year. It's good to be at home with your family [6]___ that time of the year.*

Tony: *Right. And we'll have a good time [7]___ New Year's Eve – just like the old days.*

Mum: *Wonderful! So what time can we expect you [8]___ Thursday? Will you be arriving late [9]___ night?*

Tony: *I'll probably leave London [10]___ lunchtime, so that means I'll get to you [11]___ about 6.00.*

Mum: *So you'll be with us [12]___ the evening. Dad and the children will be pleased.*

2 Complete the statements. Use *at*, *in* and *on*.

Example: *I'll be away <u>on</u> Thursday.*

1 *The meeting will start ___ 10.00.*

2 *I took a short holiday ___ January.*

3 *Columbus sailed across the Atlantic ___ 1492.*

4 *We flew to Malta late ___ Saturday.*

5 *Are you doing anything special ___ your birthday?*

6 *The telephone was invented ___ the nineteenth century.*

7 *I'll be in New York ___ this time next week.*

8 *We always go to France ___ the summer.*

9 *I won't be away for long. I'll be home ___ three days.*

10 *The President is arriving ___ midday.*

11 *Ann usually watches TV ___ the evening.*

12 *What are you doing ___ Wednesday evening?*

13 *We'll be at a party ___ New Year's Eve.*

14 *We'll be away for a week ___ New Year.*

15 *Hurry! We have to leave ___ an hour's time.*

16 *The climbers reached the top ___ the fifth day.*

17 *Tom left home ___ the age of 15.*

18 *We finished the job ___ less than a week.*

19 *I haven't got any money ___ the moment.*

3 Complete the conversation. Use *at*, *in* or *on* or nothing (✗).

● *Hello, Fred. I was trying to call you ✗ last weekend.*

○ *Did you call <u>on</u> Saturday?*

● *Yes, that's right. I phoned [1]___ Saturday morning and again [2]___ lunchtime.*

○ *I'm sorry, but I was out. I always go sailing [3]___ Saturdays.*

● *So I suppose that means you're going sailing again [4]___ Saturday [5]___ this weekend too.*

○ *I'm afraid so. What's the problem?*

● *Well, I'd like your help with a new computer that I bought [6]___ last week.*

○ *Sure. No problem. I can help you [7]___ Sunday night.*

● *Ah, but I'll be away all day until late. You see, I visit my parents [8]___ each Sunday.*

○ *I see. Well, what about [9]___ the evening? I'm free after I finish work [10]___ 5.30. In fact, I don't usually do much [11]___ the week these days, and I'm free [12]___ nearly every evening.*

● *Well, I have to go out [13]___ tonight, but could we get together [14]___ tomorrow evening?*

○ *Fine. I'm free [15]___ the evening tomorrow too. I'll come round to your place [16]___ 7.00.*

● *Thanks. That'll be really great!*

4 Complete the statements. Use these phrases.

at times, at a time, at one time, in time, on time

Example: *Don't be late. Make sure you're there <u>on time.</u>*

1 *The runners left in groups every two minutes. They left six _____*

2 *I enjoy life most of the time, but _____ I'd like to go back to the old days.*

3 We arrived just _____ The shop was just going to close.

4 There are factories everywhere here now, but _____ there were just green fields.

5 The trains always leave _____ They're never late.

5 Write the times in words. Use *past* and *to*.

Examples: *12.15 – a quarter past one*
10.41 – nineteen minutes to eleven

1 *3.10 –* _____

2 *7.50 –* _____

3 *9.30 –* _____

4 *2.45 –* _____

5 *5.15 –* _____

6 *1.13 –* _____

7 *11.31–* _____

8 *12.59 –* _____

6 Rewrite the diary notes as full statements. Use the present continuous.

You work for a busy company director. Remind him of his activities in the next two weeks.

Example: *On Monday the 26th you're travelling to New York at 8.30 in the morning.*

1 _____
   _____
   _____

2 _____
   _____
   _____
   _____

3 _____
   _____
   _____
   _____

4 _____
   _____
   _____
   _____

5 _____
   _____
   _____

6 _____
   _____

7 _____
   _____
   _____

8 _____
   _____
   _____

Diary

May

Mon, 26th May
8.30 a.m. – travel to NY

Wed, 28th May
3.45 p.m. – return to London

Fri, 30th May
all day – meet Japanese visitors from the Subarashi Corporation

Sat, 31st May
evening – speak at the goodbye party for the Managing Director

June

Mon, 2nd June
p.m. – attend the sales conference

Tues, 3rd June
am – talk at the sales conference

Thurs, 5th June
7.15 a.m. – fly to Rome

Fri, 6th June
11.45 a.m. – leave Rome for Madrid

Sat, 7th June
midday – travel back to London

I've lived here for 50 years. And I'll stay here till I die.

CROSSCHECK

for

We use *for* to say how long in any tense, in the past, present or future.
*It rained **for three hours**.*

We use *for* with the present perfect to say how long up the the present. *for* refers to the time between the start and now. (See also Unit 10.)

since

We use *since* to say how long mainly in the present perfect.
*He's lived here **since 1945**.*

We use *since* with the present perfect to say how long up to the present. *since* refers to the start. (See also Unit 10.)

ago

We use *ago* to say when something happened in the past. Count back from the present.
*Where's my book? It was here **a minute ago**!*

before

We use *before* to say when something happened in the past. Count back from another event in the past.
*I finished at 4.30, but the others had finished **two hours before**.*

during

Use *during* + noun, eg *the day*, or + noun phrase, eg *the early afternoon*.
*I'll call again **during the week**.*

while

Use *while* + verb, eg *I was training*, or + clause, eg *I was away on holiday*.
*I'll visit you **while I'm in town**.*

until/till

until/till refers to a period continuing to a point in time.
*I'll be busy **until 5.00**. (I have no free time between now and 5.00. Therefore I can't call before 5.00, but I will be able to call at 5.00.)*

by

by refers to a point in time.
*Please reply **by 5.00**. (Please call at or before 5.00. 5.00 is the latest possible time. Before 5.00 is better.)*

The Facts

Motorised road traffic is projected to at least DOUBLE on 1988 levels by the year 2025. There are more bicycles than cars in Britain, but most are little used because people won't ride them along the polluted, congested and frankly dangerous roads which characterise our towns and cities.

Exercises

1 Complete the story with *for* or *since*.

Oxford Lasers has not been in business <u>for</u> very long. In fact, the company has only existed <u>since</u> 1977. The five directors had done a lot of work on lasers at Oxford University ¹_____ several years before that. They continued to work at the University ²_____ some time after 1977 too, so their new company developed very slowly. In fact, ³_____ a while it seemed likely to close down. But ⁴_____ the introduction of new products in 1982, Oxford Lasers has grown fast. There were financial problems in the early 1990s ⁵_____ a year or two, but the company has remained a top laser producer ⁶_____ the mid-1980s. ⁷_____ a number of years it has been developing sales world-wide. It has also owned a company in the USA ⁸_____ 1985.

2 Complete the dialogues with *ago* or *before*.

Examples: ● *Tim bought a BMW two days <u>ago.</u>*
○ *He had an old Fiat <u>before,</u> didn't he?*

● *You went to Ibiza two years ¹_____ , didn't you?*
○ *That's right. We'd never been there ²_____*

● *How long ³_____ did you try to call her?*
○ *An hour ⁴_____ But she'd left ten minutes ⁵_____*

● *Lucy went away to college three years ⁶_____ , didn't she?*
○ *Yes, and it was a hard time because she hadn't been away from home very much ⁷_____*

3 Complete the statements with *during* or *while*.

Examples: *Jim Brown called <u>while</u> you were out.*
There will be a fire practice <u>during</u> the morning.

1 *What's Tom going to do _____ he's in America?*

2 *_____ the meeting, we'll discuss the sales report.*

3 *_____ you're cleaning the car, could you clean the ashtrays too?*

4 *Are you going to visit Australia _____ your trip round the world?*

5 *Somebody got into the house _____ the night.*

6 *They'd never seen anything like that _____ their whole lives!*

7 *I worked out my travel plans _____ I was waiting for the train.*

4 Complete the dialogues with *by* or *until/till*.

Examples: ● *Do you think you'll be able to finish the picture <u>by</u> tomorrow morning?*
○ *Yes, but I'll have to work <u>until</u> midnight to do it.*

● *Ann was already married ¹_____ the age of 19.*
○ *She lived at home ²_____ then, didn't she?*

● *I'm sorry, Sir. Your car won't be ready ³_____ early tomorrow afternoon.*
○ *So, if I come at 4.30, will it be ready ⁴_____ then?*
● *Oh, yes. No problem, Sir.*

○ *⁵_____ this time tomorrow, I'll be in Tokyo.*
● *How long are you going to stay there?*
○ *⁶_____ this time next week.*

● *I'm sure Tony has left the office ⁷_____ now.*
○ *I don't think so. He said he'd have to work ⁸_____ late this evening.*

5 Complete the story.

Arthur had worked in the same, large office <u>for</u> 30 years. 'I've worked here ¹_____ I was 19,' he often thought. 'And ²_____ all those years I haven't done anything very exciting.'

One day, ³_____ he was at a very boring meeting, he suddenly decided to change his life completely. He thought, 'I'll go on working ⁴_____ another six months – ⁵_____ my 50th birthday – and then I'll stop. I'll sell the house, buy a boat and go sailing.'

⁶_____ the middle of the following year he had done all these things. As he sailed among the Scottish islands on his first long trip, he thought, 'Why didn't I do this ⁷_____ ? I should have left that office ten years ⁸_____ !'

81 Preposition + noun, noun + preposition

by Shakespeare, for you, on TV, etc

Preposition + noun

Some expressions have the form preposition + noun.
These are some of the most common.

> *It's a picture **by Rembrandt**.*
> *I paid **by cheque/credit card**. (but in cash)*
> *They cut through the rock **by hand**.*

> *There's someone on the phone. It's **for you**.*
> *We're having fish **for dinner**.*
> *Let's go out **for a walk/swim/run/meal**.*
> *They've gone **for a short holiday**. (but go on holiday)*

> *I heard it **on the radio**. (but at the cinema/ theatre)*
> *He hurt her **on purpose**. (but by accident/ mistake/chance)*
> *The house is **on fire**.*
> *Sally is **on a diet**. She wants to lose six kilograms.*

> *The bus leaves at 12.00, so be there **on time**.*
> *We're going to stop for tea **on the way** there.*
> *Bill is going to Africa **on business/holiday/ safari**.*
> *They're going **on a trip/bus tour**.*

> *We're going **by car/bike/plane/train/ship/ road/air/rail/sea**, etc. (but on foot/in his car/on his bike/the bus/the plane/the train/ the ship)*

Here you are. It's a play by Shakespeare.

It's for you.

Thanks, Dad.

I've seen this on TV.

I'm going on a school trip to see it in London soon.

We're going by bus.

Romantic Flowers
by POST from GUERNSEY
for Birthdays and Anniversaries

And on this morning's Consumer Phone-In we hear from people who've had problems with faulty washing machines.

Noun + preposition

Some expressions have the form noun + preposition. These are some of the most common.

> *Tom's teacher sent the theatre a **request for** 60 tickets. (also application for/need for/reason for)*
> *He was very pleased as the theatre reduced the **price of** the tickets by 20%. (also cost of/hope of/way of)*
> *Unfortunately, there was a **problem with** the bus company. (also trouble with/matter with)*
> *There was a **rise in** the price of the bus. (also fall/increase/decrease in)*

Exercises

1 Complete the dialogues with *at, by, for, in* and *on*.

Example: ● Did you go by bus?
　　　　　　○ No, we went _in_ Steve's car.

1 ● Let's go to the beach _____ foot.
　○ No, let's go _by_ bike. It's quicker.

2 ● I saw you! You hit Sam _____ purpose!
　○ No, I didn't. I did it _____ accident!

3 ● Someone is _____ the phone. It's _____ Bob.
　○ He isn't here. He's gone out _____ a run.

4 ● I'm going to have some toast _____ breakfast.
　○ No, you aren't. It's _____ fire! Can't you smell it?

5 ● Are you here _____ holiday?
　○ No, I'm _____ a short business trip.

6 ● Can I pay _____ credit card?
　○ I'm sorry, Sir. We can only accept payment _____ cash or _____ cheque.

7 ● Is there anything good _____ TV tonight?
　○ No, and there's nothing interesting _____ the radio either.

8 ● What's the new play _____ the theatre this week?
　○ It's called 'Paris in the Spring'. It's _____ that new writer, Mark Ross.

2 Complete the statements with these words. Put a preposition before each one.

a diet, air, an artist, a school trip, a tour, a walk, dinner, his bike, my car, plane, the cinema

Example: I'm hungry. Let's stop at that restaurant _for dinner._

1 My cousins from Australia are visiting Britain. They're _____ of the country.

2 Their car is full. You'd better go _____

3 Tony's class is going _____ to Italy.

4 Tony and his friends are travelling to Italy _____

5 Can you see Rob? He's over there. He's _____

6 It's a nice day. Let's go _____ along the river.

7 They're showing a new film _____ in George Street.

8 If you want to get this package to America fast, send it _____

9 We aren't eating very much at the moment. We're _____

10 It's a wonderful picture. It's _____ who lived about 600 years ago.

3 Complete the statements with these words. Put a preposition after each one.

applications, call, difficulties, fall, hope, increase, interested, matter, need, problem, way

Example: We've had a lot of _applications for_ the job of Chief Engineer.

1 What's the _____ you? You always seem angry about something.

2 Could you please keep quiet? There's no _____ all this noise.

3 We'd better stop here for tonight. There's no _____ reaching the village before dark.

4 Prices have gone up a little this year. There's been a small _____ the cost of living.

5 Scientists have found a new _____ producing electricity cheaply.

6 There's a _____ your plan. I'm afraid it won't work.

7 The rescue team has had a _____ help. They're on their way to the accident now.

8 There has been a _____ the size of families. They're smaller nowadays.

9 I'm very _____ photography.

10 Peter had _____ his homework.

82 Adjective + preposition
He's good at Maths.

Some adjectives often take one or more prepositions. These are some of the most common.

1 *Sam is a junior accountant. He's **excited about** his first business trip next month.*

2 *He's **worried/anxious about** his accountancy exams next week.*

*He got **angry/annoyed about** a noisy party next door last night.*

*His neighbour was **sorry about** the noise.*

*He got **angry/annoyed with** his neighbour last night.*

*He sometimes gets **bored/fed up with** his work.*

*He's **afraid/nervous of** failing his exams next week.*

*His family will be **proud of** him if he passes.*

*He's **tired of** studying late every night.*

*He's not **used/accustomed to** so much hard work.*

*Luckily, he's very **interested in** what he's doing.*

3 *Sam was **amazed/surprised/shocked at/by** the number of books he had to read for the exams.*

*His boss is **pleased/happy with/about** Sam's work now.*

*He was **disappointed with/about** Sam's work at first.*

*Sam is very **careful/careless with/about** his work.*

*Sam is **responsible for** the weekly sales figures.*

*The figures are nearly **ready for** printing.*

*He's **late/early for** a meeting.*

*Sam's family feel **sorry for** him when he works late.*

*His mother thinks the work is **bad for** his eyes.*

*His father knows the work is **good for** his future.*

4 *He's **good/brilliant at** figures and Maths.*

*He's **bad/terrible/hopeless at** languages.*

*He sometimes thinks life is very **similar to** school again.*

*He sometimes thinks life is no **different from/to** school.*

Exercises

1 Complete the statements with *about, at, for, of* and *with*.

Example: *I feel very sorry _for_ Ann. The poor girl has been ill for so long.*

1 *Are you ready _____ a big surprise?*

2 *Tim is quite good _____ sport.*

3 *I'm very angry _____ Sam. He never answers my letters.*

4 *We really thought our team would win, so we were disappointed _____ the bad result.*

5 *I wish they'd be more careful _____ their work.*

6 *You must stop working day and night. It's very bad _____ you.*

7 *I'm fed up _____ eating at home all the time. Let's go out.*

8 *Tony and Lisa were so annoyed _____ the people next door that they called the police.*

2 Complete the statements with these words. Put a preposition after each one.

different, early, good, late, proud, responsible, shocked, terrible, worried

Example: ● *I was _shocked at_ the bad sales figures.*
○ *Me too. I'd expected much better sales.*

1 ● *I can't understand this Maths problem.*
○ *But it's easy! You must be really _____ Maths*

2 ● *People in Manchester are very _____ their football team.*
○ *Yes, especially as they've won the championship again.*

3 ● *The men have done the job again, but it still looks bad.*
○ *I agree. It's no _____ last time.*

4 ● *It isn't _____ small children to stay up late at night.*
○ *That's right. It means they're very tired the next day.*

5 ● *Calm down! Why are you running around like that?*
○ *Because I'm _____ a very important meeting.*

6 ● *Have you heard? Joe's a senior manager now.*
○ *Yes, I hear he's _____ the whole factory now.*

7 ● *I hope you got to the interview on time.*
○ *Yes, I did. In fact, I was twenty minutes _____ it.*

8 ● *Have Robin and Steve reached Australia in their little boat yet?*
○ *No. They're two weeks late, and we're very _____ them.*

3 Write a statement using the underlined words and the words in brackets.

Example: *Ann reads a lot about sailing. (interested)*
She's _interested in sailing._

1 *Bob is going to give away his old computer games. (tired)*
He's _____

2 *Working at night was strange at first, but it's all right now. (used)*
I'm _____

3 *Mrs Elfin shouted at her children. (angry)*
She was _____

4 *Peter isn't sure if his first business trip will go well. (anxious)*
He's _____

5 *The airline staff felt bad because of the long delay at the airport. (sorry)*
They were _____

6 *Bill decided to turn the radio programme off. (bored)*
He was _____

7 *Old Mrs Price doesn't like going out alone. (nervous)*
She's _____

8 *It was a fantastic surprise to see the huge number of people at the concert. (amazed)*
We were _____

She applied for several jobs.   He stole $600 from her.

Verb + preposition

Some verbs often take one or more prepositions.
These are some of the most common.

1   Claire **looked for** a job before she left college.
She **asked for** details of lots of jobs.
She **applied for** several jobs.
She **applied to** several companies.
She **waited** hopefully **for** the replies, but they
were all negative.

She **heard about** a good job in New York.
She **talked about** it with her friend.
She **asked about** the company at the US Embassy.
She **thought about** the job a lot.

In the end, she **wrote to** the company in
New York.
They **replied to** her letter immediately.
2   They **talked to** her on the phone.

look + different prepositions has different meanings.
   Look at this photo. It's beautiful.
   I'm **looking for** my glasses. Can you see them?
   Could you **look after** the baby for a few minutes?

think and *dream* + different prepositions have different meanings.

Claire **thought about** the job carefully.	I've just **thought of** a great idea!
When I **dream about** the crash, I always wake up.	Harry **dreams of** becoming rich one day.

Verb + object + preposition

Some verbs often take an object and then a preposition.
These are some of the most common.

   The company **invited her to** an interview.
   They **provided her with** air tickets.
3   When she got to New York, she **asked somebody
   for** directions to the company.

At the interview, she **asked them about** the job.
They **told her about** the pay and conditions.
She accepted the job, and they **congratulated her
on** her decision.

4   She also **had a bad experience in** New York. A thief
robbed her of her money. He **stole $600 from** her.
Fortunately, she had **insured herself against** theft.
She **blamed herself for** the theft because she had
left her purse on a restaurant table.
She **described the purse to** the police, but they
never found it.

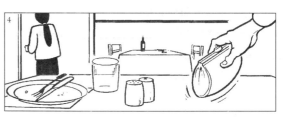

Exercises

1 Complete the statements with *about, for,* and *to.*

Example: *A boy came to the door and asked __for__ a glass of water.*

1 *Danny dreams _____ being famous one day.*

2 *I'll wait _____ you outside the cinema.*

3 *Ann is on the phone. Could you talk _____ her, please?*

4 *They're very bad. They take ages to reply _____ letters.*

5 *The family talked _____ their plans every night.*

2 Complete the dialogues with the correct forms of the verbs and prepositions.

Example: ● *There's Mark Blake. He's famous!*
　　　　　○ *Mark Blake? I've never __heard of__ him!*
　　　　　(hear)

1 ● *Hello, I'm Terry Grant.*
　○ *Hello. I've often _____ you. It's nice to meet you at last. (hear)*

2 ● *I hear you're looking for a new job.*
　○ *That's right. I've _____ several companies. (apply)*

3 ● *What sort of job are you _____ (apply)*
　○ *I'm trying to get a job in sales.*

4 ● *Have you found an answer to the problem yet?*
　○ *No. I've been _____ it for ages, but I haven't got any ideas. (think)*

5 ● *Can you see what to do about the problem?*
　○ *Well, yes, I've suddenly _____ a new idea! (think)*

6 ● *Who waters the plants when you're away?*
　○ *My neighbours _____ them. (look)*

7 ● *What sort of bike would you like?*
　○ *One like this! Come and _____ it. (look)*

8 ● *Oh, no! I've lost my wallet.*
　○ *Don't worry. I'll help you _____ it. (look)*

3 Complete the statements with these verbs. Add prepositions.

ask, congratulate, insure, provide, tell

Example: *Companies need to __insure__ themselves __against__ injuries to their staff.*

1 *The old man _____ us _____ some money, so we gave him £1.*

2 *Mrs Brett, we'd all like to _____ you _____ reaching the fantastic age of 100.*

3 *We _____ all visitors to the company _____ identity cards.*

4 *There's a reporter here. He wants to _____ you some questions _____ your plans for a new factory.*

5 *The reporter said, 'Could you please _____ me _____ your ideas for a new factory in town?'*

4 Complete the statements. Write the words in order and put the verbs in the correct forms. Add prepositions.

Example: *Yesterday a thief __stole my wallet from my pocket.__ (my/my/steal/pocket/wallet)*

1 *Tim couldn't understand, so he _____*
　_____
　(the/help/ask/teacher)

2 *We phoned the doctor, and we _____*
　_____
　(him/the/tell/accident)

3 *It wasn't Tony's fault, but they still _____*
　_____
　(him/the/crash/blame)

4 *The police are coming soon, so you can _____*
　_____
　(them/man/describe/the)

5 *It's my birthday next week, and I'm _____*
　_____
　(my/my/invite/all/party/friends)

84 Phrasal verbs

come in, sit down, give out, pick up, turn over, etc

You can turn over your papers and begin.

A phrasal verb is a verb + adverb. Some phrasal verbs do not have an object, but most do.

Subject	Verb + adverb	Subject	Verb + adverb	Object
The boys	**came in**.	*The teacher*	**gave out**	*the exam papers.*
They	**sat down**.	*The boys*	**picked up**	*their pens.*

An object can usually go before or after the adverb in a phrasal verb. Compare the following.

   *The boys **put down their pens**.*   *The boys **put their pens down**.*

But when the object is a pronoun, it must go before the adverb.

   *The boys put **them** down.* (their pens)
   *He put **them** away in his bag.* (the exam papers)

In a phrasal verb, the adverb completes the meaning of the verb. Some phrasal verbs are easy to understand and learn. They mean exactly what you expect, eg *pick up/put down, give out/take in* and *sit down/stand up*.

Others are not so easy to understand. Their meaning is not clear from the verb and the adverb together. Compare the following. The first example is clear, but the second is not.

   *They **turned over** the papers.*
   *Another boy **turned up**.* (arrived)

We use phrasal verbs a lot, so you have to learn them as you meet them. Write down the meanings when they are not clear. Here are some more examples.

   *The car **broke down**.* (stopped working)
   He was too tired to do any more and
   *he **gave up**.* (stopped trying to do something)
   *The man **made off** with my bike.* (ran away)
   *The weather is **picking up**.* (getting better)

CLEAN IT UP · CLEAN IT UP · CLEAN IT UP · CLEAN IT UP ·

Exercises

1 Complete the statements with these phrasal verbs.

come in, give out, pick up, put away, sit down, turn over, turn up

Example: *I can't find my book now, but I know it'll* <u>*turn up*</u> *later.*

1 *Could you _____ all the rubbish on the floor, please? It looks very untidy.*

2 *I'm going to _____ sets of working clothes to all the new trainees.*

3 *Please _____ on the chairs over there.*

4 *We always have to _____ our papers when we finish work and leave our desks clean.*

5 *_____ the paper and start the exam, please.*

6 *Don't wait outside the door. Please _____*

2 Complete the statements with these phrasal verbs without objects.

Moving
come in, come back, go away, go out, move on, turn round
Resting
get up, lie down, wake up

Example: *Please* <u>*come in.*</u> *The door is open.*

1 *I'm tired. I'm going to _____ and rest.*

2 *If you _____ and live somewhere else, we may we may not see you again.*

3 *Let's _____ and get some fresh air for an hour.*

4 *This place is horrible. Let's _____ and stay in the next town.*

5 *You can go home now, but please _____ to the office by 2.00.*

6 *I don't _____ immediately in the morning. I lie in bed and plan my day.*

7 *That coat looks good on you, but does it look all right from the back? _____ slowly and let me see.*

8 *Pat was so tired that she couldn't _____ She didn't open her eyes for ten minutes.*

3 Complete the statements with these phrasal verbs without objects.

pay in/take out (eg money at the bank)
put on/take off (eg clothes)
put up/bring down (eg shop prices)
switch on/switch off (eg lights)
turn up/turn down (eg radio volume)

Example: *It's getting dark. I'll* <u>*switch on*</u> *the lights.*

1 *Could you _____ £50 for me? I need some money for the weekend.*

2 *Look. They've _____ the price of these computers. They're only $950 now.*

3 *Could you _____ the TV, please? It's too loud.*

4 *Tom _____ his dirty boots before he went into the house.*

5 *It was raining, so I _____ a coat when I went out.*

6 *Oh, no! The Government is_____ the price of petrol again!*

4 Complete the statements. Change the noun objects into pronoun objects.

Example: *Bob told me to give out the clothes, so I* <u>*gave them out.*</u>

1 *Ann wanted Tom to pick up the rubbish, so she* _____

2 *Dad asked us to switch off the TV, so we* _____

3 *My boss told me to put away my papers, so I* _____

4 *Sue asked the men to put down the cases, so they* _____

5 *Steve wanted his brother to turn up the stereo, so he* _____

6 *Mum told Tina to turn over the chicken legs, so she* _____

7 *The boss asked us to pay in the money at the bank, so we* _____

FUN RIDE TURNS TO DANGER

An enjoyable day out at Britain's biggest fun park, Alton Towers, turned to danger yesterday. It happened when high winds hit the Skyride cable-cars and stopped them in mid-air.

Specially trained firemen safely brought 59 people down from several cable-cars 30 metres above the ground. They successfully used their climbing techniques and equipment to climb along the cables and enter the cars.

Although some passengers needed first-aid when they reached the ground, nobody had to go to hospital.

FORMS

There are eight different word classes in English. They are:

Verb:	*hit, stop, use, climb*
Adverb:	*yesterday, successfully, down, safely*
Noun:	*day, Alton Towers, danger*
Adjective:	*enjoyable, high, special*
Pronoun:	*they, them, nobody*
Determiner:	*a/an, the, their, some*
Preposition:	*at, from, above, along*
Linking word:	*and, although, when*

We often use one word in different ways. It may be just a different word class with a similar meaning.

> *Did they **climb**?* (verb)
> *It's a long **climb**.* (noun)
> *Some needed **first aid**.* (part of a noun)
> *We climbed along **first**.* (adverb)

Or a word may have different meanings.

> ***High** winds hit the cable-cars.* (adjective = strong)
> *The tower is 30 metres **high**.* (adjective = off the ground)
> *The price of tickets is too **high**.* (adjective = expensive)

CROSSCHECK

There are different kinds of determiners and pronouns.

Determiners

Articles: *a/an, the*

Quantifiers: *some, a lot of, no* (+ noun)
Demonstratives: *this, those* (+ noun)
Possessives: *my, your* (+ noun)

Use a determiner before a noun.

> ***The** car was in the street.*
> *They brought down **all** the people.*
> *I took **that** photo.*
>
> *Is it **my** newspaper or **your** newspaper?*

Pronouns

Personal: *I, he, she* (subject)
          me, him, her (object)
Quantifiers: *some, a lot, nobody* (+ verb)
Demonstratives: *this, those* (+ verb)
Possessives: *mine, yours* (+ verb)

Use a pronoun instead of a determiner + noun.

> ***It** was in the street.*
> ***Nobody** had to go to hospital.*
> ***That** is one of the cable-car passengers.*
>
> *Is it **mine** or **yours**?*

Exercises

1 Label the words in *italics* with these word classes.

Adjective, Adverb, Determiner, Linking word, Noun, Preposition, Pronoun, Verb

<u>*Noun*</u>   An ordinary English *family*

[1]*We* are an ordinary [2]*English* family – a mother, [3]*father* and [4]*two* children – [5]*and* we [6]*live* very [7]*ordinarily* in a small town [8]*near* London.

1 _____   5 _____
2 _____   6 _____
3 _____   7 _____
4 _____   8 _____

2 Complete the paragraph. Use the correct forms of these nouns.

bathroom, bedroom, dining-room, dish, flower, food, garden, house, kitchen, living-room, shop, television, time, vegetable, visitor

An ordinary English home

Upstairs in our <u>house</u> *there are three* [1]_____ *and a* [2]_____ *Downstairs there is a* [3]_____ *, where we sometimes watch* [4]_____ *Then there is a* [5]_____ *, but we only eat there when we have* [6]_____ *When there are only four of us, we usually eat in the* [7]_____ *It's easier to serve* [8]_____ *there and clear away the dirty* [9]_____ *Outside, there is a large* [10]_____ *We spend a lot of* [11]_____ *out there, so we keep it looking nice with lots of* [12]_____ *We also grow our own* [13]_____ *They taste better than the ones from the* [14]_____ *!*

3 Complete the paragraph. Use the correct forms of these verbs in the present simple.

be, cook, drive, drop, get, have, have to, leave, make, take, work

Ordinary weekday mornings

In the morning, I always <u>make</u> *tea for everybody. Then Rosie* [1]_____ *breakfast while Peter and Lisa*

[2]_____ *ready for school. We all* [3]_____ *the house at 8.00. Rosie* [4]_____ *always the driver. First she* [5]_____ *me at the station because I* [6]_____ *in London and I* [7]_____ *catch the 8.20 train. Next she* [8]_____ *the children to school. Then she* [9]_____ *back into town, where she* [10]_____ *a job at a bank.*

4 Complete the conversation with adjectives or adverbs.

Another ordinary morning

Peter: *I* <u>really</u> *don't want to go to school* <u>today.</u> *I'm* <u>ill</u> *! (ill, really, today)*

Lisa: *You're* [1]_____ *saying that because you've got a* [2]_____ *exam and you know you're going to do* [3]_____ *! (badly, big, only)*

Mum: *I think Lisa is* [4]_____ *You look* [5]_____ *, Peter. So finish your breakfast as* [6]_____ *as you can, and let's go. It's* [7]_____ *8.00. (fast, fine, nearly, right)*

Dad: *Yes, come on, everybody. Let's go* [8]_____ *or I'll be* [9]_____ *for the train, and I* [10]_____ *mustn't miss it this morning. (certainly, late, quickly)*

5 Complete the story with pronouns, determiners or prepositions.

Finally … a very unusual day

Last weekend <u>we</u> *took Peter and Lisa* <u>to</u> *Alton Towers.* [1]_____ *was* [2]_____ *nice day, but rather windy. (a, it, to, we)*

When [3]_____ *arrived,* [4]_____ *decided to take* [5]_____ *cable-car. Soon after* [6]_____ *started,* [7]_____ *wind got worse. Then* [8]_____ [9]_____ *cable-car system stopped and* [10]_____ *cars stopped moving. (a, it, the, the, the, we, we, whole)*

[11]_____ *was over* [12]_____ *deep valley.* [13]_____ *people* [14]_____ *our car waited calmly, but* [15]_____ *child kept crying. (a, in, most, one, ours)*

[16]_____ *hour later,* [17]_____ *group* [18]_____ *rescuers climbed* [19]_____ [20]_____ *cable to help* [21]_____ *.* [22]_____ *helped* [23]_____ *climb down* [24]_____ [25]_____ *ground. (a, along, an, of, the, the, they, to, us, us)*

199

Sentence types

A statement gives information. A question requests information or action. An order requires action. An exclamation expresses an emotion. (See Units 23/24 for more on question forms. See Unit 1 for more on orders.)

In writing, a sentence starts with a capital letter, eg *You, How, Slow, Help*. It ends with a full stop (.), a question mark (?) or an exclamation mark (!).

Sentence structure

Most sentences contain different parts. These parts can include a subject, verb, object, complement and adverbial. A subject is the focus of the sentence. A verb shows an action or a state, eg *brings* and *is*. An object is the thing or person affected by the verb. A complement gives more information about the subject. An adverbial gives more information about the verb. Look at the following statements. The simplest statement contains only two parts. The longer statements contain four. (But a statement or other type of sentence can contain many more parts than this.)

1	**Subject**	**Verb**		**2**	**Subject**	**Verb**	**Complement**
	Tom	*is driving.*			*Tom*	*is*	*the driver.*
3	**Subject**	**Verb**	**Object**	**4**	**Subject**	**Verb**	**Adverbial**
	Tom	*is driving*	*his new car.*		*Tom*	*is driving*	*dangerously.*
5	**Subject**	**Verb**	**Object**	**Adverbial**			
	Tom	*is driving*	*his new car*	*dangerously.*			

All of these statements have a subject and a verb. They are the most important parts. In statements the subject goes before the verb. (See Unit 23 for word order in questions.) If there is an object or a complement, this goes after the verb.

In statements 4 and 5 the adverb comes at the end of the sentence, but it can also come in other places. (See Unit 71.)

> *Unfortunately, he's probably going to stop us **at the side of the road now.***

Exercises

1 Label the sentences with the following.

Exclamation, Order, Question, Statement

Example: *Are you all right?* <u>*Question*</u>

1 *How much money have you got?* _____
2 *Take these letters to the post office.*

   _____

3 *Fantastic!* _____
4 *John's birthday is next week.* _____
5 *We all understand what we've got to do, don't we?*

   _____

6 *I don't like this sort of music.* _____
7 *Absolutely amazing!* _____
8 *Don't spend any more time on this job.*

   _____

2 Label the sentence parts with the following.

Adverb (A), Adverb phrase (AP), Complement (C),
Object (O), Subject (S), Verb (V)

Example:
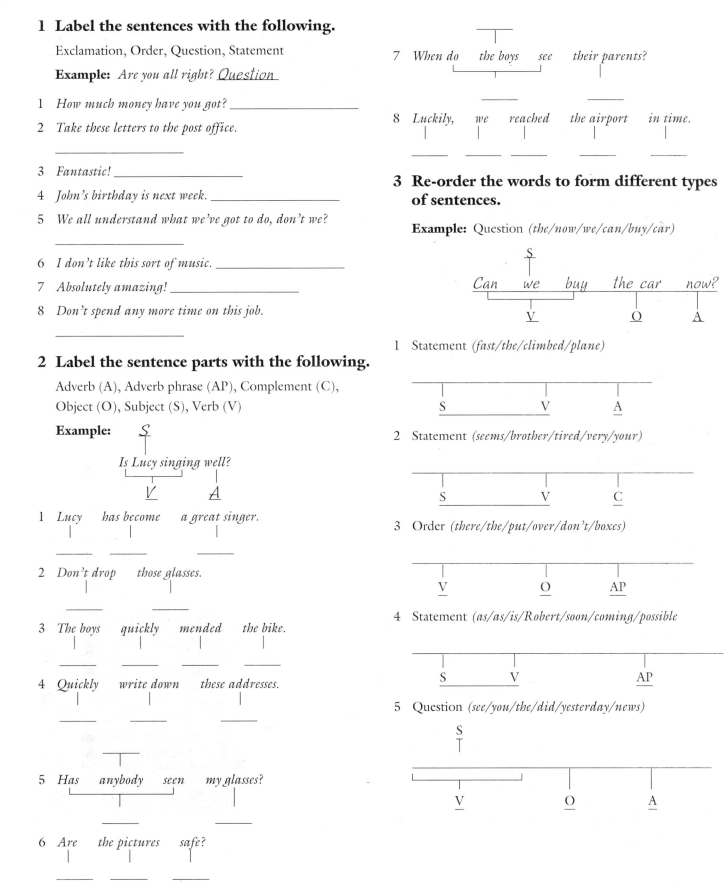

7 *When do   the boys   see   their parents?*

8 *Luckily,   we   reached   the airport   in time.*

3 Re-order the words to form different types of sentences.

Example: Question *(the/now/we/can/buy/car)*

   Can   we   buy   the car   now?
     V   O   A

1 Statement *(fast/the/climbed/plane)*
     S   V   A

2 Statement *(seems/brother/tired/very/your)*
     S   V   C

3 Order *(there/the/put/over/don't/boxes)*
     V   O   AP

4 Statement *(as/as/is/Robert/soon/coming/possible*
     S   V   AP

5 Question *(see/you/the/did/yesterday/news)*
     S
     V   O   A

201

87 Connecting clauses

and, but, or, so, because, if, when, even though, who, to, for

FORMS

Two main clauses

Ann has got a case, and Jan has got a bag.
They can take a bus, or they can take a taxi. They have to choose.
The taxi is faster, but it is more expensive.
They are late, so they will take a taxi.

Main clause + sub-clause

They need the taxi because they are late.
If they arrive late, they will miss their plane.

Two main clauses

A main clause has a verb and can be a complete sentence.

Ann went by bus.   Jan went by taxi.

The words *and*, *but*, *or* and *so* connect two main clauses. *and* adds one thing to another. *but* sets one thing against another. *or* expresses one possibility instead of another. *so* introduces a result.

Main clause		Main clause
Ann went by bus,	**and**	*Jan went by taxi.*
The taxi was faster,	**but**	*it was more expensive.*
You can take a bus,	**or**	*you can take a taxi.*
There are no buses,	**so**	*we'll have to take a taxi.*

In writing, we usually put a comma (,) between two main clauses, especially long clauses. Compare *and* and *or* in these negative sentences.

*They **didn't take** a taxi, **and** they **didn't take** a bus.*
*They **didn't take** a taxi **or** a bus.*

Main clause + sub-clause

We often put a sub-clause with a main clause. A sub-clause has a verb like a main clause. But it is not a complete idea. It adds to a main clause.

Main clause	Sub-clause
They need a taxi	***because they're late.***

We can use a sub-clause by itself in a short answer to a question.

● *Why are they late?* ○ ***Because Jan's watch was wrong.***

Here are some other types of sub-clauses. Most sub-clauses can go before the main clause (but not relative clauses). When we put the sub-clause first, we usually put a comma (,) between the two clauses.

***If you ask Alex**, he'll go to the party.* (conditional)
*Someone came to the door **when I was working in the garden**.* (similar to *while* and *as*)
***Even though Tom's leg hurt**, he managed to run.* (similar to *although* and *though*)
*Bill jumped into the river **to save the child**.* (similar to *in order to* and *so as to*)
*She's the girl **who won the prize**.* (similar to *that* and *which*)

Note that *because* introduces a reason and *so* introduces a result.

***Because they're late**, they need a taxi.*
*They're late, **so they need a taxi**.*

WELCOME TO THE NEW SEASON'S CATALOGUE

It will soon be spring and to celebrate we've put together a marvellous new collection of home storage items.

You don't have to be
crazy
to work here,
but it helps!

Because we are certain you'll just love this special new taste, we'll give you your money back if you don't (see side of packet for details).

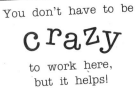

And my next guest is the woman who used to sit in my chair on this programme.

'If everybody minded their own business,' said the Duchess in a hoarse growl, 'the world would go round a deal faster than it does.'

(Alice's Adventures in Wonderland, Lewis Carroll, 1832 – 1898)

20th, 22nd, 24th April
FIDELIO by Beethoven

Although 'Fidelio' is the only opera Beethoven ever wrote, it remains the ultimate expression of his genius.

URGENT: Motor Insurance Expiry Warning

Dear Mrs Oliver

Motor Policy No: 22042904/8207
Renewal Date: 01/01/00

I wrote to you recently with details of your motor insurance premium for the coming year. So far I have not received your instructions to renew, so this is a reminder that your cover expires at noon on the renewal date.

Exercises

1 Connect the clauses with *and*, *but*, *or* or *so*.

Example: *You can buy <u>or</u> rent the apartment.*

1 *I'm tired _____ I'm hungry too.*

2 *The train was late, _____ we couldn't get to the meeting on time.*

3 *The Prince was rich, _____ he wasn't happy.*

4 *You can take the money now, _____ you can take it later.*

2 Connect clauses 1–4 and a–d with *and*, *but*, *or* or *so*.

Example: *We usually eat at 8.00,*
<u>*but we're eating at 7.30 tonight.*</u>

a *he can go at 4.00.*

b *he seems very tired at the moment.*

c *he's got to come by taxi instead.*

d *he owns a house in Scotland.*

1 *Ben has an apartment in London, _____*
_____

2 *Tom's car is at the garage for repairs, _____*
_____

3 *Sam can see the film at 1.45, _____*
_____

4 *John is usually very energetic, _____*
_____

3 Rewrite the *so* statements using *because/as*.

Example: *It was dark, so we couldn't see much.*
<u>*We couldn't see much because/as it*</u>
<u>*was dark.*</u>

1 *I was very tired, so I went to bed.*
_____

2 *My car is old, so I'm getting a new one.*
_____
_____

3 *I have to go out now, so I'll call you later.*
_____
_____

4 Rewrite the *but* statements using *even though/although*.

Example: *The engine is new, but it's already going wrong.*
<u>*The engine is already going wrong*</u>
<u>*even though/though it's new.*</u>

1 *Sally is young, but she does her job well.*
_____
_____

2 *The film is old, but it's still very popular.*
_____
_____

3 *Their new house was expensive, but it looks terrible.*
_____
_____

5 Connect the clauses with *because, if, when, even though* or *who* in the correct position.

Examples: *_____ Mary would lend you £100 <u>if</u> you asked her.*
<u>*When*</u> *I got home, _____ everybody was eating.*

1 *_____ I'd known about Ann's illness _____ I wouldn't have bothered her.*

2 *_____ Mr Hardy is the man _____ bought my company.*

3 *_____ I phoned home _____ I got to the office.*

4 *_____ Harry worked all day _____ he still couldn't finish the job.*

5 *_____ Annie ran home _____ she was afraid of the dark.*

6 *_____ Tony gets this note, _____ I'll already be in Canada.*

7 *_____ Dr Ross still works very hard _____ he's nearly 70.*

8 *_____ Tony has looked after our old car so well, _____ I think we should give it to him as a present.*

88 Connecting sentences

and, but, or, so   In addition, However, Alternatively, As a result

Sentence connectors instead of *and, but, or* and *so*

We use *and, but, or* and *so* to link parts of sentences. (See also Unit 87.)

> The day was warm **and** sunny.
> Harry found some bread, **but** no butter.

We also often want to connect the ideas in two separate sentences. In spoken English, we often use *and, but, or* and *so*.

> He's very good at football. **And** he's a great runner too.

In formal and written English, we usually avoid *and, but, or* and *so* at the start of a sentence. Instead, we can use connectors like these. (Note that we put a comma (,) after these sentence connectors.)

> ***In addition/Furthermore***, we note your required ... (instead of *and*)
> ***However***, we cannot meet that schedule. (instead of *but*)
> ***Alternatively/Instead***, we can offer you the ... (instead of *or*)
> ***As a result/consequence***, we are now out of stock. (instead of *so*)

Sentence connectors with pronouns

Subject pronouns often refer to things outside their own sentence.

> The children are tired. **They**'d better go to bed.

We often use demonstrative pronouns in the same way.

> ● *Let's have a rest.*   ○ ***That***'s a good idea.

Many sentence connectors include demonstrative pronouns or nouns. Some sentence connectors can be with or without demonstrative pronouns or nouns.

> ***In addition to*** *this/your colour requirement, we note your ...*
> ***As a result of*** *this/the heavy demand, we are now out of stock.*
> ***Instead of*** *that/the K52, they will take the K53.*

Some sentence connectors must include a pronoun or noun.

> ***Because of this***, *we are now of out stock.*
> ***Due to the heavy demand***, *we are now out of stock.*
> ***Despite this***, *we can promise delivery by ...*
> ***In spite of that***, *we can promise delivery by ...*
> ***Except for the K52***, *we have stock of all models.*
> ***Apart from that***, *we have stock of all models.*

Exercises

1 Change the informal spoken statements to formal statements from a business report. Use full verb forms and change *and*, *but*, *or* or *so* to the following.

Alternatively, As a result, However, In addition

Example: *We're unable to meet the schedule, so we won't get the contract.*
<u>We are</u> *unable to meet the schedule.*
<u>As a result, we will not get</u> *the contract.*

1 *It's possible to up-date our present model, or it's possibly the right time for a completely new model.*
_____ *possible to up-date our present model.*
_____ *possibly the right time for a completely new model.*

2 *We've reached this year's production target already, and we've managed to cut waste by 8%.*
_____ *this year's production target already. _____*
_____ *to cut waste by 8%.*

3 *We're cutting most costs successfully, but we're failing to hold down the cost of wages.*
_____ *most costs successfully.*
_____ *to hold down the cost of wages.*

4 *We haven't tried selling to America up till now, so we don't yet know if it'll be a good market for us.*
_____ *selling to America up till now. _____*
_____ *if _____ a good market for us.*

2 Write nothing (✗) or one of these words to complete the connectors.

for, from, of, to

1 *Apart <u>from</u> this*   5 *Except _____ this*
2 *As a result _____ this*   6 *In addition _____ this*
3 *Despite _____ this*   7 *In spite _____ this*
4 *Due _____ this*   8 *Instead _____ this*

3 Choose the right connecting statements from a–g to complete the teacher's reports 1–6.

Example: *Susan has not worked hard this year. Despite this, <u>she has done enough to pass the year.</u>*

a *she has behaved badly in class all year.*
b *she could go on to do extra Science.*
c *she has achieved a Grade A.*
d *she has found it difficult to improve.*
e *she has done enough to pass the year.*
f *she has often failed to complete her homework.*
g *she must learn to do some hard work.*

1 *Sally is very intelligent and has worked extremely well. As a result, _____*
_____
_____

2 *Lisa has worked very well in class. However, _____*
_____
_____
_____

3 *Tessa has failed to produce any good work. In addition,*
_____
_____
_____

4 *Lucy is clever, but she seems to spend her time thinking about pop music. Instead, _____*
_____
_____

5 *Kate has tried hard this year. In spite of this, _____*
_____
_____

6 *Denise is very talented at both Maths and Science. She may decide to take Higher Maths. Alternatively, _____*
_____
_____

Appendix 1 Irregular verbs

These common irregular verbs have the following forms.

A Verbs with no change

Infinitive	Past tense	Past participle
cost	*cost*	*cost*
cut	*cut*	*cut*
hit	*hit*	*hit*
hurt	*hurt*	*hurt*
let	*let*	*let*
put	*put*	*put*
set	*set*	*set*
shut	*shut*	*shut*
spread	*spread*	*spread*

B Verbs with one change

Infinitive	Past tense	Past participle
beat	*beat*	*beaten*
bring	*brought*	*brought*
build	*built*	*built*
burn	*burnt/burned*	*burnt/burned*
buy	*bought*	*bought*
catch	*caught*	*caught*
deal	*dealt*	*dealt*
dream	*dreamt/dreamed*	*dreamt/dreamed*
feel	*felt*	*felt*
fight	*fought*	*fought*
find	*found*	*found*
get	*got*	*got*
have * (see below)	*had*	*had*
hear	*heard*	*heard*
hold	*held*	*held*
keep	*kept*	*kept*
lay	*laid*	*laid*
lead	*led*	*led*
learn	*learnt/learned*	*learnt/learned*
leave	*left*	*left*
lend	*lent*	*lent*
lose	*lost*	*lost*
make	*made*	*made*
mean	*meant*	*meant*
meet	*met*	*met*
pay	*paid*	*paid*

*Note that the 3rd person singular of *have* in the present simple is *he/she/it has.*

read (sounds like *need*)	*read* (sounds like r*e*d)	*read* (sounds like r*e*d)
say	*said*	*said*
sell	*sold*	*sold*
send	*sent*	*sent*
sit	*sat*	*sat*
shoot	*shot*	*shot*
sleep	*slept*	*slept*
slide	*slid*	*slid*
smell	*smelt/smelled*	*smelt/smelled*
spell	*spelt/spelled*	*spelt/spelled*
spend	*spent*	*spent*
stand	*stood*	*stood*
swing	*swung*	*swung*
teach	*taught*	*taught*
tell	*told*	*told*
think	*thought*	*thought*
understand	*understood*	*understood*
win	*won*	*won*

C Verbs with two changes

Infinitive	**Past tense**	**Past participle**
*be** (see below)	*was/were*	*been*
become	*became*	*become*
begin	*began*	*begun*
bite	*bit*	*bitten*
blow	*blew*	*blown*
break	*broke*	*broken*
choose	*chose*	*chosen*
come	*came*	*come*
*do** (see below)	*did*	*done*
draw	*drew*	*drawn*
drink	*drank*	*drunk*
drive	*drove*	*driven*
eat	*ate*	*eaten*
fall	*fell*	*fallen*
fly	*flew*	*flown*
forget	*forgot*	*forgotten*
give	*gave*	*given*
go	*went*	*gone*
grow	*grew*	*grown*
hide	*hid*	*hidden*

*Note that *be* in the present simple is *I am*, *he/she/it is* and *you/we/they are*.
*Note that the 3rd person singular of *do* in the present simple is *he/she/it does*.

know	*knew*	*known*
lie	*lay*	*lain*
ride	*rode*	*ridden*
ring	*rang*	*rung*
rise	*rose*	*risen*
run	*ran*	*run*
see	*saw*	*seen*
shake	*shook*	*shaken*
show	*showed*	*shown*
sing	*sang*	*sung*
sink	*sank*	*sunk*
speak	*spoke*	*spoken*
steal	*stole*	*stolen*
swim	*swam*	*swum*
take	*took*	*taken*
throw	*threw*	*thrown*
wake	*woke*	*woken*
wear	*wore*	*worn*
write	*wrote*	*written*

Appendix 2 Some spelling rules

These spelling rules deal with spelling changes with grammatical word endings.

A Some spelling terms

To study this Appendix you need to know the terms **vowel** and **consonant**.

Vowel letters are *a, e, i, o* and *u*.

Vowel sounds are sounds written with two or more vowel letters, eg
ai, au, ea, ee, ei, ie, oa, oo, ou, etc.

Consonants are the other letters of the alphabet and their sounds, eg *b, c, d, f, g,* etc.

A **short vowel** is, eg *e* in *get* and *o* in *got*.

A **long vowel** is, eg *ee* in *keep, ea* in *heat, oo* in *soon* and *ou* in *route*.

You also need to know the term **syllable**. This is a unit of sound within a word.
stand (1 syllable)   *un•der* (2 syllables)   *un•der•stand* (3 syllables)
mis•un•der•stand (4 syllables)   *mis•un•der•stand•ing* (5 syllables)

B Word endings

English adds the following grammatical word endings to words.

Noun + s + s	Verb + ing	Verb + ed	Verb + er	Adjective + est	Adjective + ly	Adjective
cars	looks	look**ing**	looked	quick**er**	quick**est**	quick**ly**
planes	works	work**ing**	work**ed**	slow**er**	slow**est**	slow**ly**
(Plural)	(3rd person present simple)	(Present participle)	(Past simple, past participle)	(Comparative)	(Superlative)	(Adverb)

Sometimes there is a spelling change when we add an ending to a word. There are clear rules for these changes – see sections below.

C Noun and verb endings with *es*

Add *es* when the word ends in *s, ss, sh, ch* and *x*.

bus	boss	dish	match	box
bus**es**	boss**es**	dish**es**	match**es**	box**es**

Many verbs and nouns end in an *e* which we do not say. But if the silent *e* comes after *c, s, x* or
z, just add *s*. We then sound the *e + s* together.

race	practise	axe	organize
race**s**	practise**s**	axe**s**	organize**s**

After other consonants, we do not sound the silent *e* – see Section D below.

bikes	scenes	tapes	votes	consumes

We add *es* after some nouns ending in *o*, but not others. Compare the following.

cargoes	heroes	potatoes	tomatoes	volcanoes
discos	studios	photos	radios	stereos

Note also the verbs *go → goes* and *do → does*.

Some nouns which end in *f* or *fe* change their endings to *ves*.

knife	life	loaf	shelf	wife
knives	lives	loaves	shelves	wives

D Words that end in silent *e*

After final, silent *e* just add *s*.

bikes	*scenes*	*tapes*	*votes*	(Plural nouns)
consumes	*hopes*	*rules*	*types*	(3rd person present simple)

But see Section C for pronunciation of words like these.

races   *practises*   *axes*   *organizes*

Leave out *e* and add *ing* to form the present participle.

dance	*handle*	*hope*	*smile*	*write*
dancing	*handling*	*hoping*	*smiling*	*writing*

After *e* just add *d* for regular past tense and past participle forms.

consumed   *hoped*   *ruled*   *typed*

Just add *r* and *st* for comparative and superlative forms.

brave	*large*	*rude*	*wide*
braver	*larger*	*ruder*	*wider*
bravest	*largest*	*rudest*	*widest*

Just add *ly* to most adjectives for adverb forms.

bravely   *largely*   *rudely*   *widely*

But if an adjective ends in *le*, leave out *e* and just add *y*.

able	*capable*	*horrible*	*probable*
ably	*capably*	*horribly*	*probably*

Note these special *ly* cases.

day	*due*	*true*	*whole*
daily	*duly*	*truly*	*wholly*

E Words that double the final consonant

Words that end in one short vowel + one consonant often double that consonant before *ing*, *ed*, *er* and *est*.

plan	*chop*	*permit*	(Verb)
planning	*chopping*	*permitting*	(Present participle)
planned	*chopped*	*permitted*	(Past simple, past participle)
fat	*wet*	*thin*	(Adjective)
fatter	*wetter*	*thinner*	(Comparative)
fattest	*wettest*	*thinnest*	(Superlative)

Most words like *occur*, with two syllables or more, double the last consonant when the last syllable is stressed. Compare the following.

oc<u>cur</u>	<u>frigh</u>ten	per<u>mit</u>	<u>ben</u>efit
occurring	*frightening*	*permitted*	*benefited*

But words which end in one vowel + *l* are different in British English (though not American English). They all double the *l*.

quarrel	*quarrelling*	(Present participle)
travel	*travelled*	(Past simple, past participle)
beautiful	*beautifully*	(Adverb)

F Words that end in *y*

Before *s*, *y* changes to *ie* and becomes *ies*.

body	*copy*	*family*	*sky*	(Noun)
bodies	*copies*	*families*	*skies*	(Plural)
apply	*empty*	*study*	*try*	(Verb)
applies	*empties*	*studies*	*tries*	(3rd person present simple)

Before *ed*, *y* changes to *ie* and becomes *ied*.

applied   *emptied*   *studied*   *tried*   (Past simple, past participle)

Before *er* and *est*, *y* changes to *i* and becomes *ier* or *iest*.

happy	*lucky*	*pretty*	*silly*	(Adjective)
happier	*luckier*	*prettier*	*sillier*	(Comparative)
happiest	*luckiest*	*prettiest*	*silliest*	(Superlative)

But a *y* ending does not change before *ing*.

applying   *emptying*   *studying*   *trying*   (Present participle)

Most words with a vowel + *y* ending (*ay*, *ey*, *oy*) do not change at all.

play	*grey*	*boy*
plays	*greyer*	*boys*
playing	*greyest*	
played		

But note these special cases.

day	*lay*	*pay*	*say*
daily	*laid*	*paid*	*said*

G Words that end in *ie*

A few verbs end in *ie*. With these, *ie* changes to *y* and becomes *ying*.

die	*lie*	*tie*
dying	*lying*	*tying*

Appendix 3 Punctuation

A Types

Study the punctuation in the following.

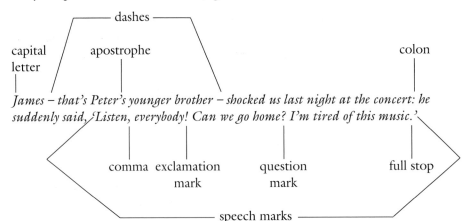

B Apostrophe (...')

Use this:

● in short forms of verbs: ***It's*** *cold.* (***It's*** *= It is)*   *I **don't** want to go out.* (***don't*** *= do not)*
Be careful with the different meanings of *'s* and *'d*: ***He's*** *working.* (***He's*** *= He is)*
He's *finished.* (***He's*** *= He has)*   ***We'd*** *finished by 5.00.* (***We'd*** *= We had)*
We'd *like to go home now.* (***We'd*** *= We would)*

● in short forms of other words, mainly years: *I met Joe in June '89.*

● to show possession after nouns: *I'm **Peter's** younger brother.*

A possessive apostrophe goes after a plural noun with *s*: *We can use my **parents'** car.*

Possessive adjectives and pronouns do not take apostrophes: *This is my coat, and this is hers.*

Be careful with *its* (possessive adjective) and *it's* (*it is/it has*): *Look at the fish. **It's** opening and closing **its** mouth.*

C Capital letter (*I, P, J, L,* etc)

Use this:

● for the 1st person singular: ***I***

● for the name of a person, place, geographical name, country, nationality: ***J****ames,*
T*he* ***P****alace* ***H****otel,* ***L****ondon, the* ***R****iver* ***N****ile,* ***C****anada,* ***C****anadian*

● for abbreviations: *the* **UN** *(the United Nations), the* **USA** *(the United States of America)*

D Colon (:)

Use this:

● to introduce a list of things: *Remember to bring the following: thick jacket, walking boots, leeping bag.*

● to lead from a general heading into a particular example: *Summer camp: equipment*

● to show a connection between two ideas: *I've got the answer: 2,301.   You should take a coat: it's going to rain.*

E Comma (,)

Use this:

- between separate clauses in one sentence: *We were shocked, but Peter just smiled.*
- to separate other parts of a sentence, eg connectors and sentence adverbs: *We were tired.* ***However,*** *we had to keep running.* ***Surprisingly,*** *it got easier as we continued.*
- between words in lists: *I bought some bread, butter, cheese and tomatoes.   It was a lovely, warm, sunny day for a picnic.*
- to introduce direct speech in a story: *Bob arrived and said, 'Hello.'*

F Dash (–)

Use this:

- to show an extra idea added to a sentence: *I met Carol* **– she's the one in a blue dress –** *when we were both students. She's going to France next month* **– or at least that's what she told me**.

G Exclamation mark (!)

Use this:

- to show strong feeling in written form: *'I'm so happy!'   'That was really stupid!' 'Listen! I've got an idea!'   'Help!'*

This takes the place of a full stop – see below.

H Full stop (.)

Use this:

- to show the end of a statement: *The men are not due to go home this week. They will return next week.*
- in abbreviations (optional): *I work for the B.B.C.   It's 10 a.m.   Have you seen Mrs. Jones?*

I Question mark (?)

Use this:

- to end a sentence in question form: *Can they do the job?   They can do it, can't they?* This takes the place of a full stop – see above.

J Speech marks ('…')

These are also called quotation marks or inverted commas.

Use these:

- to mark direct speech in a story: *Ann turned to Bob and said, 'Hi.'*
  You can also use speech marks in double form: *Ann turned to Bob and said, "Hi."*
- to mark something for special attention: *The letters 'Dr' stand for 'Doctor'.*

Appendix 4 Numbers

A Whole numbers

Write	Say
101	*a hundred and one*
199	*a hundred and ninety-nine*
235	*two hundred and thirty-five*
1,001	*a thousand and one*
1,135	*one thousand, one hundred and thirty-five*
1,000,001	*a million and one*
1,135,199	*one million, one hundred and thirty-five thousand, one hundred and ninety-nine*

Compare the following.

a hundred BUT *exactly one hundred*

about a hundred BUT *exactly one hundred and twelve*

B Telephone numbers

Write	Say
521 301377	*five two one … three oh one … three seven seven* OR *five two one … three zero one … three double seven*
999 775666	*nine nine nine … seven seven five … six six six* OR *treble nine … double seven five … treble six*

C Decimals

Write	Say
31.3166	*thirty-one point three one six six*
33.3333	*thirty-three point three recurring*

D Fractions

Write		Say			
$\frac{1}{2}$	$1\frac{1}{2}$	*a half*	OR	*one half*	*one and a half*
$\frac{1}{3}$	$2\frac{2}{3}$	*a third*	OR	*one third*	*two and two-thirds*
$\frac{1}{4}$	$5\frac{3}{4}$	*a quarter*	OR	*one quarter*	*five and three quarters*
$\frac{1}{5}$	$7\frac{4}{5}$	*a fifth*	OR	*one fifth*	*seven and four-fifths*
$\frac{1}{6}$	$9\frac{5}{6}$	*a sixth*	OR	*one sixth*	*nine and five-sixths*
$\frac{1}{10}$	$10\frac{7}{10}$	*a tenth*	OR	*one tenth*	*ten and seven-tenths*

E Mathematical terms

Write	Say
$7 + 2 = 9$	*seven plus/add/and two equals/is nine*
$9 - 3 = 6$	*nine minus/take away three equals/is six*
$6 \times 3 = 18$	*six times/multiplied by three equals/is eighteen*
$18 \div 2 = 9$	*eighteen divided by two equals/is nine*

F Ordinal numbers

Write (eg in dates)	Write or say	Write (eg in dates)	Write or say
1st	first	20th	twentieth
2nd	second	21st	twenty-first
3rd	third	22nd	twenty-second
4th	fourth	23rd	twenty-third
5th	fifth	24th	twenty-fourth
6th	sixth	...	
7th	seventh	30th	thirtieth
8th	eighth	40th	fortieth
9th	ninth	50th	fiftieth
10th	tenth	60th	sixtieth
11th	eleventh	70th	seventieth
12th	twelfth	80th	eightieth
13th	thirteenth	90th	ninetieth
14th	fourteenth	100th	hundredth
15th	fifteenth	101st	hundred and first
...			
19th	nineteenth	...	

Appendix 5 Days, dates and times

A Days and months – abbreviations

Note that the short forms of days and months may have a full stop, eg *Mon.* and *Oct.*

Days		Months			
Full	Short	Full	Short	Full	Short
Monday	*Mon*	*January*	*Jan*	*July*	*Jul*
Tuesday	*Tue/Tues*	*February*	*Feb*	*August*	*Aug*
Wednesday	*Wed*	*March*	*Mar*	*September*	*Sep*
Thursday	*Thu/Thur/Thurs*	*April*	*Apr*	*October*	*Oct*
Friday	*Fri*	*May*	*–*	*November*	*Nov*
Saturday	*Sat*	*June*	*Jun*	*December*	*Dec*
Sunday	*Sun*				

B Dates – word order

Write	Say
1st January	*the first of January*
January 1st	*January the first*

C Dates – abbreviations

Write	Say
Monday, 21st January	*Monday, the twenty-first of January*
Mon, 21st Jan	
Mon, 21 Jan	

D Dates in numbers

Write	Say
30/6	*the thirtieth of June*
31/12/94	*the thirty-first of December, 1994*

E Times

Write	Say
10.00	*ten o'clock*
10 a.m.	*ten a.m./ten o'clock* (in the morning)
3.00 p.m.	*three p.m./three o'clock* (in the afternoon)
10.00 p.m.	*ten p.m./ten o'clock* (at night)
12 a.m./12 p.m.	*midday/midnight*
1.15/1.30/1.45	*a quarter past one/half past one/a quarter to two* OR *one fifteen/one thirty/one forty-five*
2.10/2.20/2.40	*ten past two/twenty past two/twenty to three* OR *two ten/two twenty/two forty*
3.13/3.59	*thirteen minutes past three/one minute to four* OR *three thirteen/three fifty-nine*

Index

(The numbers in the index refer to the units, not the pages.)

Answer key

Unit 1

Exercise 1
1 *Be*
2 *don't be*
3 *Be*
4 *Don't be*
5 *Be*
6 *Don't be*
7 *Be*
8 *Don't be*

Exercise 2
1 *Don't play*
2 *Take*
3 *Turn off*
4 *Don't talk*
5 *Don't forget*
6 *press*
7 *Don't drive*
8 *Write*

Exercise 3
1 *put in*
2 *place/put*
3 *press/push*
4 *choose*
5 *place/put*
6 *press/push*
7 *take*
8 *enjoy*

Exercise 4
1 *go*
2 *Turn*
3 *Turn*
4 *Take*
5 *Pass*
6 *Follow   turn*
7 *Cross   turn*
8 *Go   take*

Unit 2

Exercise 1
1 *live*
2 *like*
3 *cries*
4 *start*
5 *goes*
6 *fetches*
7 *has*

Exercise 2
1 *want   love*
2 *use   doesn't work*
3 *doesn't get   eats*
4 *don't like   don't enjoy*
5 *doesn't swim   goes*
6 *don't drink   keeps*
7 *doesn't drive   walks*

Exercise 3
1 *Does Tom drive?*
2 *Do you know Ann Smith?*
3 *Does the TV work?*
4 *Do you go out much?*
5 *Does Marie speak French?*
6 *Do Fred and Mary live near here?*

Exercise 4
1 *How does Tom go to work?*
2 *When does Sally visit her parents?*
3 *Where do they go on holiday every year?*
4 *What time do you/I get home in the evening?*
5 *Why do you/we always make mistakes?*
6 *How long do the children watch TV after school?*
7 *What does the cat have for lunch?*

Unit 3

Exercise 1
1 *are*
2 *Is*
3 *is*
4 *Am*
5 *Are*
6 *is*
7 *Are*
8 *am   is   are*

Exercise 2
1 *I'm*
2 *he's*
3 *they're*
4 *you're*
5 *I'm not*
6 *he isn't/he's not*
7 *they aren't/they're not*
8 *you aren't/you're not*

Exercise 3
1 *I'm not 80 kilos. I'm 85 kilos.*
2 *isn't in Berlin. He's in Paris.*
3 *aren't 1 metre 75. You're 1 metre 80.*
4 *aren't at home. They're at school.*

Exercise 4
1 *Yes, she is.*
2 *No, you aren't. You're very late.*
3 *No, it isn't. It's 30th April.*
4 *Yes, there are.*
5 *No, I'm not. I'm only 28.*

Exercise 5
1 *How old is he? He's 25.*
2 *What's his job? He's a designer.*
3 *Where is his office? It's on the second floor.*
4 *How many people are there? There are six.*
5 *Which is his desk? It's the one by the window.*

Unit 4

Exercise 1
1 *I'm going.*
2 *You aren't going./ You're not going.*
3 *He isn't going./He's not going.*
4 *They're going.*
5 *It isn't going./It's not going.*

Exercise 2
1 *'m not feeling*
2 *'re going*
3 *aren't working.*
4 *is ringing   isn't answering*
5 *'m looking for   isn't working   's visiting*
6 *'s having*
7 *aren't watching   're listening*

Exercise 3
1 *are the children doing?   They're playing*
2 *Are you enjoying   am.*
3 *is Bill training   He's trying*
4 *Is Sally going   isn't.*
5 *are we flying? We're doing*
6 *Are the boys washing aren't   They're cutting*
7 *'s the cat eating? It's eating*

Exercise 4
1 *'s getting*
2 *are choosing*
3 *Are you writing*
4 *'m planning*
5 *'re leaving*
6 *are you cutting*
7 *is making*

Exercise 5
1 *'m working*
2 *'re building*
3 *are*
4 *studying*
5 *'m not*
6 *'m training*
7 *is*
8 *going*
9 *'s starting*

Unit 5

Exercise 1
1 *Are you going*
2 *Are you doing*
3 *is staying*
4 *'m taking*
5 *aren't doing*
6 *aren't going*
7 *are you planning*
8 *'re having*

Exercise 2
1 *don't need*
2 *look*
3 *do you say*
4 *don't like*
5 *Does the bus stop*
6 *doesn't do*
7 *does he leave*
8 *goes*
9 *walk*
10 *don't mind.*
11 *Do you know*

Exercise 3
1 *'re*
2 *don't*

3 *is*
4 *Are*
5 *does*
6 *do*
7 *isn't*
8 *doesn't*
9 *Do*
10 *aren't*

Exercise 4

1 *'m making*
2 *'m staying*
3 *do*
4 *get up*
5 *start*
6 *eat*
7 *owns*
8 *'m living*
9 *takes*
10 *train*
11 *'s finishing*
12 *'m writing*

Unit 6

Exercise 1

1 *asked*
2 *was/were*
3 *broke*
4 *called*
5 *did*
6 *drove*
7 *ate*
8 *found*
9 *went*
10 *had*
11 *invited*
12 *jumped*
13 *kept*
14 *left*
15 *met*
16 *needed*
17 *opened*
18 *ran*
19 *saw*
20 *woke up*

be, break, do, drive, eat, find, go, have, keep, leave, meet, run, see and *wake up* are irregular verbs.
be, do and *have* can be main verbs and auxiliary verbs.

Exercise 2

1 *saw*
2 *jumped*

---

3 *ran*
4 *ate/had*
5 *had*
6 *left*
7 *drove*

Exercise 3

1 *found my old suit didn't find my new one.*
2 *cleaned her red shoes didn't clean her black ones.*
3 *called their mother didn't call their sister.*

Exercise 4

1 *Did Tim and Fred visit Paris too?*
  No, they didn't.
2 *Did Ann run well too?*
  Yes, she did.
3 *Did they have a French test too?*
  No, they didn't.
4 *Did Peter practise the piano too?*
  Yes, he did.

Exercise 5

1 *When did she go there?*
2 *How did she go?*
3 *Why did she go?*
4 *What time did she get there?*
5 *Who did she meet?*
6 *Where did they meet?*

Unit 7

Exercise 1

1 *was   were*
2 *were   was   were*
3 *were   was   was*
4 *were   was   was*

Exercise 2

1 *was*
2 *Was*
3 *was.*
4 *were*
5 *were*
6 *was*
7 *wasn't*
8 *weren't*
9 *were*

Exercise 3

1 *How old was the house?*
  About 100 years old.

---

2 *How many bedrooms were there?*
  Four.
3 *How big was the living-room?*
  12 x 5 metres.
4 *Where was the kitchen?*
  At the back of the house.
5 *What was outside?*
  A garden with a stream.
6 *What was the only problem?*
  The price.
7 *How much was the house?*
  £200,000.

Exercise 4

1 *are   are*
2 *was   isn't*
3 *were   're*
4 *weren't   was*
5 *was   is   is*

Unit 8

Exercise 1

1 *was calling*
2 *were swimming*
3 *was watching*
4 *were having*
5 *was getting*
6 *were riding*

Exercise 2

1 *were   swimming were swimming Were they swimming weren't.   were swimming*
2 *Was   listening wasn't.   was watching was he watching? was watching*
3 *were   riding their bikes?   were riding*
4 *was   calling? was calling*

Exercise 3

1 *were you doing*
2 *was he running*
3 *was driving   broke down.*
4 *opened   was shining*

---

5 *were working   rang*
6 *hit   was trying*
7 *was trying   crashed*

Exercise 4

1 *was*
2 *were singing.*
3 *was walking*
4 *noticed*
5 *was playing*
6 *called*
7 *looked*
8 *shouted*
9 *invited*
10 *were playing*
11 *stopped*
12 *were eating*
13 *decided*
14 *happened.*
15 *was getting*
16 *started*
17 *fell*
18 *were watching*
19 *laughed*
20 *felt*

Unit 9

Exercise 1

1 *asked*
2 *been*
3 *chosen*
4 *done*
5 *eaten*
6 *found*
7 *given*
8 *had*
9 *invited*
10 *joined*
11 *kept*
12 *left*
13 *made*
14 *needed*
15 *opened*
16 *put*
17 *run*
18 *started*
19 *taken*
20 *woken up*

be, choose, do, eat, find, give, have, keep, leave, make, put, run, take and *wake up* are irregular verbs.
be, do and *have* can be main verbs and auxiliary verbs.

Exercise 2

1 found
2 bought
3 started
4 joined
5 made
6 met
7 been
8 invited

Exercise 3

1 've broken
2 have caught
3 has painted
4 have arrived
5 has won
6 has got

Exercise 4

1 has joined the school drama group, hasn't joined the tennis club.
2 has made a cake, hasn't made any sandwiches.
3 have brought their books, haven't brought their pens.
4 have chosen the carpets for their new house, haven't chosen any furniture.
5 've washed the car, haven't washed the children's bikes.
6 've invited Alan to the party, haven't invited Joe.

Exercise 5

1 Have the boys done their French homework too?
   No, they haven't.
2 Has Mark been busy all day too?
   Yes, he has.
3 Have you learnt to fly too?
   Yes, I have.
4 Has Sally brought her books too?
   No, she hasn't.

Exercise 6

1 How long has Emma lived in London?
2 Why have you come so late?
3 What have you done with my skirt?
4 Where has Andy put the bike?
5 How many kilometres have you driven today?

Exercise 7

1 Yes, she's just gone to Rome.
2 No, I haven't met them yet.
3 Yes, he's just bought some chocolate.
4 No, we haven't finished work yet.
5 No, they haven't come home yet.
6 Yes, I've just bought some.
7 Yes, I've just put them in your briefcase.

Exercise 8

1 But you still haven't called him.
2 We've already bought the tickets.
3 But you still haven't packed your bag.
4 She's already got £50.
5 It's already doing 300 kph.
6 But I still haven't had a reply.

Unit 10

Exercise 1

1 This land has belonged to Mr Hill since 1950.
2 Sally has had the same car for five years.
3 We've lived in this house since I was 25.

Exercise 2

1 have they had   Since
2 has he worked   For
3 have they wanted   Since
4 has he lived   For

Exercise 3

1 He hasn't seen Susan for three weeks.
2 They haven't met since Claire's wedding.
3 We haven't had fish for dinner for months.

Exercise 4

1 Have you ever studied English before?
   Yes, I've studied English once.
2 How many times has he seen Superman?
   He's seen it seven times.
3 Have they ever tried Indian food?
   Yes, they've tried it a few times.
4 How often has it rained today?
   It's rained twice today.

Exercise 5

1 Have   been   has gone
2 's gone
3 has   been

Unit 11

Exercise 1

1 did you do?
2 went
3 looked
4 Did you find
5 weren't
6 was
7 didn't call
8 didn't want
9 did you do
10 phoned

Exercise 2

1 have you put   haven't seen
2 Have you packed   've left
3 Has Dad given   hasn't.
4 've brought   has gone

Exercise 3

1 asked   asked
2 was/were   been
3 cut   cut
4 did   done
5 found   found
6 went   gone
7 had   had
8 invited   invited
9 joined   joined
10 kept   kept

be, cut, do, find, go, have and keep are irregular verbs.
be, do and have can be main verbs and auxiliary verbs.

Exercise 4

1 has
2 didn't
3 hasn't
4 Did
5 haven't
6 Has
7 did
8 have

Exercise 5

1 haven't written
2 has been
3 have begun
4 've had
5 told
6 's let
7 got
8 've found
9 signed
10 gave

Unit 12

Exercise 1

1 've been working
2 've been playing
3 has been using
4 've been doing
5 's been studying

Exercise 2

1 hasn't been spending   's been saving
2 haven't been going   've been going
3 hasn't been doing   's been listening

Exercise 3

1 have you been doing
2 has he been getting on
3 Has he been learning
4 Have you been eating
5 have they been working

Exercise 4

1 has Pam been doing
  She's been looking for
  a new job.
  has she been doing
  Since last month./For
  a month.
2 have Nick and Andy
  been doing
  They've been training
  for the London
  Marathon.
  have they been doing
  For three months.

Unit 13

Exercise 1

1 had gone.
2 had taken
3 had eaten
4 'd changed
5 'd seen
6 had bought
7 'd left
8 'd started

Exercise 2

1 'd already arranged
2 'd never seen
3 had just started
4 'd recently heard
  about
5 still hadn't repaired
6 had already spent
7 had only had

Exercise 3

1 arrived   had gone.
2 had got away
  closed
3 'd crossed   were
  able
4 left   'd done
5 turned back
  'd run out of

Exercise 4

1 We drove out of town
  when we'd loaded the
  jeep.
2 We stopped for a rest
  when we'd driven into
  the hills.
3 We started again
  when we'd had a good
  rest.

4 We stopped for the
  night when we'd been
  on the road for ten
  hours.
5 We started to cook
  dinner when we'd
  unpacked the jeep.
6 We went to sleep when
  we'd finished dinner.

Unit 14

Exercise 1

1 'm going to wash it
  after lunch.
2 's going to clean them
  now.
3 're going to mend
  them this evening.
4 's going to have it in
  a minute.

Exercise 2

1 's going to rain.
  're going to get
2 's not going to get
  's going to miss
3 're going to run
  out of
  're not going to reach
4 's not going to give up
  's going to finish

Exercise 3

1 Is Sam going to pass
  his exams?
  Yes, he is.
2 Are your parents
  going to take you out?
  No, they aren't.
3 Are you going to
  watch TV this
  evening?
  Yes, I am.
4 Is Sally going to buy a
  newspaper?
  No, she isn't.

Exercise 4

1 Where is she going to
  put them?
2 When are they going
  to move out?
3 How many are you
  going to do?
4 What is he going to
  see?

Unit 15

Exercise 1

1 won't find
2 will cross
3 won't open
4 'll do
5 won't be

Exercise 2

1 'll buy
2 won't be
3 'll wash
4 'll close
5 won't make
6 won't forget

Exercise 3

1 He'll get
2 She'll give
3 I'll carry
4 He'll be
5 I'll cut

Exercise 4

1 Will Ann be ten next
  week?
  Yes, she will.
2 Will the boys like their
  new school?
  No, they won't.
3 Will Mr Hall arrive
  tonight?
  Yes, he will.
4 Will next term start
  on 15th April?
  No, it won't.

Exercise 5

1 'll phone
2 won't be
3 Will everybody want
4 will.
5 will we need
6 'll have to
7 Will we need
8 won't.
9 'll have
10 won't rain.

Unit 16

Exercise 1

1 At 10.00 he'll be
  doing Art.
2 At 10.45 he'll be
  learning French.

3 At 11.20 he'll be
  studying Maths.
4 At 12.20 he'll be
  doing English.
5 At 1.05 he'll be
  having lunch.

Exercise 2

1 'll be meeting the
  Sales Manager.
2 'll be visiting the
  factory.
3 'll be having meetings
  with the sales team.
4 'll be showing visitors
  round London all
  day.
5 'll be spending the day
  in Paris.

Exercise 3

1 When will he be flying
  to Florida?
  Next Monday.
2 How long will he be
  riding across
  America?
  For two months.
3 Where will he be
  arriving in ten weeks?
  In California.
4 Where will he be going
  from there?
  To Alaska.

Unit 17

Exercise 1

1 'll have written a
  book of short stories.
2 'll have produced a
  play in London.
3 'll have published a
  best-seller novel.
4 'll have won an
  important
  international prize.
5 'll have made a lot of
  money.

Exercise 2

1 won't have finished
2 will have sold
3 'll have gone
4 'll have got
5 won't have had

Exercise 3

1 *What will they have finished*
   They'll have put in the windows, but they won't have fitted the doors.
2 *What will they have finished*
   They'll have done the wiring, but they won't have laid the floors.
3 *What will they have finished*
   They'll have plastered the walls, but they won't have painted the house.

Unit 18

Exercise 1

1 *'re going to crash.*
   'll be
2 *Are we going to eat*
   're going to go
3 *'ll have*
4 *Will you answer*
   'll probably be
5 *'ll be   are you going to leave*
   'm going to study
6 *will the meeting start?*
   won't be

Exercise 2

1 *'re taking*
2 *reaches*
3 *'re flying*
4 *takes off*
5 *arrives*
6 *are staying*

Exercise 3

1 *'ll be flying   will you be doing?*
   'll be working
2 *'ll pass*
   won't do
3 *will Sam be*
   will have
   'll be talking
4 *'ll be waiting*
   'll have

Exercise 4

1 *will have laid*

2 *will be working*
3 *will be working*
4 *'ll be taking*
5 *'ll have left   'll be training*
6 *will be arriving*
   won't have finished

Unit 19

Exercise 1

1 *Have you got*
   haven't got   's got
   hasn't got
2 *'s got*
   Has he got
   hasn't.

Exercise 2

1 *Do you have*
   don't have   has
   doesn't have
2 *has*
   Does she have
   doesn't.
3 *Did you have*
   did   didn't have
   had
4 *do you have?*
   don't have   haven't had
   did you have?
5 *has*
   has he had
   's had   doesn't have

Exercise 3

1 *have got*
2 *hasn't got*
3 *'ve got*
4 *'ve had*
5 *'ve   had.*
6 *didn't have*
7 *had*
8 *'ve got*
9 *'ve got*
10 *'s had*

Exercise 4

1 *has a look*
2 *has a chat*
3 *have time*
4 *have coffee*
5 *has a game*
6 *has a swim*
7 *have lunch*
8 *have a rest*
9 *has a run*
10 *has a chance*

Unit 20

Exercise 1

1 *know*
   drives
2 *start?*
   begins
3 *like*
   watches
4 *have*
   has

Exercise 2

1 *finishes*
2 *'m listening*
3 *hope*
4 *is he making*
5 *does she go*
6 *Are you enjoying*

Exercise 3

1 *cost   cost   cost*
2 *cut   cut   cut*
3 *hit   hit   hit*
4 *let   let   let*
5 *read   read   read*
6 *learn   learnt   learnt*
7 *make   made   made*
8 *pay   paid   paid*
9 *get   got   got*
10 *ride   rode   ridden*
11 *take   took   taken*
12 *wear   wore   worn*
13 *see   saw   seen*
14 *give   gave   given*

Exercise 4

1 *cut*
   cut
2 *make*
   made
3 *ride*
   ride   rode
4 *let*
   let   hit   got

Exercise 5

1 *done?*
   made
2 *seen*
   given
3 *read*
   learnt
4 *hit*
   cut

Unit 21

Exercise 1

1 *'m*
2 *is*
3 *'ll be*
4 *has been*
5 *were*
6 *'ve been*
7 *Are*
8 *was*

Exercise 2

1 *do*
   don't
2 *Do*
   don't
3 *did*
   didn't
4 *does*
   don't
5 *Did*
   didn't
6 *Does*
   doesn't

Exercise 3

1 *Have*
   haven't   haven't
2 *hasn't*
3 *Have*
   've   haven't
4 *hadn't*
5 *'ll have*
6 *has*
   's
7 *won't have*
8 *'d*

Exercise 4

1 *Hasn't Paul come home yet?*
2 *Why didn't they call the police?*
3 *Aren't you enjoying the film?*
4 *Why don't you agree with me?*
5 *Isn't Rosie going to the wedding?*
6 *Which questions haven't they answered yet?*
7 *Don't you have to go home now?*
8 *Which parts don't we have to learn?*

Exercise 5

1 have you?
2 doesn't he?
3 weren't they?
4 do you?
5 didn't he?
6 haven't they?
7 does he?
8 wasn't she?
9 are you?
10 did he?

Exercise 6

1 Neither/Nor do we.
2 So does Alan.
3 Neither/Nor have I.
4 Neither/Nor did Lisa.
5 So have her brothers.
6 Neither/Nor is she.
7 Neither/Nor had we.
8 So did the van.
9 Neither/Nor are you.
10 So has Andy.

Exercise 7

1 What are you having
for lunch?
We're having chicken.
What did you have for
lunch?
We had chicken.
2 How much work is he
doing?
He's doing doing ten
hours.
How much work did
he do?
He did ten hours.
How much work has
he done?
He's done ten hours.
3 Why are they being so
slow with their work?
Because they're being
careful.
Why were they so slow
with their work?
Because they were
careful.
Why have they been so
slow with their work?
Because they've been
careful.

Unit 22

Exercise 1

1 You're

2 He's
3 I'm
4 What's
5 We'll
6 he's   he'll
7 you'd
8 she'd   she'd
9 They've
10 I'd

Exercise 2

1 don't
2 isn't
3 hasn't
4 won't
5 Don't   didn't
6 'm not
7 isn't   doesn't
8 hadn't   wouldn't
9 haven't
10 wasn't

Exercise 3

1 don't
2 'm
3 's
4 've
5 'd
6 'd
7 haven't
8 'm
9 Don't
10 're
11 won't
12 doesn't
13 'll
14 'll
15 'll
16 's

Exercise 4

1 we have
2 are not
3 do not
4 I am
5 they are
6 will not
7 we are
8 have not

Exercise 5

1 we had
2 you would
3 it is
4 he has
5 He is
6 I would

Unit 23

Exercise 1

1 Does Bob like football
too?
2 Is Lucy good at
cooking too?
3 Has Dad had dinner
too?
4 Did Jim cook some
meat too?
5 Are you going out
tonight too?

Exercise 2

1 Does he have to go now
too?
2 Must she finish the
letters too?
3 Can he swim fast too?
4 Should we train every
evening too?
5 Will we have to write
to all our friends too?

Exercise 3

1 Have they been
married for long?
2 Did they move to
Manchester at that
time?
3 Have they got any
children?
4 Do the children go to
school?
5 Is she starting school
soon?

Exercise 4

1 Why? Isn't it a good
one?
2 Really? Don't you like
flying?
3 Why? Hasn't he gone
to college yet?
4 Really? Aren't they
going to bed soon?
5 Why? Didn't she buy
one yesterday?

Unit 24

Exercise 1

1 Where
2 Whose
3 How long
4 How many

5 Which
6 When
7 Why
8 What

Exercise 2

1 How old are you?
I'm ...
2 What's your address?
It's ...
3 What does your father
do?
He's a/an ...
4 How many brothers
and sisters have you
got?
I've got ...
5 Why are you learning
English?
Because ...

Exercise 3

1 Why hasn't Tom
answered my letter?
2 What haven't we
done?
3 Why won't they be able
to go on holiday?
4 Where didn't we go?
5 Why isn't Ann going
to go out tonight?
6 Why don't you like this
television programme?

Exercise 4

1 Who called the police?
2 What went wrong?
3 What did Bob find by
the door?
4 Who did Tom phone?
5 What did the car run
over?
6 Who saw Peter?
7 What did Julie eat?

Unit 25

Exercise 1

1 won't you?
2 has it?
3 aren't they?
4 didn't it?
5 is she?
6 was he?
7 can he?
8 shouldn't he?
9 need we?
10 might she?

11 *won't he?*
12 *have you?*
13 *won't they?*
14 *has it?*
15 *is it?*
16 *wasn't it?*
17 *doesn't he?*
18 *didn't you?*
19 *don't you?*
20 *didn't she?*

Exercise 2

1 *didn't it?*
2 *were they?*
3 *aren't you?*
4 *do you?*
5 *is she?*
6 *haven't you?*
7 *will they?*

Exercise 3

1 *isn't it?*
2 *are there?*
3 *are they?*
4 *have I?*
5 *didn't you?*
6 *won't we?*

Exercise 4

1 *didn't I?*
2 *haven't you?*
3 *weren't they?*
4 *aren't we?*
5 *does it?*
6 *don't we?*
7 *is there?*

Unit 26

Exercise 1

1 *I haven't.*
2 *I do.*
3 *I'm not.*
4 *we should.*
5 *I would.*
6 *there aren't.*
7 *I haven't.*
8 *he is.*
9 *I can't.*
10 *I did.*
11 *I must.*

Exercise 2

1 *I'm not.*
2 *I haven't.*
3 *I wasn't.*
4 *I didn't.*
5 *I was.*

6 *I was.*
7 *I did.*
8 *I was.*
9 *I did.*
10 *I was.*

Exercise 3

1 *Yes, I am./No, I'm not.*
2 *Yes, I do./No, I don't.*
3 *Yes, it is./No, it isn't.*
4 *Yes, I am./No, I'm not.*
5 *Yes, they do./No, they don't.*
6 *Yes, they do./No, they don't.*
7 *Yes, I do./No, I don't.*
8 *Yes, I will./No, I won't.*
9 *Yes, I have./No, I haven't.*
10 *Yes, I would./No, I wouldn't.*

Unit 27

Exercise 1

1 *Do you know what date it is today?*
2 *Could you tell me when Ann is coming home?*
3 *Do you have any idea why Tom has gone?*
4 *Can you say how long you'll be away?*
5 *Can you tell me where they've gone?*

Exercise 2

1 *Do you know if/whether they have had lunch?*
2 *Can you say if/whether you'll be home tonight?*
3 *Do you have any idea if/whether the team are going to win?*
4 *Can you tell us if/whether we're having a test this week?*

Exercise 3

1 *Can you tell me if/whether Tom goes to school?*
2 *Can you say if/whether the ring cost a lot?*
3 *Do you have any idea if/whether they play tennis?*
4 *Could you tell us when the bus went?*
5 *Do you know how the engine works?*
6 *Can you tell me where they always go?*

Exercise 4

1 *Why do you think he arrives late?*
2 *Do you think they're going to finish today?*
3 *How far do you think they walked?*
4 *Do you think we've made a mistake?*
5 *Where do you think you will live when you go to college?*

Unit 28

Exercise 1

1 *Neither/Nor do I*
2 *So am I*
3 *So am I.*
4 *So did I*
5 *Neither/Nor did I*
6 *So did I*
7 *Neither/Nor could I*
8 *So was I.*
9 *So is mine.*
10 *So does mine.*
11 *So is mine.*

Exercise 2

1 *neither/nor is Ted.*
2 *so is Sally.*
3 *so does Claire.*
4 *so does Ken.*
5 *so can Ted.*
6 *neither/nor can Claire.*

Exercise 3

1 *I expect so.*
2 *I suppose so.*
3 *I don't think so.*
4 *I'm afraid not.*
5 *I guess not.*
6 *I think so.*

Unit 29

Exercise 1

1 *can see*
2 *can go*
3 *can't walk*
4 *can't catch*

Exercise 2

1 *can   could*
2 *can   couldn't*
3 *couldn't   can't*
4 *could   couldn't*

Exercise 3

1 *could hear*
2 *could remember*
3 *could understand*
4 *could feel*

Exercise 4

1 *could*
2 *could*
3 *were able to*
4 *was able to*
5 *could*

Exercise 5

1 *were able to*
2 *could*
3 *can*
4 *couldn't*
5 *be able to*
6 *can't*
7 *were able to*
8 *couldn't*

Exercise 6

1 *can't have*
2 *could have*
3 *can't have*
4 *could have*

Unit 30

Exercise 1

1 *can*
2 *Could*
3 *Would*
4 *can*
5 *May*
6 *Could*

Exercise 2

1 *Can I borrow your book?*

2 *Can you lend me your pen?*
3 *Could you tell me your address?*
4 *Would you take a seat, please?*
5 *May I put your bag away?*
6 *Would all passengers remain in their seats until the plane stops?*

Exercise 3

1 *Yes, you can go now.*
2 *No, you can't park here.*
3 *Yes, you can pass the bus.*
4 *No, you can't turn round here.*

Exercise 4

1 would
2 Would
3 could
4 Can
5 can
6 can't

Unit 31

Exercise 1

1 *ought*
2 *should*
3 *ought*
4 *should*
5 *should.*

Exercise 2

1 *ought*
2 *oughtn't*
3 *should*
4 *oughtn't*
5 *shouldn't*
6 *should*
7 *should*
8 *ought*

Exercise 3

1 *'d better*
2 *'d better not*
3 *'d better not*
4 *'d better*

Exercise 4

1 *You ought to do more exercise.*

---

2 *You'd better see a dentist.*
3 *You shouldn't watch TV so much.*
4 *You oughtn't to use the phone so much.*
5 *You'd better not go out yet.*
6 *You should go to the beach.*

Exercise 5

1 *He should have gone to the doctor.*
2 *They shouldn't have played outside.*
3 *We ought to have turned left at the traffic lights.*
4 *She oughtn't to have bought it.*

Unit 32

Exercise 1

1 *has Paul had to pay for it?*
2 *will Emma have to go to London?*
3 *did the Smith family have to go last week?*
4 *does Ann have to change all her plans?*
5 *have Ed and Sue had to live in the flat?*

Exercise 2

1 *must rest for a week Mr Robbins.'*
2 *have to pay immediately.*
3 *must check in one hour before the flight.*
4 *must complete a registration form.*
5 *must be home by 6.00.'*
6 *has to go to the police station.*

Exercise 3

1 *must*
2 *has to*
3 *must*
4 *had to*
5 *must*
6 *have to*
7 *must*

Exercise 4

1 *mustn't*
2 *don't have to*
3 *mustn't*
4 *mustn't*
5 *doesn't have to*
6 *don't have to*

Unit 33

Exercise 1

1 *needn't*
2 *mustn't*
3 *mustn't*
4 *needn't*
5 *mustn't*
6 *needn't*

Exercise 2

1 *I have to work late.*
2 *Where do they have to go?*
3 *Does she need to go so soon?*
4 *Do you have to work tomorrow?*
5 *I don't need to do my homework.*
6 *Why do they need to learn French?*

Exercise 3

1 *Do you need to*
2 *needn't*
3 *need to*
4 *need to*
5 *needn't*
6 *need to*
7 *mustn't*
8 *do we need to*
9 *need to*
10 *mustn't*

Exercise 4

1 *didn't need to*
2 *needn't have*
3 *needn't have*
4 *didn't need to*
5 *didn't need to*
6 *needn't have*

Unit 34

Exercise 1

1 *may/might*
2 *may/might*
3 *may/might not*

---

4 *may/might*
5 *may/might not*
6 *may/might not*

Exercise 2

1 *He can't be under 60. He may/might be about 64 or 65. He must be 65 because he's just retired from work.*
2 *It must be Julian because that looks like his jacket. It may/might not be him. He's walking towards some other people. It can't be Rod. Rod is taller.*

Exercise 3

1 *can't be doing*
2 *can't be playing*
3 *must be practising*

Exercise 4

1 *can't have dropped*
2 *may/might have left*
3 *must have put*

Unit 35

Exercise 1

1 *could*
2 *had to/needed to*
3 *was able to*
4 *had to/needed to*
5 *didn't need to/have to*
6 *had to/needed to*
7 *couldn't*
8 *had to*
9 *could*
10 *needed*
11 *couldn't*
12 *couldn't/wasn't able to*
13 *was able to*

Exercise 2

1 *can't have*
2 *may/might/could have*
3 *may/might/could have*
4 *may/might/could have*
5 *must have*

Exercise 3

1 wouldn't have
2 should have
3 needn't have
4 could have
5 would have
6 'd have
7 shouldn't have
8 'd have

Unit 36

Exercise 1

1 can't   Can
2 could
3 couldn't.
4 Could
5 were able to
6 Was he able to

Exercise 2

1 Can I borrow your book?
2 Can I help you?
3 Could you get the red file, please?
4 Would you like a cup of tea?
5 Could I have your name, please?
6 Can you lend me some money?
7 Could I have a day off next week, please?
8 May I park my car outside the entrance?

Exercise 3

1 You should go to the dentist.
2 They oughtn't to watch TV.
3 You'd better get some glasses.
4 He ought to find a better job.
5 He'd better not miss the next test.
6 He shouldn't go out yet.

Exercise 4

1 mustn't   must
2 mustn't   'll have to
3 must   must
4 can't/mustn't   must/have to

Exercise 5

1 don't need to/needn't
2 didn't need/have to
3 don't have to   have to
4 had to   didn't have/need to
5 don't need to/needn't need/have to
6 have to   had to

Exercise 6

1 will
2 may
3 may not.
4 'll
5 could
6 might
7 won't

Exercise 7

1 must be meeting Stephen Fisher.
2 may be at the City Hotel   may be at the Ritz Grill.
3 can't be in Birmingham.   must be travelling to Liverpool or Manchester.

Exercise 8

1 should/ought to have
2 can't/couldn't have
3 shouldn't/oughtn't to have
4 needn't have
5 'd have

Unit 37

Exercise 1

1 is made
2 is produced
3 are provided
4 are brought
5 is put
6 are delivered

Exercise 2

1 was built
2 were used
3 were flown
4 were found
5 were carried

6 were begun
7 were provided
8 was employed

Exercise 3

1 First the new factory was built.
2 Then the new Superbike 2,000 was designed.
3 The design wasn't shown to anyone.
4 1,000 were bought in the first year.

Exercise 4

1 When was oil first used?
It was first used thousands of years ago.
2 Was it burned for light?
Yes, it was.
3 When was far more oil needed?
It was needed about 100 years ago.
4 Was more oil found at that time?
Yes, it was.
5 How many barrels of oil are pumped every day now?
Nearly 50 million barrels of oil are pumped.

Unit 38

Exercise 1

1 We were being called by someone.
2 They are being pulled down next week.
3 The work wasn't being done efficiently.
4 She was being looked after by Sue.
5 It's being serviced at the garage.

Exercise 2

1 Many new houses have been built.
2 It hadn't been driven for 20 years.
3 We've been left behind.

4 We hadn't been told about it.

Exercise 3

1 Up to five books can be borrowed.
2 Books should be returned on time.
3 Protective clothing must be worn at all times.
4 Food mustn't be eaten in the office.

Exercise 4

1 have/get the window mended now.
2 have/get these films printed soon.
3 have/get this wall rebuilt tomorrow.

Exercise 5

1 This castle was built in 1760.
2 Tony was being pulled along the road.
3 The match won't be won by Alan. It'll be won by Jim.
4 Contracts should always be read before they're signed.
5 A memo has been written and it's being read.

Unit 39

Exercise 1

1 to play
2 to give
3 to see
4 to be
5 to win
6 to move
7 to climb
8 to learn

Exercise 2

1 watching
2 losing
3 buying
4 eating
5 saying
6 waiting
7 smoking
8 walking.

Exercise 3

1 to spend
2 arriving.
3 to have
4 to save
5 smoking.
6 going?
7 to see
8 doing
9 going
10 to go
11 walking

Exercise 4

1 not to mind what he said.
2 not making so much noise?
3 not having the money to repay Sam.
4 not to go out with the others.
5 not to talk to Bill any more.

Unit 40

Exercise 1

1 to be
2 to take
3 to form
4 to provide
5 to ask/asking

Exercise 2

1 getting up
2 to go
3 to check
4 swimming
   swimming
5 reading
6 to do
7 to visit
8 playing
9 to know
10 to live

Exercise 3

1 to post
2 to buy
3 asking
4 hearing
5 saying
6 saying
7 to get
8 to do

Exercise 4

1 to get
   using
2 writing   signing
   to do
3 correcting.
   to do

Exercise 5

1 mean to say those terrible things to Emma.
2 to develop a new kind of engine.
3 remember having fights with other children.
4 stop making so much noise late at night.
5 to tell you that your son has done badly in his exams.
6 stop to buy some things for dinner at this supermarket.
7 throwing your work away and starting again.
8 to telephone you this morning, but I didn't.
9 needs painting.

Exercise 6

1 training
2 to find
3 doing
4 to do
5 thinking
6 passing
7 leaving
8 to take
9 to say.
10 to catch up
11 to study

Unit 41

Exercise 1

1 Alan to be quiet.
2 Rob not to drive so fast.
3 me not to take photos.
4 her son to take his medicine after lunch.
5 everybody to try the cake.
6 the man to stop.

Exercise 2

1 Tina not to buy the dress.
2 the climbers to turn back.
3 our boat to roll over.
4 you buy now and pay later.
5 the boys run five kilometres.
6 us go out.

Exercise 3

1 to buy that car.
2 Tom to get the job.
3 Mrs Jones to leave her cases (there).
4 to see the contract.
5 our friends (to) cut down a tree.
6 you to see your present yet.

Exercise 4

1 to swim
2 to have
3 to help
4 to get
5 (to) buy
6 talk

Unit 42

Exercise 1

1 for breaking
2 on paying
3 about moving
4 to going
5 like doing
6 of joining

Exercise 2

1 You can't prevent me from winning.
2 Ben's father punished him for breaking the window.
3 I must warn you about going sailing in this wind.
4 I can't forgive her for hitting my child.
5 You can't blame him for leaving that terrible job.
6 We can't stop the dogs (from) fighting.

Exercise 3

1 capable of hurting
2 excited about going
3 fond of visiting
4 interested in studying
5 pleased about passing
6 fed up with hearing
7 bad at cooking.

Exercise 4

1 thought about going
2 decided against doing
3 discouraged us from choosing
4 enthusiastic to see
5 looking forward to showing
6 tired of working
7 thank her for asking

Unit 43

Exercise 1

1 the oil light comes on.
2 it becomes ice.
3 it soon goes bad.
4 the lights come on.
5 the machinery soon breaks down.

Exercise 2

1 arrives,
2 will tell
3 won't let
4 don't try
5 'll call
6 will lend
7 won't listen
8 don't come

Exercise 3

1 If the police come, they'll ask about Tom.
2 If you enter the race, you'll probably win.
3 If the party goes on till late, we'll go home early.
4 If you call the office at 2.00, Tony will be there.
5 If Ann doesn't call, I'll be worried.
6 If you finish the job today, you won't have to come tomorrow.

Exercise 4

1 *won't be able*
2 *is*
3 *decide*
4 *will come.*
5 *will you join*
6 *organize*
7 *go*
8 *'ll have*
9 *'ll come*
10 *isn't*
11 *find*
12 *'ll cost*
13 *don't act*
14 *will take*
15 *'ll miss*

Unit 44

Exercise 1

1 *had*
2 *'d go*
3 *lost*
4 *followed*
5 *'d be*
6 *wouldn't believe*
7 *'d stay*
8 *didn't get*

Exercise 2

1 *Ann would be pleased if Tom called.*
2 *If you didn't visit us again, we'd be very sad.*
3 *I'd get fit quite fast if I worked out at the gym.*
4 *Barry wouldn't argue so much if he had more friends.*
5 *The team would win more games if they trained harder.*

Exercise 3

1 *'d waste*
2 *'d become*
3 *'d enjoy*
4 *might never see*

Exercise 4

1 *Where would they stay if they visited Turkey? They'd stay in cheap hotels.*
2 *Who would we see if we complained at the Head Office? You'd talk to the Sales Manager.*
3 *How would you travel if you visited Scotland? I'd go by car.*
4 *What would they do if they left school now? They'd get jobs.*

Unit 45

Exercise 1

1 *'d have loved*
2 *'d gone*
3 *hadn't shown*
4 *had been*
5 *'d saved   'd have had*
6 *wouldn't have asked   hadn't been*

Exercise 2

1 *If Jim had asked us, we'd have lent him our car.*
2 *If I hadn't written down her phone number, I'd have forgotten.*
3 *The car wouldn't have crashed if Tom had kept to the speed limit.*
4 *I'd have forgotten to buy Ann's present if you hadn't reminded me.*

Exercise 3

1 *If we'd had a map, we'd have found the house.*
2 *If the bus hadn't arrived late, we'd have missed it.*
3 *If they hadn't opened the box, they wouldn't have found the books.*
4 *If the tree had fallen on the car, the driver would have been hurt.*
5 *If I'd turned back, I wouldn't have got lost.*

Exercise 4

1 *he might have won the race.*
2 *they could have caught the thieves.*
3 *we'd have got home an hour ago.*

Unit 46

Exercise 1

1 *they're sitting by their fire.*
2 *it's hot there and he's sitting by their new pool.*

Exercise 2

1 *He said he was working outside London that month.*
2 *He told me he'd finished his college course the year before.*
3 *He said he hadn't been to see his parents for ages.*
4 *He told me he'd arrived home with his family the day before.*
5 *He said they were going back to London the next day.*
6 *He told me they couldn't stay for long as he had to get back to work.*
7 *He said they might come back the following year. He didn't know.*
8 *He told me he'd write soon and send me a photo of the family.*
9 *He said I should stay with them when I had time.*

Exercise 3

1 *But you said you loved this music.*
2 *But you told me he wouldn't sell his bike.*
3 *But you said you would call her.*
4 *But you told me it was on today.*

5 *But you said they'd lose the match.*
6 *But you told me she'd be at home tonight.*
7 *But you said they wouldn't send you anything.*
8 *But you told me they couldn't swim at all.*

Unit 47

Exercise 1

1 *we're going for our holiday this year.   if we're going to visit them again.*
2 *we're doing this winter.   if we're taking a skiing holiday again.*

Exercise 2

1 *Jim asked me if I'd sold my terrible old car.*
2 *Jim asked me if I still lived with my parents.*
3 *Jim asked me if I was going to visit London soon.*
4 *I asked him if there was room for me to stay with him.*
5 *I asked him if I could have his phone number.*
6 *I asked him if he'd met his wife at college.*

Exercise 3

1 *They asked him where he came from.*
2 *They asked him how long he'd been in Britain.*
3 *They asked him why he'd decided to go there.*
4 *They asked him how long he was going to stay.*
5 *They asked him where he was living.*

Exercise 4

1   A Swedish student asked me if I knew the way to the station.
2   A Turkish student asked me if I could help him/her find a flat.
3   A Lebanese student asked me which was the best travel agency.

Unit 48

Exercise 1

1   The girl asked me to open the door.
2   Carol instructed the new assistant not to use the photocopier.
3   Tom invited us to come for dinner on Saturday.
4   Celia reminded me not to be late for the party.
5   Ann asked everybody not to make so much noise.
6   Mrs Davis told Tony to give his name to the receptionist.
7   Bob warned Emma not to touch the red button.
8   The manager reminded her assistant to post the letters.

Exercise 2

1   They agreed to meet at 7.30.
2   He promised to be there on time.
3   She threatened not to wait if he was late.
4   He offered to get there an hour early.
5   She threatened she'd leave if he wasn't there at 7.30.
6   He promised not to be late.

Exercise 3

1   Maria suggested going parachuting.

2   Barry insisted going at that moment/ immediately.
3   Barry admitted feeling scared.
4   Maria apologized for suggesting parachuting.
5   Barry insisted on jumping.

Unit 49

Exercise 1

1   an
2   an
3   a
4   an
5   a
6   an
7   a
8   an
9   an
10 a
11 a
12 an

Exercise 2

1   a letter
2   an umbrella
3   some paint(s)
4   some glasses
5   an egg
6   a taxi

Exercise 3

1   Do
2   Is
3   are
4   Does
5   is
6   is
7   Are
8   are

Exercise 4

1   some
2   x
3   some
4   x
5   some
6   some

Exercise 5

1   Colleges are places to study.
2   A large plane can carry a heavy load.

3   Nowadays, students need to learn to use computers.
4   A car uses more energy per person than a train or bus.

Exercise 6

1   some
2   x
3   x
4   a
5   an
6   some
7   some
8   some
9   a
10 an

Unit 50

Exercise 1

1   police
2   cattle.
3   contents
4   scissors?
5   clothes
6   glasses
7   shorts.
8   sheep.

Exercise 2

1   is
2   Does
3   are
4   Is
5   are
6   is
7   is
8   is
9   Does
10 are

Exercise 3

1   children
2   person
3   foot
4   teeth.
5   tooth
6   people.
7   women
8   child

Exercise 4

1   knives
2   matches
3   potatoes
4   loaves

5   photos.
6   wives
7   batteries.
8   lives.
9   roofs

Unit 51

Exercise 1

1   apples
2   bananas
3   beans
4   biscuits
5   carrots
6   eggs
7   olives
8   onions
9   oranges
10 peas
11 potatoes
12 tomatoes
13 apple juice
14 bread
15 butter
16 cheese
17 cooking oil
18 milk
19 mineral water
20 rice
21 salt
22 soup
23 sugar
24 tea

Exercise 2

1   meat.
2   vegetables.
3   beans
4   onions.
5   rice
6   bread
7   bread rolls
8   tomatoes
9   olive oil
10 list

Exercise 3

1   some
2   information
3   ideas
4   is
5   furniture
6   some
7   a
8   luggage?
9   hair.
10 any

Exercise 4

1 e a packet of tea.
2 i a carton of milk.
3 d a five-litre bottle of cooking oil.
4 a a roll of kitchen paper.
5 f three loaves of bread.
6 h four cans of Pepsi.
7 c a box of matches.
8 g a two-kilo bag of potatoes.
9 b a piece of cheese.

Unit 52

Exercise 1

1 an
2 a
3 an
4 a
5 an
6 a
7 an   a
8 an   a

Exercise 2

1 ¹a
   ²a
2 ¹a   ²a
   ³the
   ⁴The   ⁵the
3 ¹a   ²the
   ³an   ⁴The   ⁵the
   ⁶a   ⁷The   ⁸an
4 ¹a
   ²the
   ³the
5 ¹the
   ²a   ³a   ⁴the
   ⁵the   ⁶the

Exercise 3

1 ¹a   ²the   ³a
   ⁴the   ⁵the   ⁶a
2 ¹a   ²a   ³the   ⁴a
   ⁵the   ⁶a   ⁷an
   ⁸the   ⁹the   ¹⁰the
   ¹¹the   ¹²The   ¹³the
   ¹⁴the   ¹⁵the
   ¹⁶a/the   ¹⁷the
   ¹⁸the   ¹⁹The   ²⁰an

Exercise 4

1 the beach.
2 The sun

3 the sky
4 The birds
5 the
6 trees
7 the
8 fields
9 the
10 wind.
11 the
12 sea
13 the
14 waves
15 the
16 sand.
17 the world

Exercise 5

1 the
   a
2 the
   a
3 the
   a
4 a
   the
5 a
   the
6 the
   a
7 the
   a
8 the
   a
9 a
   the
10 the
    a

Exercise 6

1 A reporter answered when I phoned the newspaper.
2 Joe fell and knocked a vase over.
3 The police officer stopped me for driving too fast.
4 The ship can travel from Britain to the USA in four days.
5 When I was away, I brought a present for my parents.
6 I picked the phone up and called my sister.
7 Sarah wrote a long letter to her father.

Unit 53

Exercise 1

1 d A camera is for taking pictures.
2 e A pen is for writing.
3 a A fork is for picking up food.
4 b A file is for holding papers.
5 g A diary is for noting dates of meetings, etc.
6 f A fridge is for keeping food cold.
7 c An answering machine is for taking phone messages.

Exercise 2

1 g Bell invented the telephone.
2 d Otis invented the lift/elevator.
3 b Marconi invented the radio.
4 f Biro invented the ballpoint pen.
5 a Edison invented the electric lamp.
6 c Dunlop invented the modern car tyre.
7 e Singer invented the sewing machine.

Exercise 3

1 I don't like black coffee.
2 I like fast cars.
3 I don't mind homework.
4 I don't like loud rock music.
5 I like swimming.
6 I don't mind tennis.

Exercise 4

1 the horse
2 companies
3 the salt
4 The books
5 Money
6 water.
7 Elephants
8 The phone

Exercise 5

1 the poor.
2 the unemployed
3 the old
4 The young
5 The blind

Exercise 6

1 the Australians
2 the British
3 the Chinese
4 the Danes/Danish
5 the Egyptians
6 the French
7 the Indonesians
8 the Japanese
9 the Kuwaitis
10 the Dutch
11 the Portuguese
12 the Spanish
13 the Russians
14 the Turks/Turkish
15 the Americans
16 the Venezuelans

Exercise 7

1 The   the
2 x   x
3 x   the   the
4 x   the   the
5 The   the   x   the   the

Exercise 8

1 the
2 the
3 x
4 the
5 x
6 x
7 x
8 the
9 x
10 the
11 x
12 x
13 the
14 the
15 the

Unit 54

Exercise 1

1 those
2 That
3 these
4 this

5 *those   that*
  those
  this

Exercise 2

1 *this   this*
2 *this*
  that
3 *this*
  this   That
4 *This   these*
  This
5 *these.*
  those
  those

Exercise 3

1 *these ones*
  *Those ones   These
  ones*
2 *that   one*
  this one
  that one
3 *these ones*
  those ones
  these ones

Exercise 4

1 *one*
  the one
2 *ones*
  the   ones
3 *the one   the one*
4 *ones   the   ones*
  the   ones
5 *the one   the one*
  the one   the ones

Unit 55

Exercise 1

1 *some*
2 *any*
3 *some*
4 *any*
5 *some*
6 *any*
7 *some*

Exercise 2

1 *some   any.*
  some
2 *some*
  any   some
3 *some   any*
  some
4 *some*
  any

Exercise 3

1 *anything*
  anything   something
2 *anything?*
  somebody/something
3 *anybody*
  some
4 *somebody*
  any/some
5 *something*
  anything
6 *any*
  anybody

Exercise 4

1 *any colour*
2 *anybody*
3 *anything*
4 *anybody*
5 *anywhere*

Unit 56

Exercise 1

1 *Are there any
  potatoes?
  Yes, there are some in
  the bag.*
2 *Is there any coffee?
  No, there isn't. I'll buy
  some.*
3 *Is there a large pan?
  No, there isn't. I'll buy
  one.*
4 *Are there any carrots?
  No, there aren't. I'll
  buy some.*
5 *Is there any butter?
  Yes, there's some in the
  fridge.*
6 *Is there a teapot?
  Yes, there's one on the
  shelf.*

Exercise 2

1 *There wasn't*
2 *There was*
3 *There weren't*
4 *There were*
5 *There was*
6 *There were*
7 *There was*

Exercise 3

1 *There are   They*
2 *There wasn't   it*
3 *There weren't   they*

4 *There's   him?*
5 *There aren't   them*
6 *There isn't   it*

Exercise 4

1 *It's good/lovely to*
2 *It's not worth*
3 *It's no use*
4 *It was sad that*
5 *It was sad that*

Unit 57

Exercise 1

1 *a lot of/lots of
  much*
2 *a lot of/lots of
  many*
3 *much   much*
4 *a lot of/lots of
  much*
5 *many
  many   a lot of/lots
  of*
6 *much
  A lot.*
7 *many
  many.*
8 *much
  much.*

Exercise 2

1 *a little   a few*
2 *little   little*
3 *Few   a few*
4 *a little   a few*
5 *a few   little*
6 *a little   a few*
7 *few   little*
8 *a little
  a few*

Exercise 3

1 *little*
2 *many*
3 *a few*
4 *many*
5 *a lot of/lots of*
6 *much*
7 *a lot*
8 *much.*
9 *little*
10 *a little*

Unit 58

Exercise 1

1 *a few of them.*
2 *all of them.*
3 *some of them.*
4 *most of them.*
5 *a few of them.*

Exercise 2

1 *Both of you*
2 *Half of them*
3 *All/Most of you*
4 *Both of them*
5 *a few of us   most of
  us*

Exercise 3

1 *neither of*
2 *none of*
3 *any of*
4 *either of*
5 *None of*
6 *Neither of*
7 *any of*
8 *either of*
9 *either of*
10 *any of   none of*

Exercise 4

1 *both*
2 *every*
3 *all*
4 *all*
5 *each*
6 *Each*
7 *Every*

Unit 59

Exercise 1

1 *Bill*
2 *Bill*
3 *Paul*
4 *the practice*
5 *Paul*
6 *Bill*
7 *Neil*
8 *Batman film*
9 *People*
10 *Paul, Bill, Neil*

Exercise 2

1 *They're*
2 *she's*
3 *you
  We're*

4 *It's*
5 *he's*
6 *you*
  I'm
7 *You're*
  it's   I'm   I'm

Exercise 3

1 *her*
2 *you*
3 *him*
4 *them.*
5 *you*
  me   him
6 *me/us*
  you   you   her

Exercise 4

1 *He's*
2 *you*
3 *It's*
4 *you*
5 *me*
6 *We*
7 *you*
8 *me*
9 *I*
10 *it*
11 *her*
12 *They're*
13 *She*
14 *them*
15 *It's*
16 *I*

Unit 60

Exercise 1

1 *your*
2 *his*
3 *our*
4 *their*
5 *her*
6 *my*
7 *its*

Exercise 2

1 *No, it isn't his. His are older.*
2 *No, they aren't hers. Hers are newer.*
3 *No, it isn't theirs. Theirs is smaller.*
4 *No, it isn't yours. Yours is nicer.*
5 *No, they aren't ours. Ours are longer.*
6 *mine*

Exercise 3

1 *They're yours. Look, they've got your name inside.*
2 *It's his. Look, it's got his name inside.*
3 *They're theirs. Look, they've got their names inside.*
4 *It's mine. Look, it's got my name inside.*
5 *They're hers. Look, they've got her name inside.*
6 *It's ours. Look, it's got our names inside.*

Exercise 4

1 *it's*
2 *its*
3 *It's*
4 *it's*
5 *Its*
6 *it's*

Exercise 5

1 *s'*
2 *'s*
3 *'s*
4 *'s*
5 *s'*
6 *'s   's*

Unit 61

Exercise 1

1 *themselves*
2 *itself*
3 *herself*
4 *myself*
5 *himself*
6 *ourselves*
7 *yourself.*
8 *yourselves.*

Exercise 2

1 *save himself.*
2 *kill yourself*
3 *looked at herself*
4 *made myself*
5 *bought themselves*
6 *push ourselves*
7 *wash itself.*
8 *look after yourselves.*

Exercise 3

1 *me.*

2 *yourselves*
3 *herself.*
4 *us*
5 *ourselves.*
6 *them.*
7 *him*

Exercise 4

1 *No, I paid for it myself.*
2 *No, she prepares them herself.*
3 *No, he's bringing it himself.*
4 *No, they'll have to tidy it themselves.*
5 *No, we're going to clean it ourselves.*
6 *No, you're going to make it yourself.*

Unit 62

Exercise 1

1 *Ann gave her parents a present.*
2 *Nick sent a book to his niece.*
3 *Did you really buy it for me?*
4 *Could you lend Harry some money?*
5 *Susie's grandmother made her a lovely dress.*
6 *I'll take Celia some magazines next time I visit her in hospital.*
7 *Could you pass the report to the boss when he arrives?*
8 *I offered Rob a place to stay as he had nowhere else to go.*

Exercise 2

1 *No, don't sell them to Sally. Sell them to me.*
2 *No, don't take it there. Take it to the one near my house.*
3 *No, don't buy it for Sally. Buy it for her brother.*
4 *No, don't show it to him. Show it to the police.*

5 *No, don't cook it for the children. Cook it for the adults.*
6 *No, don't pay it to the teacher. Pay it to the school secretary.*
7 *No, don't by one/it for me. Buy it/one for the children.*

Exercise 3

1 *for*
2 *for*
3 *to*
4 *to*
5 *for*
6 *for*
7 *to*
8 *to*
9 *for*

Unit 63

Exercise 1

1 *some*
2 *anything*
3 *any*
4 *somewhere*
5 *anybody*
6 *some*
7 *anybody*
8 *some*
9 *anywhere.*
10 *something*

Exercise 2

1 *everybody/one*
2 *Everywhere*
3 *something*
4 *Nobody*
5 *anybody/one*
6 *anywhere*
7 *anything*

Exercise 3

1 *everywhere*
2 *anywhere*
3 *somewhere*
4 *Somebody*
5 *anyone?*
6 *anywhere*
7 *nowhere*
8 *nobody*
9 *something*
10 *anything.*

Exercise 4

1 *nothing interesting*
2 *something else*
3 *anywhere else*
4 *everywhere possible*
5 *anyone nice*
6 *nowhere else*

Unit 64

Exercise 1

1 *which/that*
2 *which/that*
3 *which/that*
4 *who/that*
5 *which/that*
6 *who/that*
7 *which/that*
8 *who/that*

Exercise 2

1 *The pilot who/that crashed his plane in the lake escaped without injury.*
2 *The student who/that broke the 10,000-metre record has got a place in the national team.*
3 *The bus which/that takes people to the airport broke down.*
4 *The file which/that has all the information is on the top shelf.*
5 *The policeman who/that rescued 15 people from a fire has received an award.*
6 *The woman who/that phoned last night wanted to speak to you.*

Exercise 3

1 *who/that scored all the goals?*
2 *which/that will pay a better salary.*
3 *who/that can repair my old car?*
4 *which/that teaches Japanese.*
5 *who/that are warm and friendly.*

6 *who/that painted that picture?*
7 *who/that was lost for five days.*
8 *who/that discovered America.*

Unit 65

Exercise 1

1 *The book which/that has all the answers has disappeared.*
2 *We climbed over the fence which/that separates the fields.*
3 *The old man who/that can't see well crashed his car.*
4 *I'm going to give the boy who/that found my camera some money.*

Exercise 2

1 *The girls who/that we met at the wedding seemed sad.*
2 *I want to go to the museum which/that you told me about.*
3 *The taxi which/that I'd ordered finally arrived.*
4 *The flowers which/that she gave us are dying.*

Exercise 3

1 *x*
2 *who/that*
3 *x*
4 *who/that*
5 *x*

Exercise 4

1 *showing*
2 *entering*
3 *finishing*
4 *standing*
5 *wearing*

Exercise 5

1 *used*
2 *being painted*
3 *being prepared*

4 *written*
5 *being mended*
6 *made*

Unit 66

Exercise 1

1 *which*
   The pyramids.
2 *who*
   Yuri Gagarin.
3 *whose*
   Marie Curie.
4 *who*
   Marco Polo.
5 *whose*
   Japan.
6 *which   whose*
   Texas.

Exercise 2

1 *He was the one whose wife had a wonderful diamond necklace.*
2 *They were the ones whose children fell in the pool.*
3 *She was the one whose hat flew off in the wind.*
4 *They were the ones whose car refused to start after the party.*
5 *They were the ones whose daughters wore lovely blue dresses.*

Exercise 3

1 *reason why their boat nearly turned over.*
2 *old hotel where they dried out their clothes.*
3 *night when the rain almost washed their tent away.*

Unit 67

Exercise 1

1 *adding*
2 *defining*
3 *defining*
4 *adding*

Exercise 2

1 *Old Professor Jones, who's nearly 70, is*

going to stop work soon.
2 *To the north of India are the Himalayas, which include the highest mountains in the world.*
3 *I bought myself some good, new clothes, which I needed for my new job.*
4 *Barry Stone, who works as a computer programmer, has built his own house.*

Exercise 3

1 *d   The baby cried all night, which meant I was tired all next day.*
2 *a   The old ship stayed in port, which saved it from the storm.*
3 *c   I was out when Peter called, which was why I didn't hear the news.*
4 *g   The company has won the contract, which is good news.*
5 *b   They've started doing road repairs, which is causing bad traffic delays.*
6 *e   The sun has come out at last, which means we can go to the beach.*
7 *f   The school is building a new gymnasium, which is going to help their basketball teams a lot.*

Unit 68

Exercise 1

1 *smells delicious.*
2 *feel tired.*
3 *get angry.*
4 *seem   happy.*
5 *sounds terrible.*

Exercise 2

1 *a boring old book*

2 *an unusual blue diamond.*
3 *an exciting new film*
4 *a strange yellow light*
5 *an interesting German clock*
6 *a lovely little baby*
7 *a pleasant green valley*
8 *a tall young man*
9 *a round plastic box*

Exercise 3
1 *He was a funny, little, old man.*
2 *It was an ugly, brown, metal box.*
3 *They were beautiful, new, Italian, silk jackets.*
4 *They were wonderful, tall, round, Chinese vases.*

Exercise 4
1 *to play with matches.*
2 *to go home.*
3 *to remember to post them.*
4 *to have you with us.*
5 *to understand.*
6 *to drive when you're tired.*

Unit 69

Exercise 1
1 *excited*
2 *confused.*
3 *annoying*
4 *fascinated*
5 *exhausted*
6 *puzzling.*
7 *surprising*
8 *amazing.*

Exercise 2
1 *astonished astonishing*
2 *shocking. shocked*
3 *embarrassing embarrassed*
4 *depressed depressing.*
5 *interesting interested*
6 *disappointed disappointing.*

7 *irritated irritating*
8 *tired tiring.*

Exercise 3
1 *satisfied.*
2 *disgusted*
3 *worrying.*
4 *horrifying*
5 *relaxed*
6 *amusing.*
7 *infuriating.*
8 *terrified.*

Unit 70

Exercise 1
1 *quickly*
2 *nice*
3 *wonderful.*
4 *safely.*
5 *warm.*
6 *warmly immediately.*
7 *hard   kind*
8 *slowly   quietly*

Exercise 2
1 *proper properly.*
2 *quiet quietly*
3 *smooth smoothly*
4 *pleasant pleasant*
5 *intelligently intelligent*
6 *badly. bad*
7 *effective effectively   effective*

Exercise 3
1 *sensibly.*
2 *easily.*
3 *safely.*
4 *successfully.*
5 *Luckily*
6 *similarly   wholly*
7 *Unfortunately really   truly*

Exercise 4
1 *late*
2 *early*

3 *straight*
4 *hard*
5 *wrong*
6 *short.*
7 *far*
8 *well*
9 *direct.*
10 *low*

Exercise 5
1 *hardly hard*
2 *highly high*
3 *near nearly*
4 *freely free*
5 *short shortly.*
6 *directly direct*

Exercise 6
1 *hard*
2 *easily.*
3 *early*
4 *late.*
5 *tired*
6 *quickly*
7 *seriously.*

Unit 71

Exercise 1
1 *Hopefully,*
2 *Stupidly,*
3 *Angrily,*
4 *Frighteningly,*
5 *Finally,*
6 *Quietly,*
7 *Sadly,*
8 *Luckily,*

Exercise 2
1 *always get*
2 *was only trying*
3 *can sometimes see*
4 *will only be*
5 *don't usually work*
6 *has clearly been failing*
7 *Have you ever been*
8 *must never talk*

Exercise 3
1 *there very soon.*

2 *in America for five years.*
3 *very heavily yesterday.*
4 *much harder since last September.*
5 *over here as soon as possible.*
6 *wrong all the time.*

Exercise 4
1 *last week*
2 *over here*
3 *Sadly*
4 *last year*
5 *definitely*
6 *this time*
7 *usually*
8 *soon*

Unit 72

Exercise 1
1 *upstairs*
2 *definitely*
3 *slowly*
4 *now*
5 *hard*
6 *always*
7 *Luckily*

Exercise 2
1 *manner*
2 *place*
3 *degree*
4 *degree*
5 *manner*
6 *time*
7 *time*
8 *time*
9 *degree*
10 *time*   •
11 *degree*
12 *time*
13 *time*
14 *place*
15 *manner*
16 *sentence*
17 *manner*
18 *time*
19 *sentence*
20 *place*
21 *manner*
22 *sentence*
23 *manner*
24 *sentence*
25 *manner*
26 *degree*
27 *time*

28 *time*
29 *time*
30 *frequency*

Exercise 3

1 *there before midday.*
2 *beautifully yesterday.*
3 *everywhere for a year.*
4 *angrily at the meeting last night.*
5 *well at college these days.*

Exercise 4

1 *I usually do the washing on Monday.*
2 *Do you ever visit your old school?*
3 *Flights to New York leave once an hour.*
4 *You have to take the medicine twice a day.*

Exercise 5

1 *Sadly, she'd already gone.*
2 *Hopefully, he'll be well soon.*
3 *Surprisingly, our children are good at Art.*
4 *Unfortunately, he isn't here to receive it.*

Exercise 6

1 *has definitely finished*
2 *'ll never visit*
3 *are always delivered*
4 *hasn't clearly understood*
5 *'ll hardly ever see*

Unit 73

Exercise 1

1 *shorter   shortest*
2 *prettier   prettiest*
3 *longer   longest*
4 *uglier   ugliest*
5 *larger   largest*
6 *bigger   biggest*
7 *smaller   smallest*
8 *nicer   nicest*
9 *cooler   coolest*
10 *easier   easiest*
11 *simpler   simplest*
12 *finer   finest*
13 *thinner   thinnest*
14 *hotter   hottest*

Exercise 2

1 *easier*
2 *simpler*
3 *nicer*
4 *hotter*
5 *longer*

Exercise 3

1 *latest*
2 *quickest*
3 *narrowest*
4 *fittest*
5 *funniest*

Exercise 4

1 *fitter   fittest*
2 *finer   finest*
3 *lowest   lower*
4 *whiter   whitest*
5 *easiest   easier*

Exercise 5

1 *more   fewer*
2 *more?*
   most
3 *less*
   least   fewest
   most

Exercise 6

1 *most talented   more talented*
2 *most expensive   less expensive?*
3 *more dangerous most dangerous*
4 *more valuable   most valuable*
5 *less interesting.*
   least interesting

Exercise 7

1 *drives more slowly*
2 *writes more excitingly*
3 *sleeps more lightly*
4 *arrives earlier*
5 *plays football less intelligently*

Exercise 8

1 *The Crystal performed the most reliably, and the Wash-Tech performed the least reliably.*
2 *The Wash-Tech ran the most economically, and the Crystal ran the most cheaply.*
3 *The Crystal finished the fastest, and the Snowline finished the least quickly.*

Unit 74

Exercise 1

1 *Sue is younger than Ann.*
2 *The Toyota is more expensive than the Honda./The Honda is less expensive than the Toyota.*
3 *Robin runs/can run faster than Jack.*
4 *Mount Egmont is more dangerous than Mount George./Mount George is less dangerous than Mount Egmont.*
5 *The journey by tunnel is shorter than the journey by sea.*

Exercise 2

1 *Yesterday was the hottest day of the year.*
2 *The XL400 is/has been the most popular car in Europe this year.*
3 *Tom and Sam were the best players in last year's team.*
4 *Some people say Casa Blanca was/is the finest film ever.*

Exercise 3

1 *A Jumbo 747 isn't nearly as fast as Concord.*
2 *Britain isn't nearly as warm as Egypt.*
3 *Silver isn't nearly as expensive as gold.*
4 *Rome isn't nearly as old as Athens.*
5 *French food is much better than English food.*

Exercise 4

1 *he*
2 *her.*
3 *she*
4 *they*
5 *them.*
6 *him*
7 *I*
8 *me.*

Unit 75

Exercise 1

1 *too young.*
2 *too quickly*
3 *too strong.*
4 *too late.*
5 *too quietly.*

Exercise 2

1 *big enough.*
2 *soon enough?*
3 *carefully enough.*
4 *hard enough.*
5 *good enough.*

Exercise 3

1 *enough A5 paper, n't   enough A4 paper.*
   too few brown envelopes.
2 *n't   enough large paper clips,   too few medium clips.*
   enough small clips.
3 *too little brown sticky tape,   n't   enough clear tape.*
   enough elastic bands.
4 *too little glue,   too few stapling machines.*
   n't   enough staples.

Exercise 4

1 *I haven't got enough money for a holiday.*
2 *This coffee is too strong for your mother.*
3 *The house is big enough for the family.*

Exercise 5

1 *It isn't warm enough to go out.*
2 *The bird was too fast to catch.*

3 We were too late to catch the bus.
4 The plane was flying just high enough to miss the mountain.

Unit 76

Exercise 1

1 a bit
2 not very
3 very
4 quite
5 not very

Exercise 2

1 much/far
2 much
3 a little
4 a little
5 far/much

Exercise 3

1 so
2 such
3 such
4 so
5 such
6 so
7 so
8 such
9 such
10 so

Exercise 4

1 e The weather was so bad (that) we gave up our holiday and went home.
2 a The students are making so much noise (that) all the neighbours are complaining.
3 d The birds are so friendly (that) they even take food from your hand.
4 h The children made such a mess (that) it took an hour to clean the room.
5 f Everybody is so busy (that) nobody is answering the phone.
6 g I haven't driven for such a long time (that) I feel quite

nervous about going on the road.
7 c After the trip we were all so tired (that) we went straight to sleep.
8 b They took such a long time to get ready (that) they nearly missed their plane.

Unit 77

Exercise 1

1 near
2 above
3 behind
4 next to
5 under
6 in
7 on
8 in front of
9 opposite
10 between

Exercise 2

1 at
2 at
3 in
4 in
5 opposite
6 in front of
7 in front of
8 between
9 Among
10 among

Exercise 3

1 past
2 across
3 into
4 through
5 along
6 round
7 towards
8 over
9 up
10 down
11 under
12 inside
13 out of
14 away from

Unit 78

Exercise 1

1 g Tom lives at

Number 25, North Street.
2 i There's a notice on the wall outside my office.
3 a Ann is buying some things in the shopping centre.
4 d Dad is having a sleep in the small bedroom.
5 c My aunt lives in a small town outside London.
6 b Come and meet all the trainees in Room 564.
7 f I want you to introduce me to everyone at the party.
8 e There are two men working up on the roof.
9 j Sally put the vase of flowers on the table.
10 h Both London and Oxford are on the River Thames.

Exercise 2

1 in the middle of
2 on the way
3 at that meeting.
4 on that wall.
5 on the bottle
6 at that desk.
7 at the entrance.
8 in the garden.
9 in a village

Exercise 3

1 at
2 on
3 at
4 on
5 on
6 at
7 at
8 at
9 at
10 in
11 in
12 in
13 on

Unit 79

Exercise 1

1 at

2 in
3 in
4 on
5 at
6 at
7 on
8 on
9 at
10 at
11 at
12 in

Exercise 2

1 at
2 in
3 in
4 on
5 on
6 in
7 at
8 in
9 in
10 at
11 in
12 on
13 on
14 at
15 in
16 on
17 at
18 in
19 at

Exercise 3

1 on
2 at
3 on
4 on
5 x
6 x
7 on
8 x
9 in
10 at
11 in
12 x
13 x
14 x
15 in
16 at

Exercise 4

1 at a time.
2 at times
3 in time.
4 at one time
5 on time.

Exercise 5

1. ten past three
2. ten to seven
3. half past nine
4. a quarter to three
5. a quarter past five
6. thirteen minutes past one
7. twenty-nine minutes to eleven
8. one minute to one

Exercise 6

1. On Wednesday the 28th you're returning to London at 3.45 in the afternoon.
2. On Friday the 30th you're meeting Japanese visitors from the Subarashi Corporation all day.
3. On Saturday the 31st you're speaking at the goodbye party for the Managing Director in the evening.
4. On Monday the 2nd you're attending the sales conference in the afternoon/evening.
5. On Tuesday the 3rd you're talking at the sales conference in the morning.
6. On Thursday the 5th you're flying to Rome at 7.15 in the morning.
7. On Friday the 6th you're leaving Rome for Madrid at 11.45 in the morning.
8. On Saturday the 7th you're travelling back to London at midday.

Unit 80

Exercise 1

1. for
2. for
3. for
4. since
5. for
6. since
7. For
8. since

Exercise 2

1. ago
2. before.
3. ago
4. ago.
5. before.
6. ago
7. before.

Exercise 3

1. while
2. During
3. While
4. during
5. during
6. during
7. while

Exercise 4

1. by
2. until/till
3. until/till
4. by
5. By
6. Until/till
7. by
8. until/till

Exercise 5

1. since
2. during
3. while
4. for
5. until/till
6. By
7. before
8. ago

Unit 81

Exercise 1

1. on
   by
2. on
   by
3. on   for
   for
4. for
   on
5. on
   on
6. by
   in   by
7. on
   on
8. at
   by

Exercise 2

1. on a tour
2. in my car.
3. on a school trip
4. by plane.
5. on his bike.
6. for a walk
7. at the cinema
8. by air
9. on a diet.
10. by an artist

Exercise 3

1. matter with
2. need for
3. hope of
4. increase in
5. way of
6. problem with
7. call for
8. fall in
9. interested in
10. difficulties with

Unit 82

Exercise 1

1. for
2. at
3. with
4. with/about
5. with/about
6. for
7. with
8. with

Exercise 2

1. terrible at
2. proud of
3. different from
4. good for
5. late for
6. responsible for
7. early for
8. worried about

Exercise 3

1. tired of his old computer games.
2. used to working at night.
3. angry with her children.
4. anxious about his first business trip.
5. sorry about the long delay at the airport.
6. bored with the radio programme.
7. nervous about going out alone.
8. amazed at the huge number of people at the concert.

Unit 83

Exercise 1

1. about
2. for
3. to
4. to
5. about

Exercise 2

1. heard about
2. applied to
3. applying for?
4. thinking about
5. thought of
6. look after
7. look at
8. look for

Exercise 3

1. asked   for
2. congratulate   on
3. provide   with
4. ask   about
5. tell   about

Exercise 4

1. asked the teacher for help.
2. told him about the accident.
3. blamed him for the crash.
4. describe the man to them.
5. inviting all my friends to my party.

Unit 84

Exercise 1

1. pick up
2. give out
3. sit down
4. put away
5. Turn over
6. come in.

Exercise 2

1 lie down
2 go away
3 go out
4 move on
5 come back
6 get up
7 Turn round
8 wake up.

Exercise 3

1 take out
2 brought down
3 turn down
4 took off
5 put on
6 putting up

Exercise 4

1 picked it up.
2 switched it off.
3 put them away.
4 put them down.
5 turned it up.
6 turned them over.
7 paid it in.

Unit 85

Exercise 1

1 Pronoun
2 Adjective
3 Noun
4 Adjective
5 Linking word
6 Verb
7 Adverb
8 Preposition

Exercise 2

1 bedrooms
2 bathroom.
3 living-room
4 television.
5 dining-room
6 visitors.
7 kitchen.
8 food
9 dishes.
10 garden.
11 time
12 flowers.
13 vegetables.
14 shop

Exercise 3

1 cooks
2 get

---

3 leave
4 is
5 drops
6 work
7 have to
8 takes
9 drives
10 has

Exercise 4

1 only
2 big
3 badly
4 right.
5 fine
6 fast
7 nearly
8 quickly
9 late
10 certainly

Exercise 5

1 It
2 a
3 we
4 we
5 a
6 it
7 the
8 the
9 whole
10 the
11 Ours
12 a
13 Most
14 in
15 one
16 An
17 a
18 of
19 along
20 the
21 us
22 They
23 us
24 to
25 the

Unit 86

Exercise 1

1 Question
2 Order
3 Exclamation
4 Statement
5 Question
6 Statement
7 Exclamation
8 Order

Exercise 2

1	S	V	C	
2	V	O		
3	S	A	V	O
4	A	V	O	
5	S			
	V	O		
6	V	S	C	
7	S			
	V	O		
8	A	S	V	C
	AP			

Exercise 3

1 The plane   climbed
   fast.
2 Your brother   seems
   very tired.
3 Don't put   the boxes
   over there.
4 Robert   is coming
   as soon as possible.
5 Did you see
   the news   yesterday?

Unit 87

Exercise 1

1 and
2 so
3 but
4 or

Exercise 2

1 and he owns a house
   in Scotland.
2 so he's got to come
   home by taxi instead.
3 or he can go at 4.00.
4 but he seems very tired
   at the moment.

Exercise 3

1 I went to bed because/
   as I was tired.
2 I'm getting a new car
   because/as mine is old.
3 I'll call you later
   because/as I have to go
   now.

Exercise 4

1 Sally does her job well
   even though/though
   she's young.
2 The film is still
   very popular even

---

though/ though it's
   old.
3 Their new house looks
   terrible even though/
   though it was
   expensive.

Exercise 5

1 If
2 who
3 when
4 Even though
5 because
6 When
7 even though
8 Because

Unit 88

Exercise 1

1 It is   Alternatively,
   it is
2 We have reached
   In addition, we have
   managed
3 We are cutting
   However, we are
   failing
4 We have not tried
   As a result, we do not
   know   it will be

Exercise 2

1 from
2 of
3 x
4 to
5 for
6 to
7 of
8 of

Exercise 3

1 she has achieved a
   Grade A.
2 she has often failed to
   complete her
   homework.
3 she has behaved badly
   in class all year.
4 she must learn to do
   some hard work.
5 she has found it
   difficult to improve.
6 she could go on to do
   extra Science.